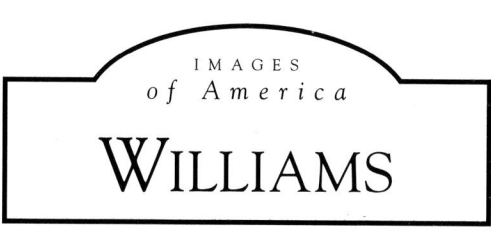

IMAGES
of America

WILLIAMS

Larry Hrenchir

10-19-2011

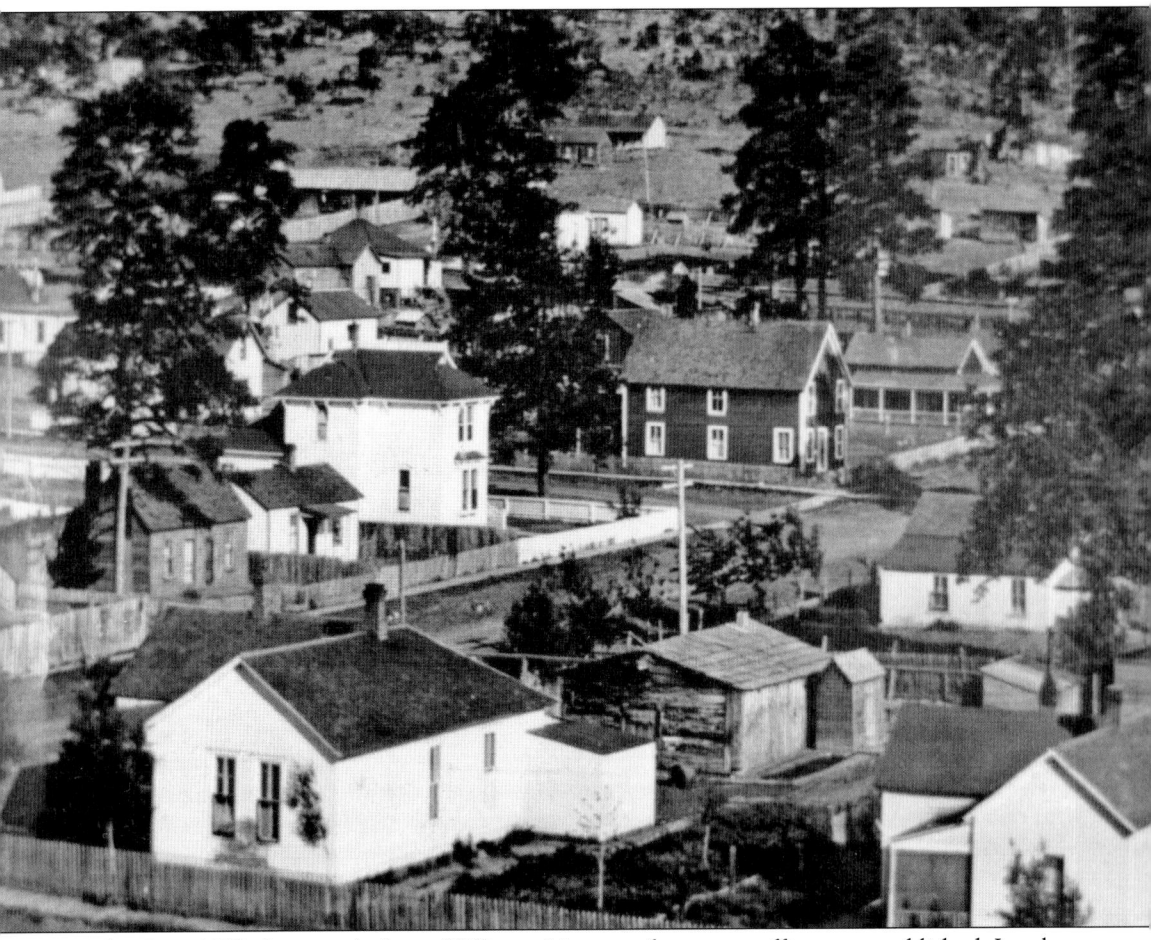

This June 1915 photograph shows Williams 34 years after a post office was established. Lumber was plentiful within the forested community, making it the material of choice for home building. After a number of fires swept through the city, however, business owners began to build with rock in order to protect their investments. (Courtesy Williams Public Library.)

ON THE COVER: The famed Bill Williams Mountain Men pose for one of many publicity shots that would be taken of them during the years since their formation in 1953. This photograph shows a number of the group's founding members, who became Arizona state ambassadors soon after the creation of the club. (Courtesy Bob Dean.)

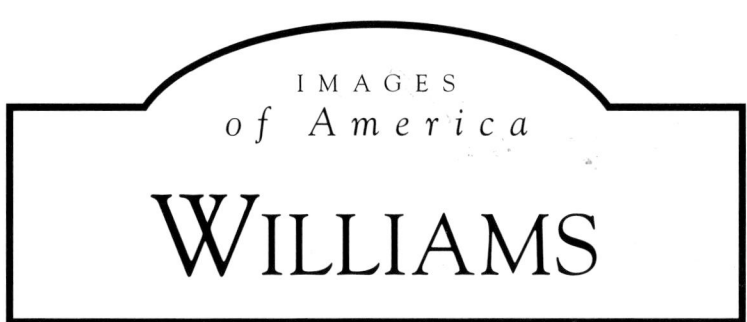

IMAGES
of America

WILLIAMS

Patrick Whitehurst

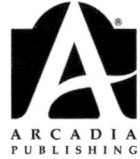

ARCADIA
PUBLISHING

Published by Arcadia Publishing
Charleston SC, Chicago IL, Portsmouth NH, San Francisco CA

Printed in the United States of America

Library of Congress Catalog Card Number: 2008926273

For all general information contact Arcadia Publishing at:
Telephone 843-853-2070
Fax 843-853-0044
E-mail sales@arcadiapublishing.com
For customer service and orders:
Toll-Free 1-888-313-2665

Visit us on the Internet at www.arcadiapublishing.com

For Williams librarian Andrea Dunn

CONTENTS

ACKNOWLEDGMENTS

The search for history can be an exciting task. As I learned when I began working on *Williams*, the past can be a very personal and treasured part of an individual's life. In seeking historic photographs for this book, I sought out various individuals in the community whose families have been in the area for generations. I placed an advertisement in the *Williams–Grand Canyon News* to solicit historic photographs. A number of individuals also assisted me in seeking out photographs that could be included in this work, such as George Garcia of the Williams Historical Society. What you now hold in your hands is the culmination of that effort.

I would like to thank Jared Jackson of Arcadia Publishing. When I first heard of Jared, I was surprised at the claims being made about him. "He's always there when you need him," they said. "He can answer all of your questions," they said. Well, they were right. Jared's assistance proved invaluable in the creation of this book.

Thanks also to Williams city manager Dennis Wells and Arizona State Railroad Museum founder Al Richmond for their knowledge and assistance, and special thanks to Andrea Dunn of the Williams Public Library, Lynda Duffy, Red Garter Bed and Bakery owner John Holst, Bob Dean of the Bill Williams Mountain Men, author Frank Barrios, Margaret Hangen and Jackie Banks with the Kaibab National Forest, publisher Doug Wells of the *Williams–Grand Canyon News*, Eddie Sandoval, Christa Rodrigue, and Clyde Polson, all of whom shared their great collections of historic photographs, stories, and their time. This project would not have been possible without their priceless assistance.

Thanks also to Colleen Whitehurst for her support. Despite her own busy life, she did whatever was necessary for me to complete this book, and for that I will always be in her debt.

INTRODUCTION

When you arrive in Williams, it is often hard to know where to look first. For many, that first glimpse of the town is what sticks in the mind forever. When we think of the community sitting in the shadow of Bill Williams Mountain, some of us remember seeing the steam engine headed out of town on its daily trek to the Grand Canyon; others may remember seeing an elk or two trotting under a canopy of tall pine trees, the proud historic district, or that famous sign that lets visitors know they are on one of the most beloved roads in U.S. history—Route 66. No matter what the view happened to look like at the time, snow-covered or hot and sunny, that first peek at this historic community is the one many remember best.

This particular stretch of the Mother Road was called Bill Williams Avenue in the early days of Williams's history, and the motor courts and tall signs were all there, harkening back to an era of two-lane traffic, roadsters, and Burma Shave. While Route 66 was established in 1926, Williams has been around since 1879. Back then, there were no roadsters, only horses and buggies. Livestock roamed the landscape.

The railroad came through soon after in 1882, creating a vein of trade and commerce through the area. Williams residents soon found themselves in a booming community filled with rail workers and sawmill employees. The Saginaw mill opened in 1894, which created a number of new jobs in the area. The sawmill would remain a fixture in Williams until its move to Flagstaff in the 1940s. As the town filled with hard-working individuals, the surge in growth meant big changes for the small community of Williams.

New businesses began to arrive, goods and merchandise became available in the community, and buildings began to appear across the landscape. Crime, however, seemed to grow also. Houses of ill repute, opium dens, and bootlegging all became a part of the Williams landscape. A rash of fires would also plague the landscape during Williams's formative years. The formation of a fire department and police force would eventually put an end to both problems.

Ranching families played a part in Williams history as well, such as the McNellys and the Pouquettes, many of whom still have roots in the community. Members of the Pouquette family owned at least three sheepherding companies in the Williams area during the early 1900s: the Pouquette Sheep Company, the Red Hill Sheep Company, and the Sitgreaves Sheep Company. Each summer, it was estimated that between 75,000 and 80,000 sheep made their presence known in town.

With the formation of the National Forest Service in 1905, public lands in Williams were preserved, to the delight of some and the dismay of others. As part of the Tusayan National Forest, large tracts of land around Williams became off-limits to ranchers and loggers. The forest around Williams would be changed to its new designation as the Kaibab National Forest in 1934.

By the 1950s, Williams had become a different place. Struggling to find their own identity, residents started the Bill Williams Mountain Men organization to honor the town's namesake. The idea paid off, for the group was so well received that they were soon made Arizona state ambassadors and attended a number of nationwide events. Travelers on Route 66 also poured into Williams, as well as tourists on their way to visit the Grand Canyon. These visitors earned Williams the nickname of the "Gateway to the Grand Canyon."

The city would continue to thrive well into the 1980s. Residents faced their next big hurdle in 1984, when Williams and Route 66 were bypassed by Interstate 40. While many worried the town would fold up upon the completion of the four-lane highway, that did not prove to be the case. The addition of the Grand Canyon Railway, as well as a renewed interest in historic Route 66, helped put Williams back in the spotlight. Today hundreds of thousands of visitors make their way through the city each year, hailing from distant countries and from as close as neighboring Flagstaff. Williams, unlike its humble beginnings, has grown to become a world-class destination all its own.

One

A Red-Headed Namesake
The Story of Bill Williams

Born in 1787 in North Carolina, William "Bill" Shirley Williams was the fourth son of Joseph Williams and was known for his shocking mane of red hair and for his amazing abilities.

Bill Williams, besides becoming a pastor, is credited with translating the Bible into a number of native languages and for brokering disputes between colonizers and native tribes. Legends galore surround his exploits. They range from daring rescues to life-and-death battles. As a famed mountain man and trapper called "Lone Elk" and "Old Bill," among other nicknames, he continuously moved west in his lifetime and is credited with finding an area of mountains in what is today northern Arizona. He performed guide duties for a number of expeditions. During a particular trapping expedition, legend has it that Bill Williams met a number of topographers who were mapping northern Arizona and told them of a particular mountain in the area, which the men subsequently named "Bill Williams Mountain."

The death of Bill Williams is a story with a number of conflicting outcomes. Some believe the notorious mountain man was killed in a Ute raid in 1849. He is more commonly thought to have perished in 1848 after a doomed expedition into the Rocky Mountains. The expedition, led by Capt. John C. Fremont of the U.S. Topographical Engineers, sought to find a passable route through the mountains to California. More than 10 men died during the trip because of a series of heavy snowstorms that hit the area. Williams himself managed to survive the ill-fated expedition. His death came shortly thereafter, however, when Williams returned to his home base of Taos, New Mexico, after salvaging what was left of the ill-fated Fremont expedition. Whether he was killed by a Ute tribe or raiders seeking his goods remains a mystery, just as his final resting place is. Some believe the mountain man is buried on Bill Williams Mountain itself. Others believe he is buried somewhere in Colorado. His real resting place, perhaps, may never be known.

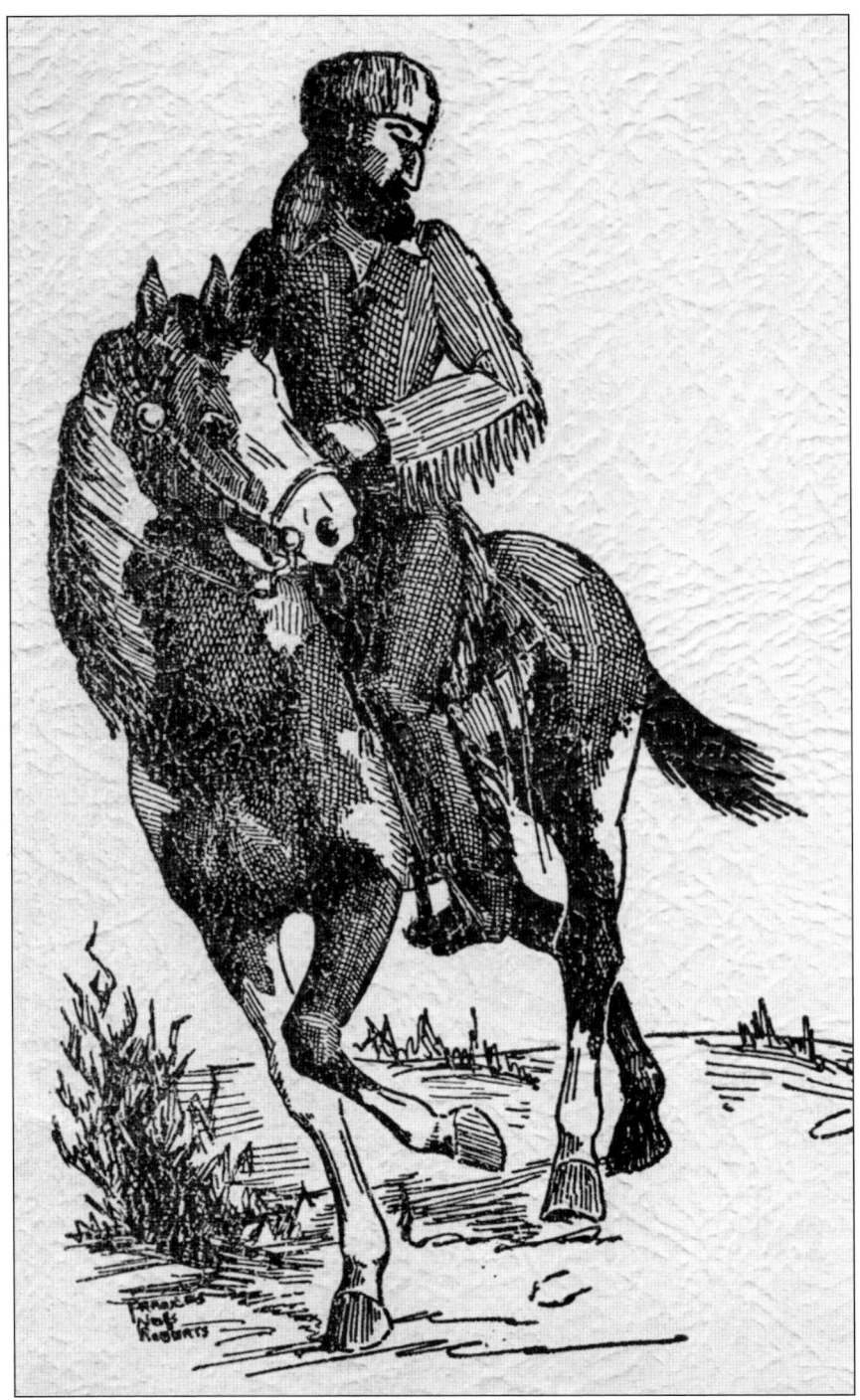

This 1957 illustration by Frances Wells Roberts for the publication *The Story of "Old Bill Williams"* shows the adventurous nature of Bill Williams and the many legends that surround the man. Born to humble beginnings in 1787, Williams would go down in history as one of the most famous pioneers to brave the Wild West. Besides being known as a famed mountain man, Williams was also a preacher for the Methodist Church. (Courtesy Wells family.)

Two

A TOWN BEGINS
WILLIAMS IS SETTLED

Founding the city of Williams was not necessarily high on Charles Thomas Rogers's priority list when he set out to find suitable grazing conditions for his cattle, but that is indeed what Rogers eventually became known for. Rogers headed west from Maine around 1853, becoming a meat seller and rancher in Prescott. Drought forced him to move on in 1878. He made his way to the Bill Williams Mountain area and stopped near the base of the mountain to allow his cattle to graze and for his wife to give birth to the newest member of the Rogers family. Rather than move any further, the family decided to stay. Their large ranch eventually became a popular spot for travelers making their way through the area. A post office was established in 1881, with Rogers as postmaster.

By 1882, things really began to change in Williams. Roughly 50 houses, three stores, and three saloons operated in the community. The Atlantic and Pacific Railroad also arrived that year. The railroads, a new sawmill, and an abundant supply of grasslands for cattle became the top three industries in the fast-growing community.

Another famous Williams icon, Cormick E. Boyce, made his home in the town in 1881. Called the "Daddy of Williams," Boyce is credited with building Williams from the land that Rogers settled. Arriving in Williams thanks to a broken wagon wheel, the young Irishman quickly became one of the town's foremost merchants. Boyce brought a strong sense of civic pride to the community. He served as postmaster in 1887 and was one of the first county supervisors when Coconino County was established in 1891.

Boyce was one of the first to build with brick in Williams, thanks to the town's lengthy history of fires. He erected the Grand Canyon Hotel in brick, which would eventually save the structure from a large fire that swept through the entire block in 1901. Boyce's private water system is also credited with helping to save his hotel from the fire's wrath.

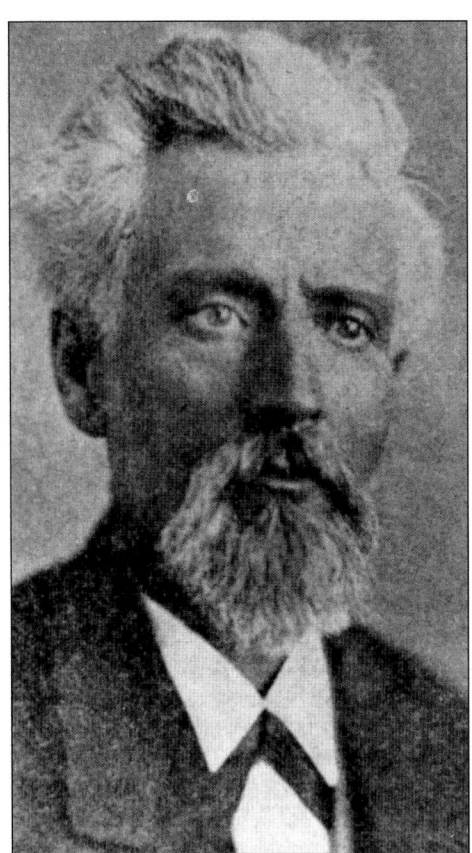

Charles Thomas Rogers (1827–1903) is credited with bringing Williams to life. Shown here in 1876, Rogers headed west from Maine in 1853, eventually settling under the shadow of the Bill Williams Mountain. His ranch, which became known as "Rogers Stop," was a popular stop for travelers making their way through the area. (Courtesy Williams Public Library.)

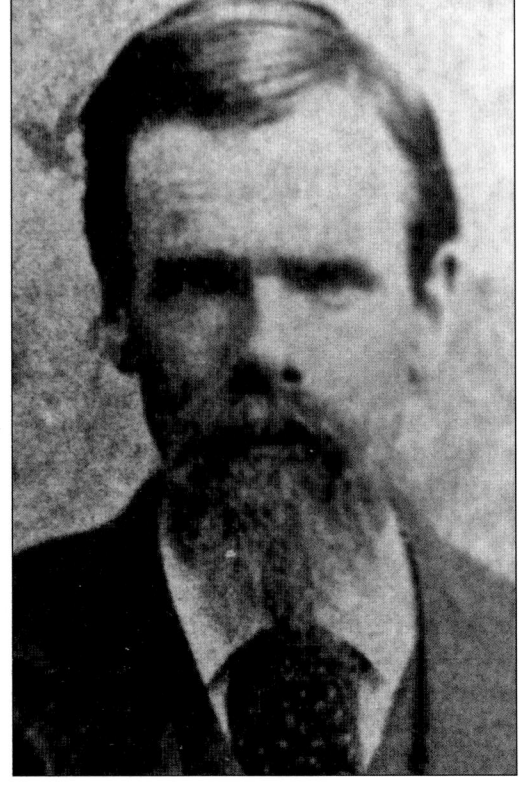

Called the "Daddy of Williams," Cormick Boyce came to Williams with a broken wagon wheel in 1881. He went on to become one of the most successful businessmen in the city. Boyce was known for his generosity. He contributed money to a number of young men in Williams who wished to open their own businesses. Boyce died in 1929 after moving to San Diego. (Courtesy Williams Public Library.)

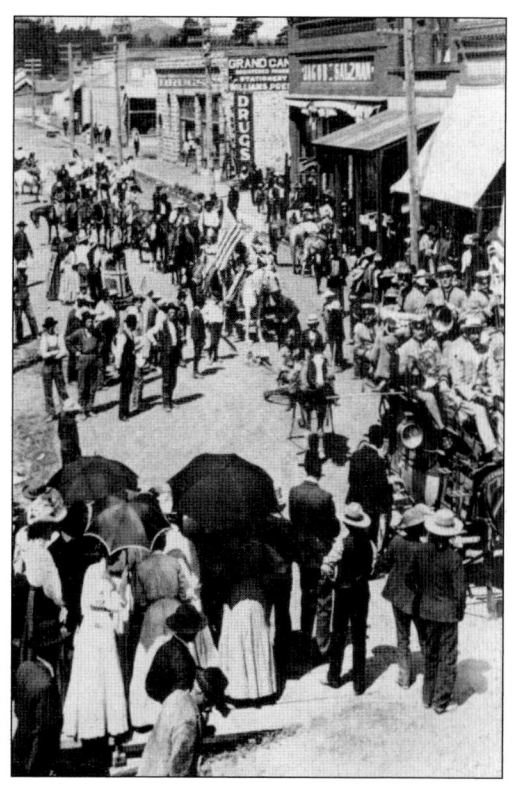

Residents of Williams have always enjoyed a good parade. Seen here in 1909 (right) and six years earlier in 1903 (below), city residents would pack the wooden sidewalks of Bill Williams Avenue during the city's annual Fourth of July parade. Despite a large fire in the area a year before the 1909 parade, the townsfolk were never deterred when it came to celebrations. The 1908 fire took out an entire city block, consuming businesses as well as 12 homes. Made up of rail workers, lumber mill employees, ranchers, and business people, Williams's residents formed a makeshift organization to fight fires when they broke out. The group was commonly referred to as the "Bucket Brigade." (Both, courtesy *Williams–Grand Canyon News*.)

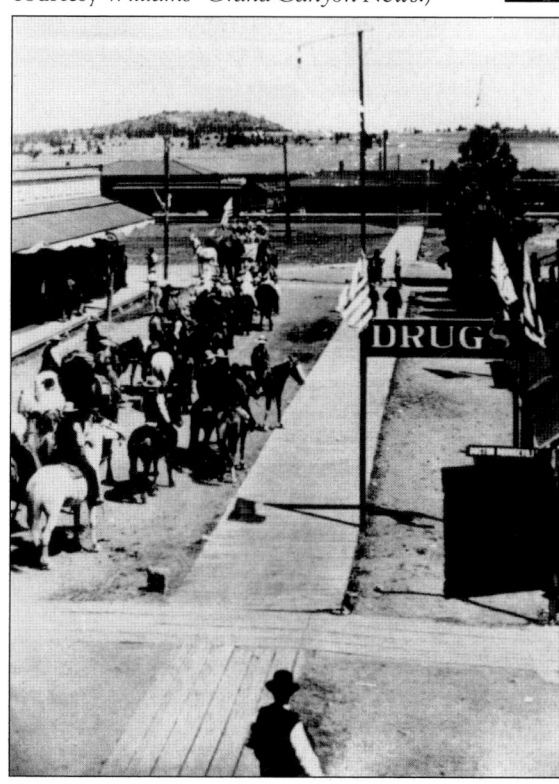

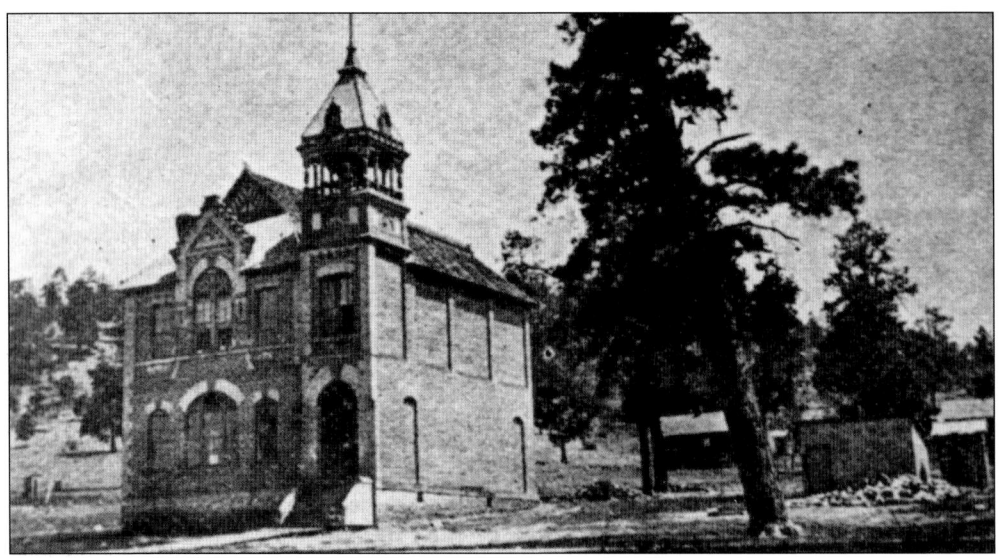

A Williams school in 1898 offers a look at the town's quick growth during its formative years. A school in the area was first established in 1882, with 23 students in attendance during that same year. Prior to the construction of a new school, students in Williams attended classes in a one-room building near the corner of Bill Williams Avenue and Second Street. (Courtesy Williams Public Library.)

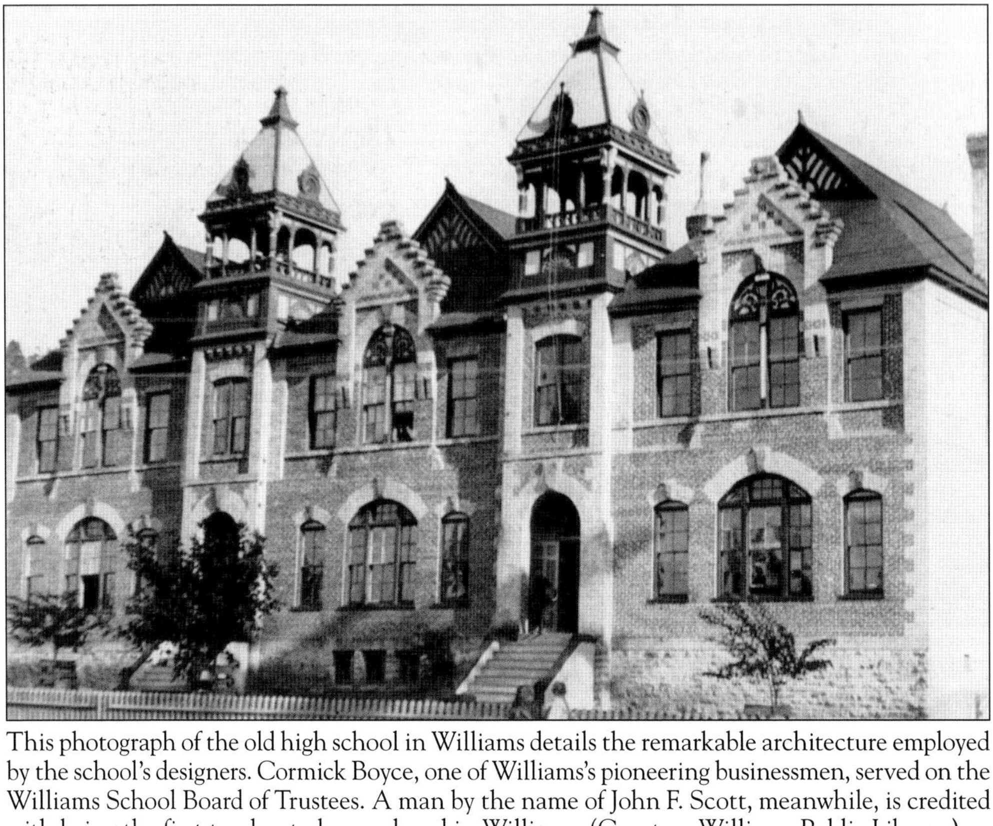

This photograph of the old high school in Williams details the remarkable architecture employed by the school's designers. Cormick Boyce, one of Williams's pioneering businessmen, served on the Williams School Board of Trustees. A man by the name of John F. Scott, meanwhile, is credited with being the first teacher to be employed in Williams. (Courtesy Williams Public Library.)

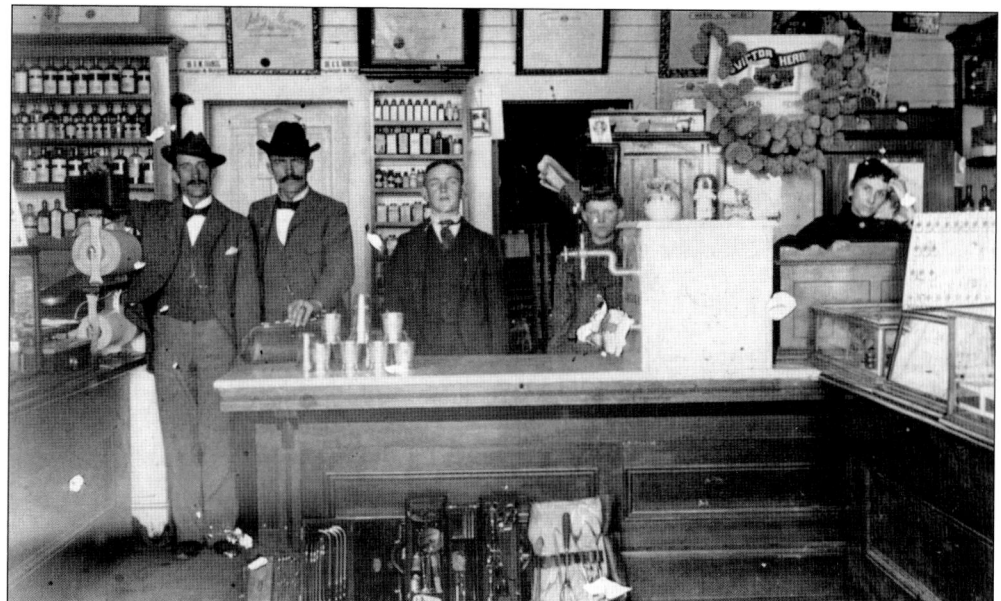

Clerks mind the store in this 1896 photograph. Businesses came and went during the heyday of Williams. Besides dry goods and other merchandise stores, saloons and brothels were also plentiful in the area, catering to an almost daily influx of new residents and travelers to the city. (Courtesy *Williams–Grand Canyon News*.)

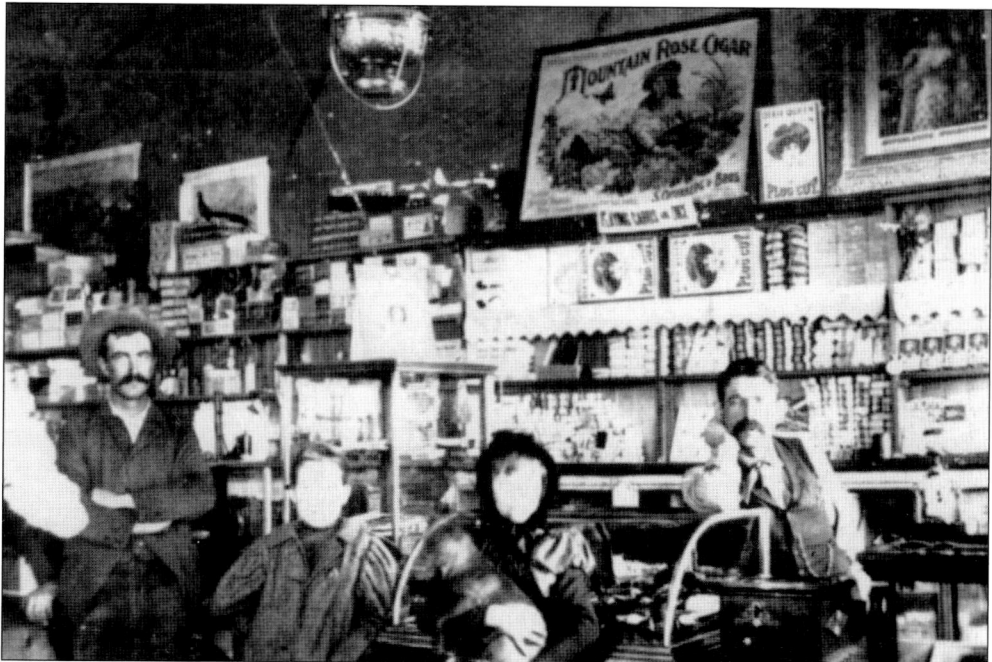

This photograph of the M. J. Kennedy General Store illustrates the variety of goods that were available in Williams at the end of the 19th century. Water, however, proved to be a scarce commodity in the area. A sample from the town pump, tested in 1895 by professors from both Harvard and Yale, proved to be the worst water sample the college professors had ever seen. (Courtesy Williams Public Library.)

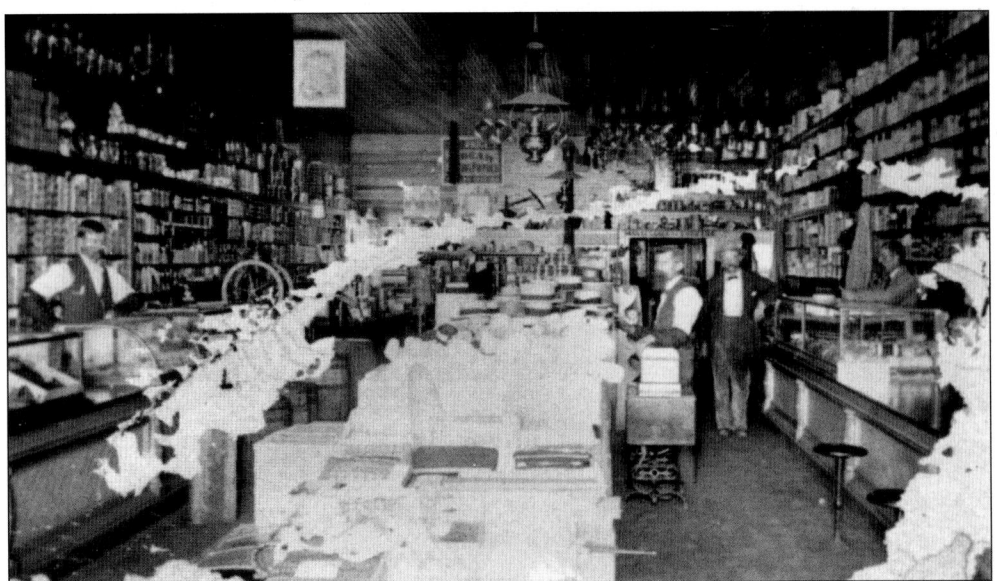

Gus Polson (center, right) and F. O. Polson (center, left) pose for a photograph inside the Polson Brothers Store in Williams. The Polson family established what is commonly thought to be one of Williams's biggest businesses and eventually moved into other endeavors as well. They created their general merchandise store in 1894. The Polsons moved into a new store in 1895, one of three general merchandise stores at the time. (Courtesy Williams Public Library.)

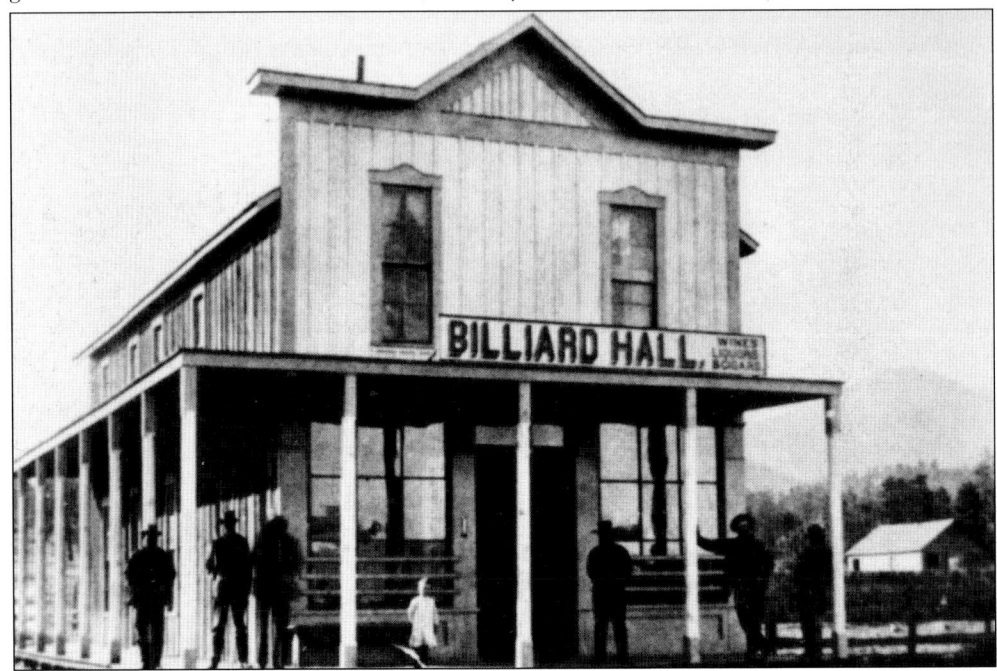

The F. R. Nellis Billiard Hall, shown here in 1880, catered to the leisurely pursuits of early settlers in Williams. That same year, the town's founder, Charles Thomas Rogers, permanently established his residency in Williams after holding properties in both Prescott and Williams. Rogers is said to have made the move in anticipation of the arrival of the railroad two years later. (Courtesy Williams Public Library.)

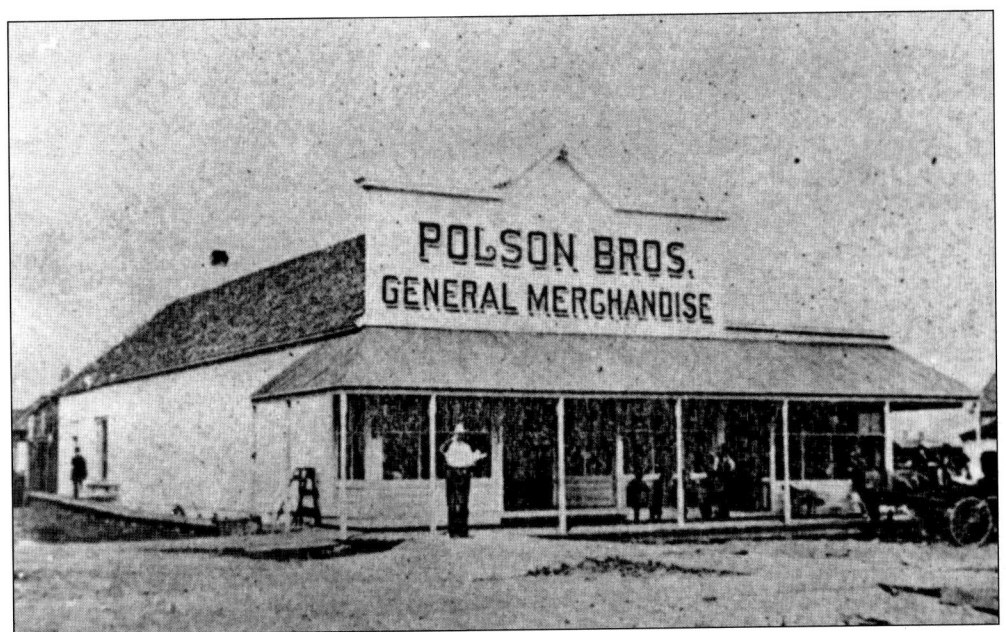

When the population of Williams reached 600, business owners began to see a measure of prosperity. The Polson brothers, whose store is shown in this 1898 photograph, would also become involved in politics. A. F. Polson became one of the members of a new city council in 1895. (Courtesy Williams Public Library.)

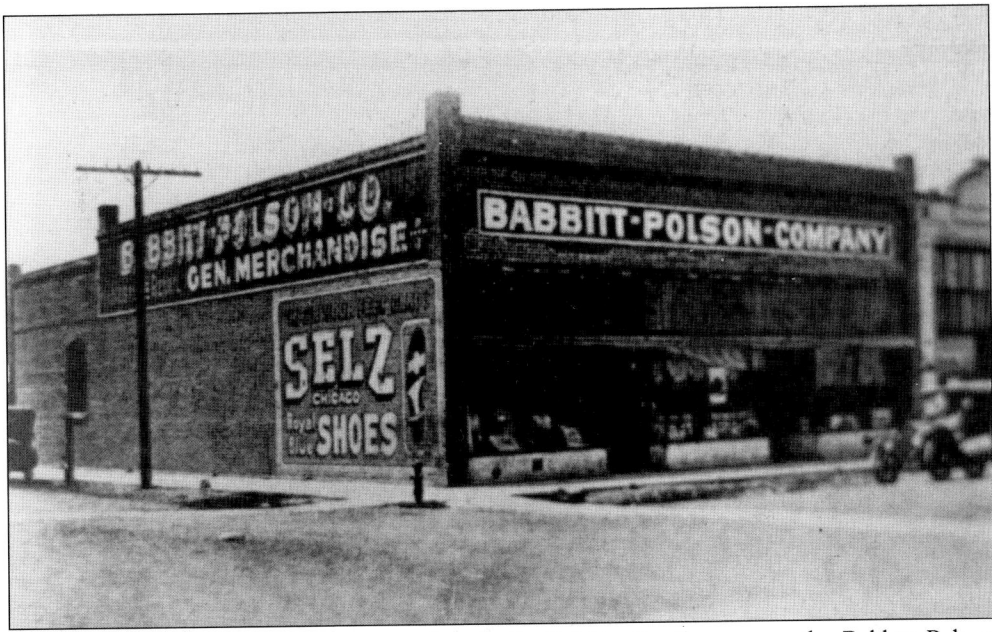

The Polson family eventually partnered with the Babbitt family to open the Babbitt-Polson Company. Though their large store would burn to the ground, merchandise and all, during the large 1908 conflagration in the downtown area, the Babbitt-Polson Company quickly rebuilt. The building in this photograph can still be seen in the downtown area. (Courtesy Williams Public Library.)

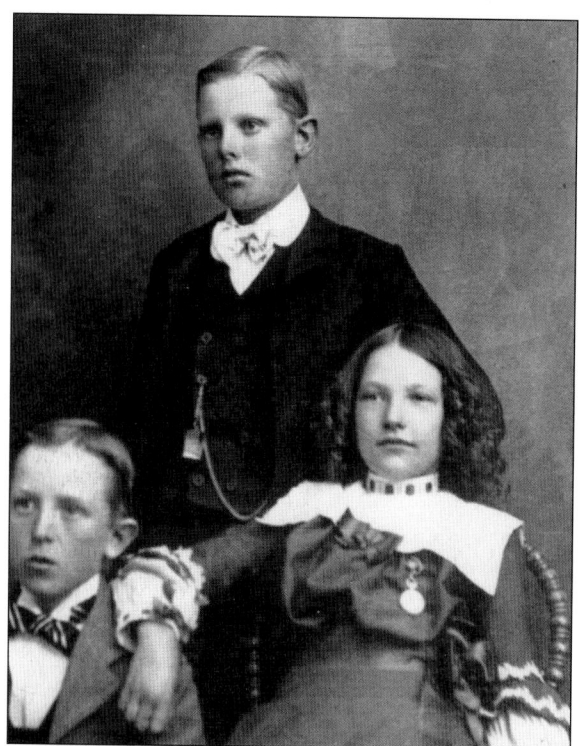

The Polson family would remain in the Williams area for generations. From left to right, Clyde, Marie, and Claude Polson, shown here in 1905, helped bring the family into the next century. Members of the Polson family can still be found in Williams to this day. (Courtesy Williams Public Library.)

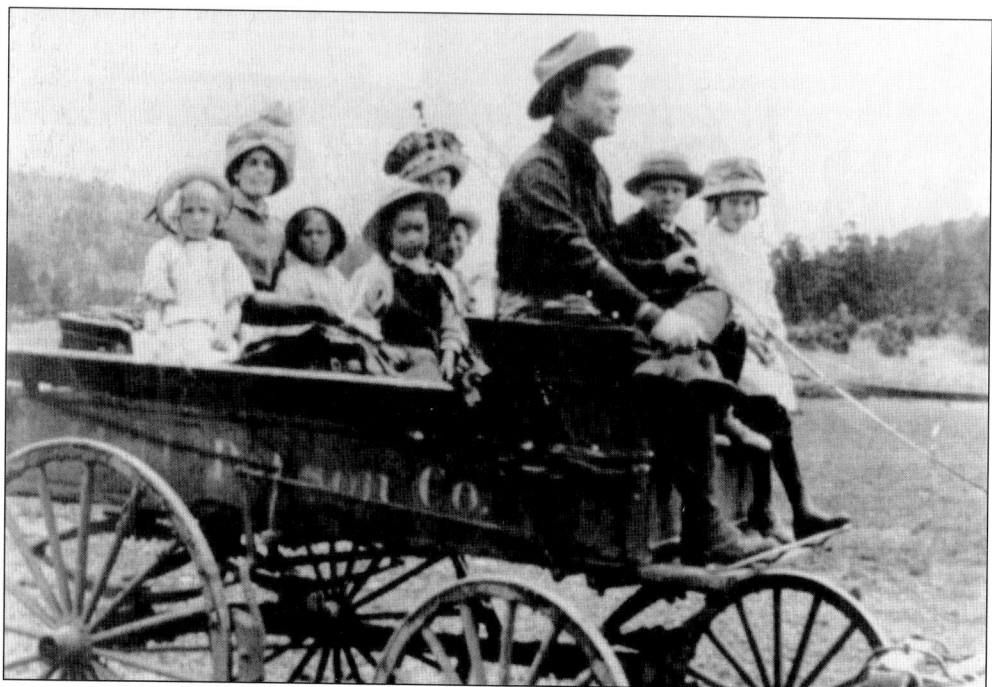

A number of happy travelers take a trip in the Babbitt-Polson wagon in 1914. The Babbitt brothers of Flagstaff, who were well-known merchandisers and livestock men at the time, went into business in 1905. They expanded into general merchandising when they joined forces with the Polson family. (Courtesy Williams Public Library.)

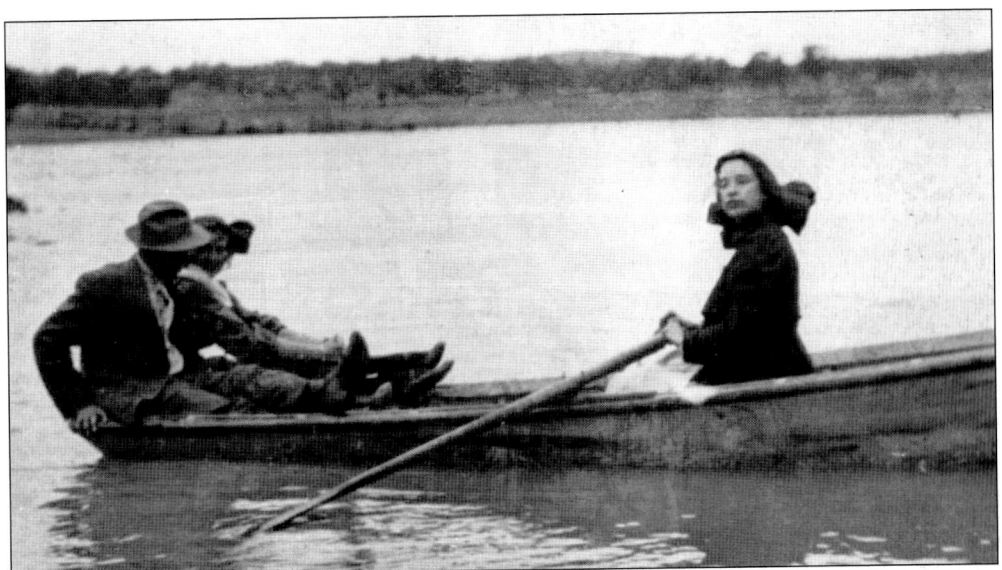

Despite a busy business to run, Clyde Polson Sr. still found time for a little rest and relaxation. Polson (left), pictured here with residents Burnette Summerson (center) and Helen Stark, drifts along on one of the many lakes that surround the Williams area. Stark, a longtime resident of Williams, lived to be over 100 years old. (Courtesy Williams Public Library.)

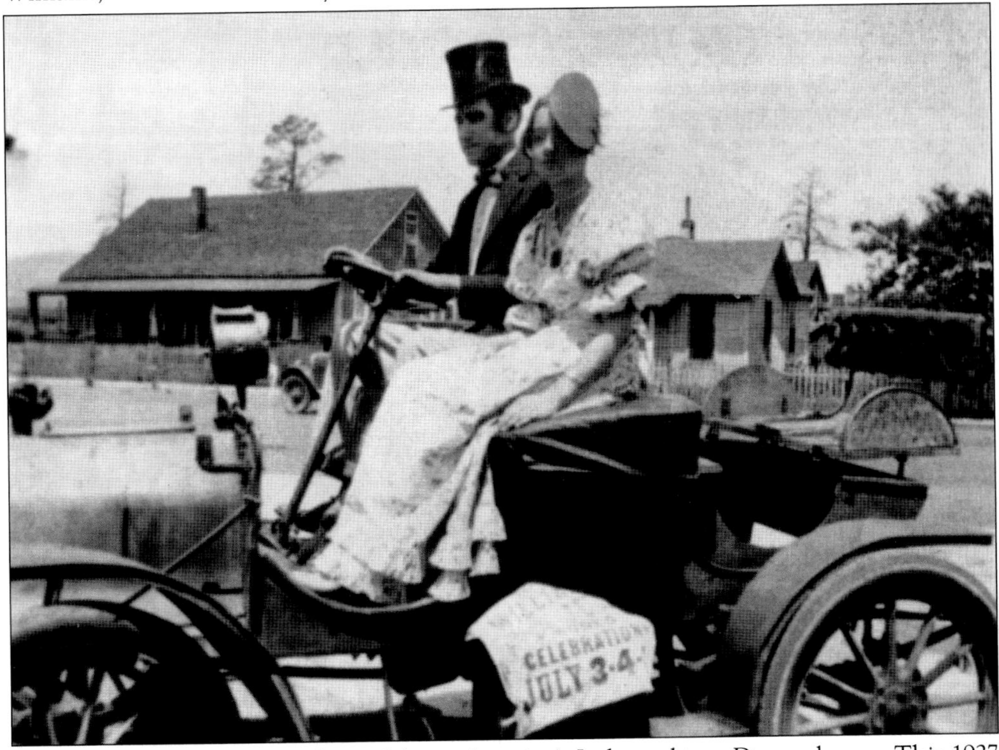

Williams residents continued to celebrate America's Independence Day each year. This 1927 photograph show a couple dressed to the nines for the annual celebration. A newspaper heralding the arrival of the Fourth of July celebration sits at the bottom of the couple's vehicle. (Courtesy Williams Public Library.)

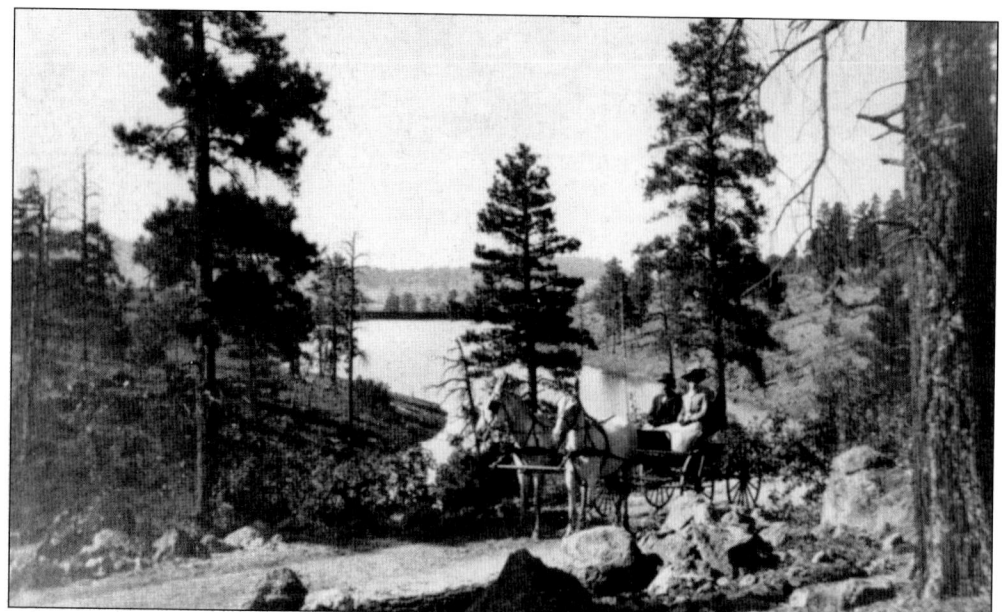

A horse-drawn carriage pulls a couple behind the Williams Dam at the beginning of the 20th century. Williams officials commissioned the erection of a number of dams, as well as the development of wells in the 1890s, though the town would continue to suffer water shortages throughout the years. (Courtesy Williams Public Library.)

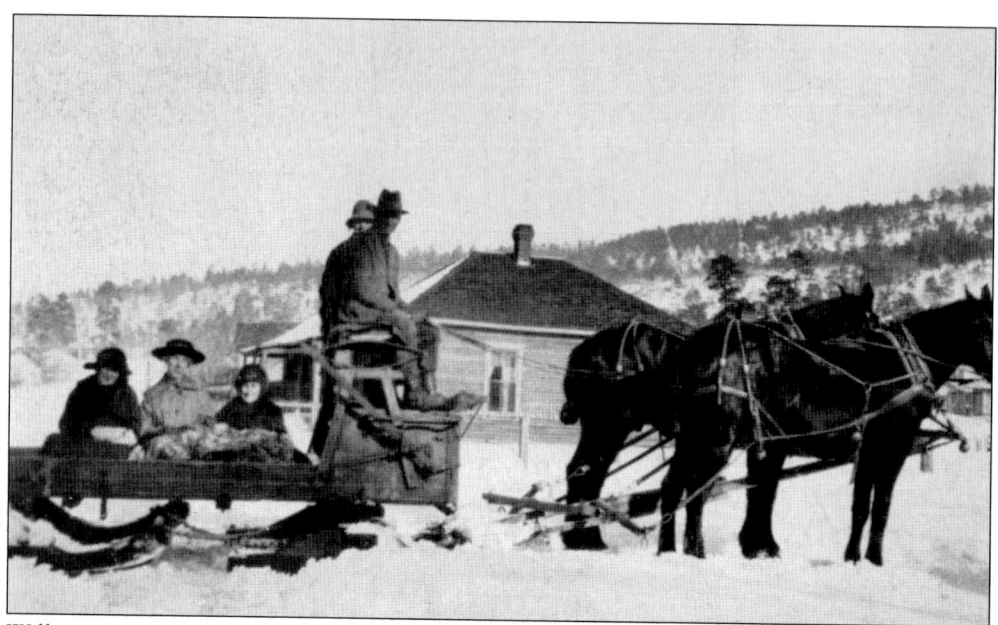

Williams residents enjoy winter by riding through town in a horse-drawn sleigh. By the beginning of the 20th century, the residents found themselves in the rare predicament of having more water than they needed. Due to heavy snows and intermittent rain in 1903, the dams filled to capacity, producing a flood that ran through the community that year. (Courtesy Williams Public Library.)

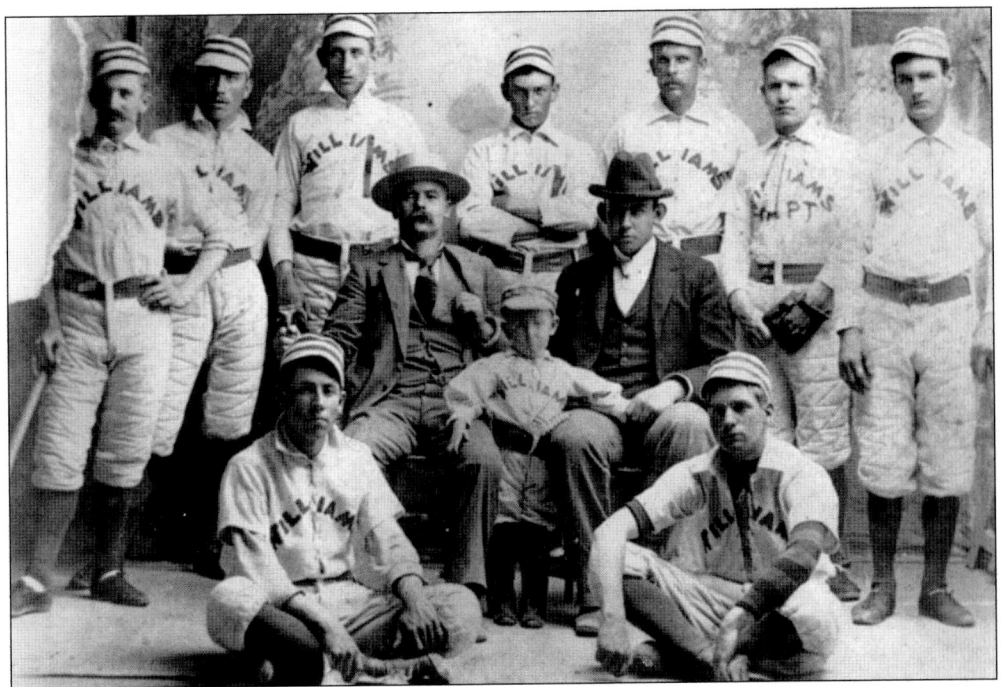

The people of Williams wasted no time when it came to America's pastime. As the popularity of baseball swept across the nation in the early 1900s, Williams residents quickly formed its own team. Longtime resident Harry McDougall is standing, third from the left. (Courtesy Williams Public Library.)

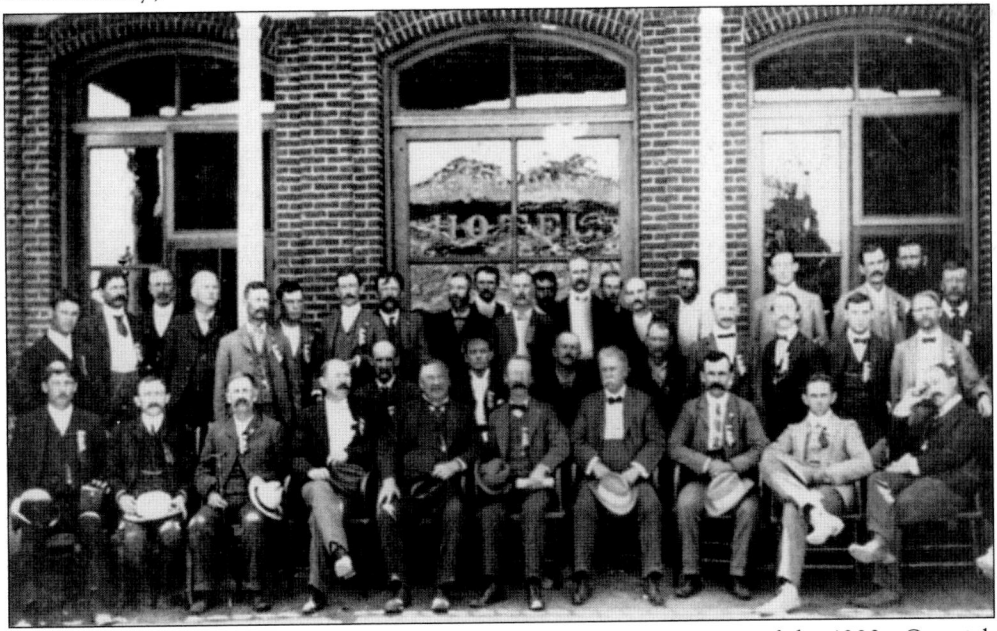

A group of men gather at the Grand Canyon Hotel at the beginning of the 1900s. Cormick Boyce, proprietor of the hotel, used his private water system to save the building from the threat of destruction when a fire swept through the downtown area in 1901. Boyce was one of the first business owners in Williams to build with brick. (Courtesy Williams Public Library.)

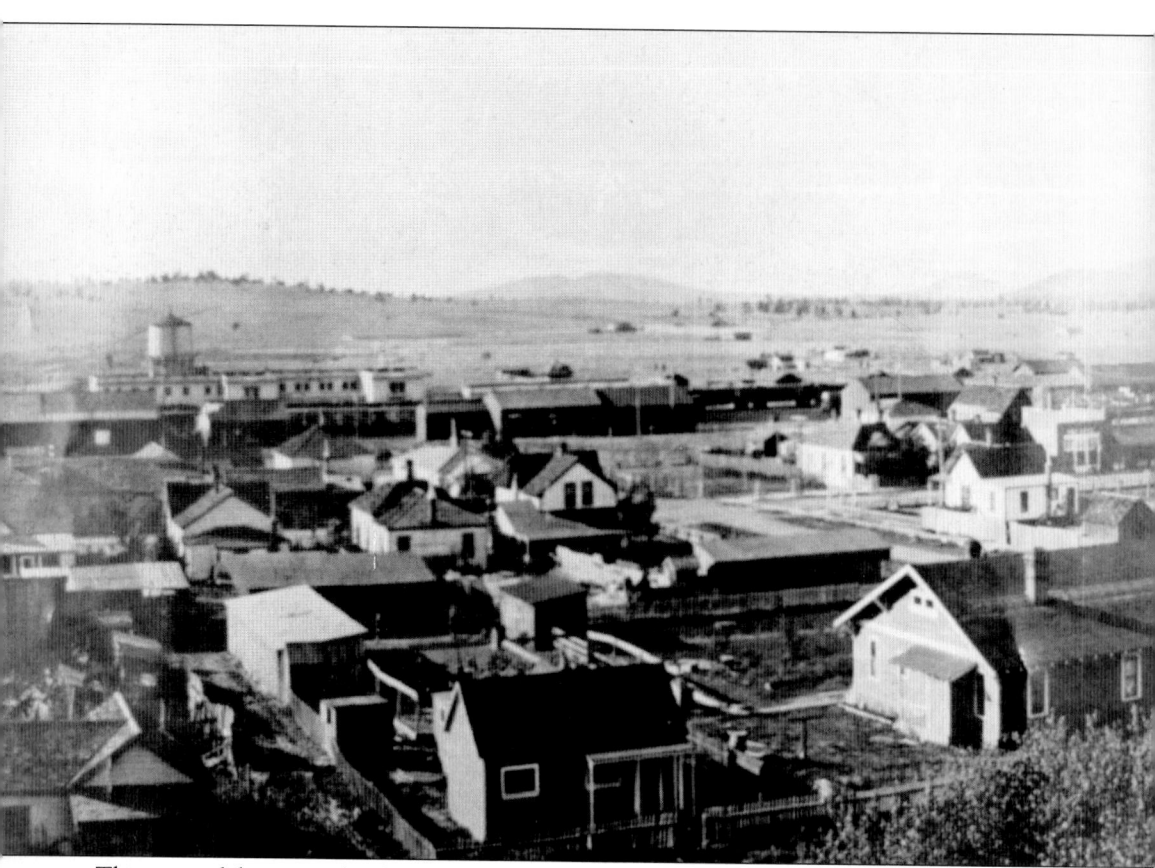

This view of the west side of Williams in 1915 shows how the town continued to thrive, despite the fact that the city still had not found a reliable source of water for residents. Water and electric utilities were taken over by the Williams Water and Electric Company in 1912, though the company

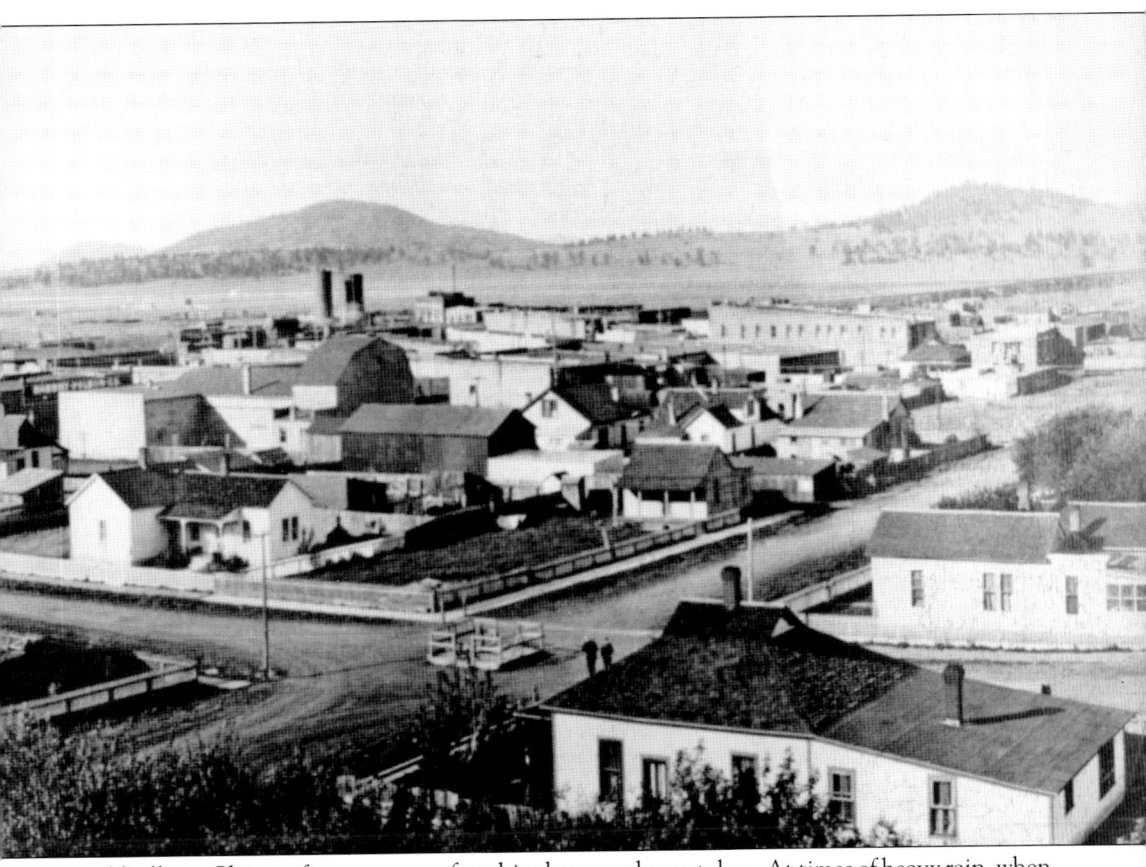

would sell to a Chicago firm one year after this photograph was taken. At times of heavy rain, when the city's reservoirs would fill to capacity, city officials often forewent the search for sustainable water, claiming Williams had enough to last for years. (Courtesy Williams Public Library.)

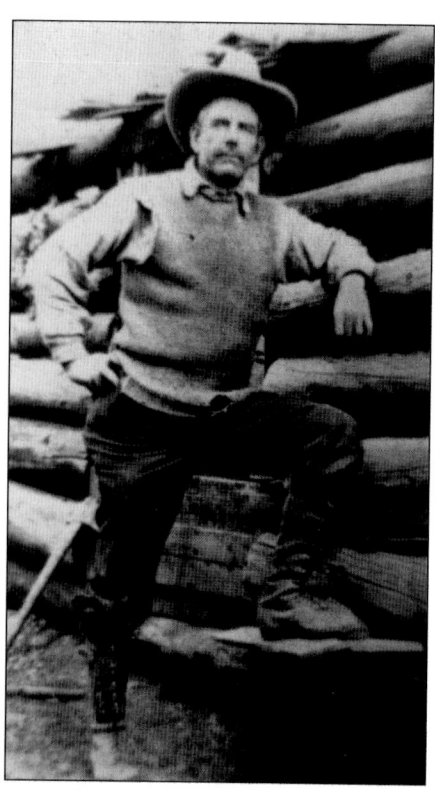

Ambrose Means (1878–1941), one of Williams's more colorful residents, spent plenty of time in Arizona. He moved to Williams in 1932 with his wife, Mirian Whiting. Besides being a tracker, guide, and roper, Means is well known as a trick rider for Buffalo Bill's Wild West Show. Means went to Africa in 1910 to lasso wild animals. He returned for a second adventure in 1913. (Courtesy Williams Public Library.)

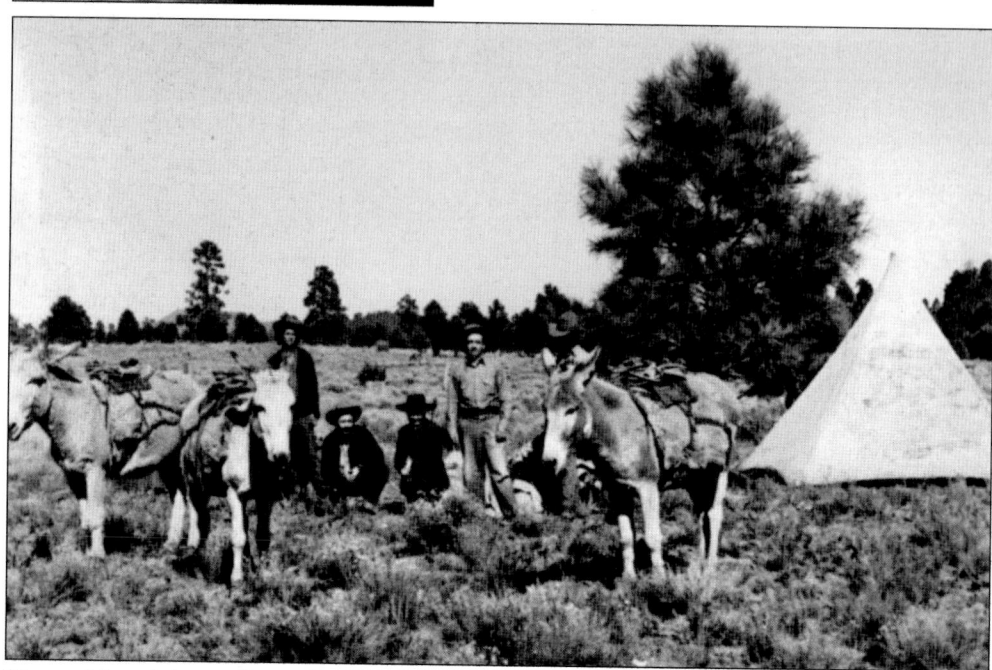

Pictured from left to right are Pierre Pouquette, Robert Pouquette, a Mrs. Francis, John Aleman, and an unidentified man at the Pouquette Ranch campsite in Williams. The Pouquette family was sheep ranchers in the Williams area, where as many as 75,000 to 80,000 head of sheep could be found in the summer months. (Courtesy Williams Public Library.)

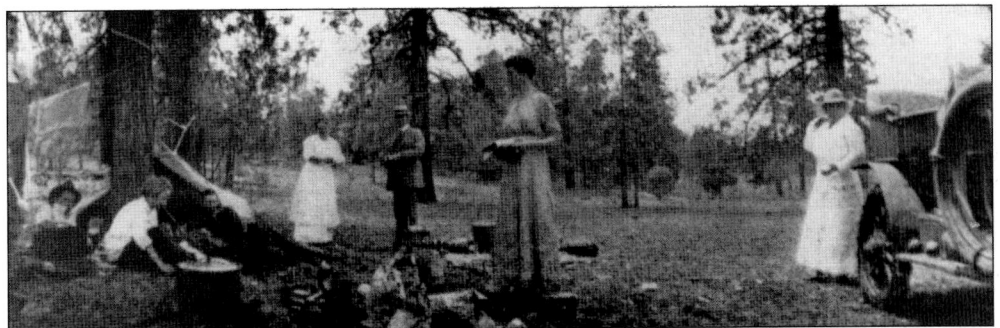

Picnickers enjoy the weather at Coleman Lake in 1916. Outdoor enthusiasts are often drawn to Williams because of its many lakes, hiking trails, and hunting opportunities, though not many dress the way they did in 1916 in preparation for an afternoon outdoors. (Courtesy Williams Public Library.)

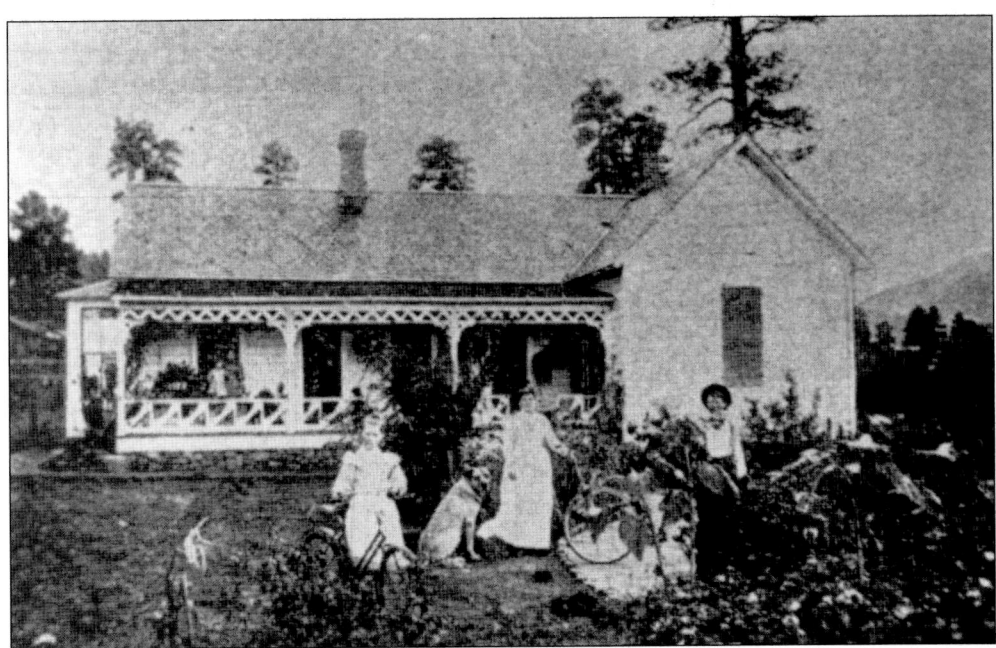

Williams's fashions mirrored that of the rest of the nation near the end of the 19th century. This photograph of Cormick Boyce's home in 1898 shows a residence and its inhabitants that would have been just as comfortable in New York City as they were in the Wild West. Cormick Boyce, besides his other endeavors, was named Williams's postmaster in 1887. (Courtesy Williams Public Library.)

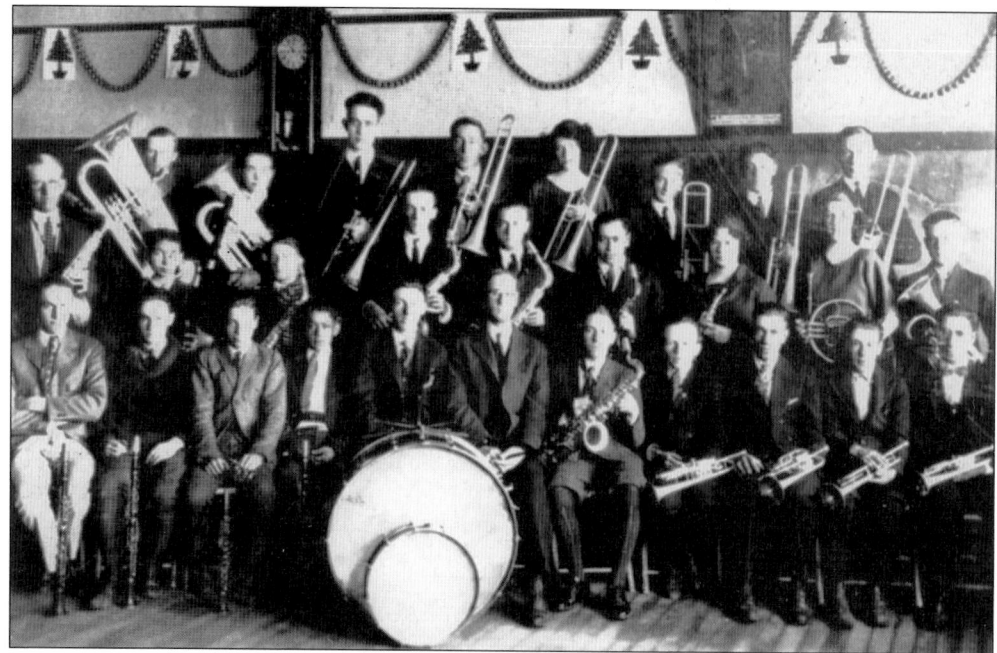

A band plays at the Williams Opera House in 1910. The first opera house in Williams was built in 1892 at the northwest corner of Grant Avenue and Second Street. Events included the Democratic Territorial Convention in 1896, prizefights, and balls. More than 650 people attended the December 1892 ball, representing cities from Albuquerque, Needles, and Flagstaff. (Courtesy Williams Public Library.)

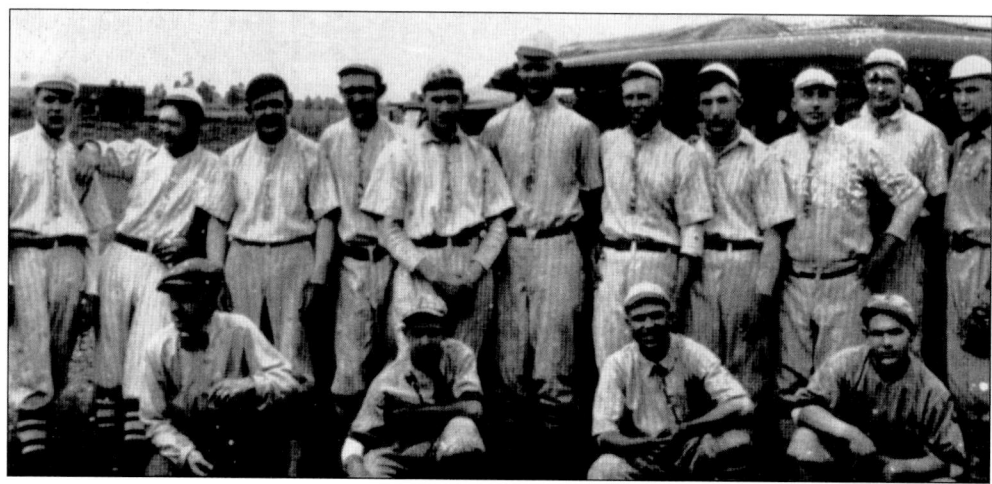

Williams High School baseball players, including Williams resident R. C. Sullivant (pictured far left), pose for this 1919 photograph. A high school in Williams was accredited by the state university in 1916. By 1920, school officials began construction of a new wing to accommodate the growing number of high school students in the city. (Courtesy Williams Public Library.)

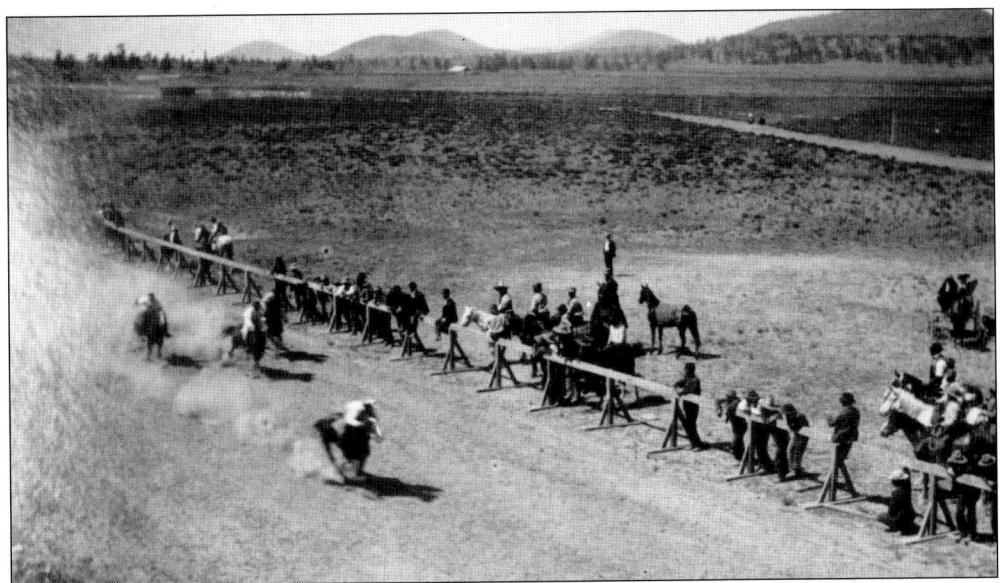

Horse racing in Williams became quite popular in the early 1900s. A number of jockeys push their horses toward the finish line as race enthusiasts cheer them on in this 1909 photograph. Williams residents were fond of sporting events in the community. A number of challenges, including horse and foot races, were typically planned each year during the community's annual Fourth of July celebrations. (Courtesy Williams Public Library.)

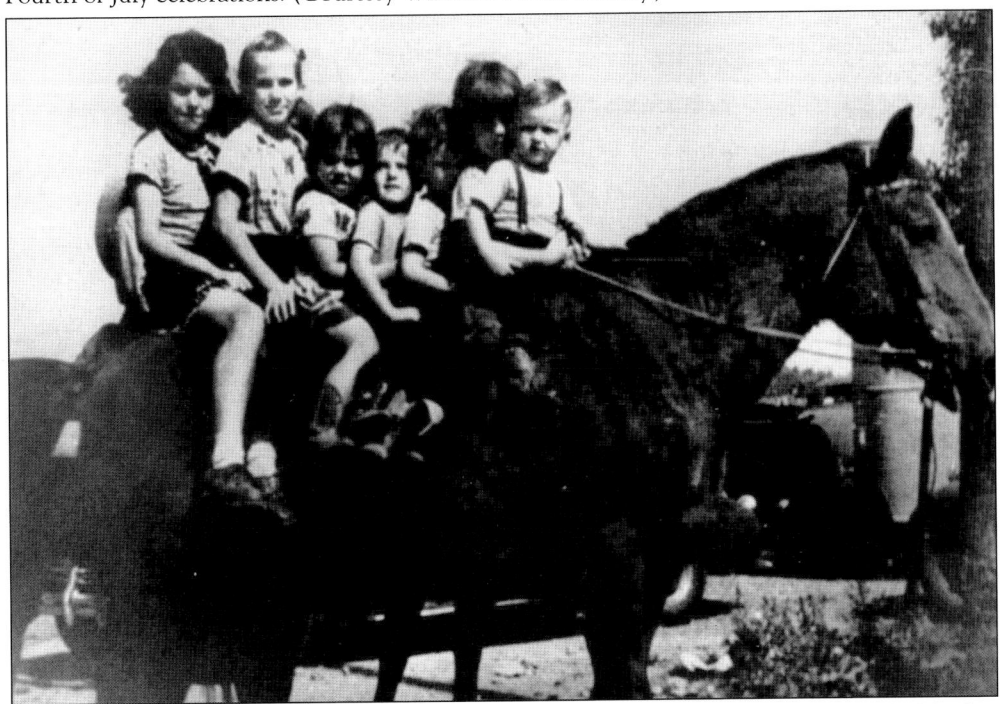

Besides the annual Fourth of July parade in downtown Williams, city residents also held other parades to honor various holidays in the community. Pictured here are Cody Means, Harriet Means, Tommy Payne, Tommy Bowden Jr., Opal Means, Jerry Payne, and other horseback riders as they prepare for the annual Labor Day parade. (Courtesy Williams Public Library.)

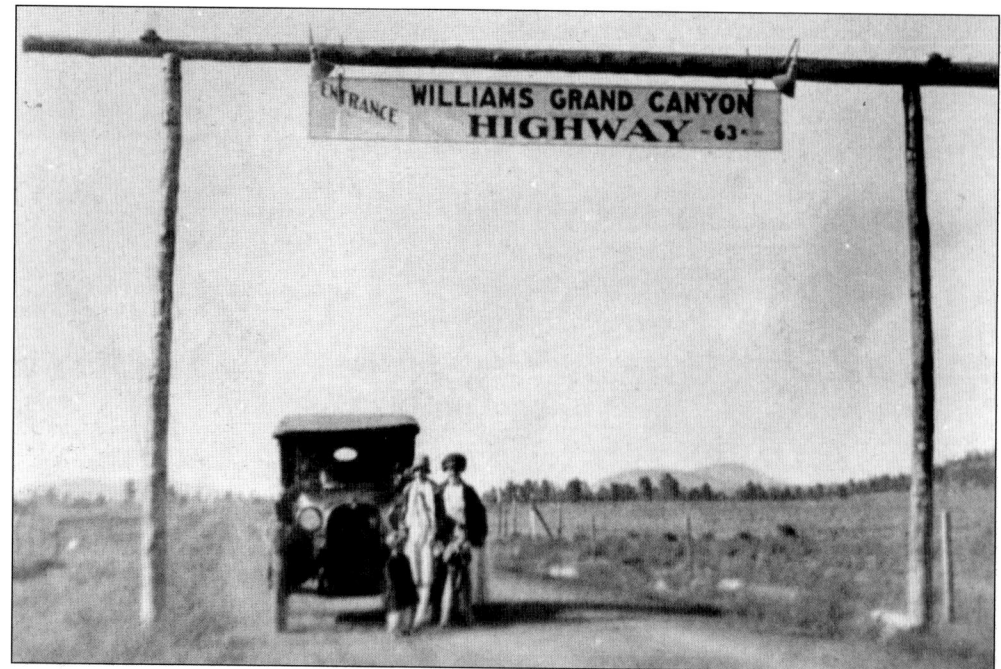

The old highway from Williams to the Grand Canyon became a well-traveled road by 1926, where it was estimated that the number of automobile travelers to the canyon matched that of railroad travelers. By the next year, automobile travelers surpassed rail travelers for the first time. The first automobile in Williams, meanwhile, was purchased in 1904. (Courtesy *Williams–Grand Canyon News*.)

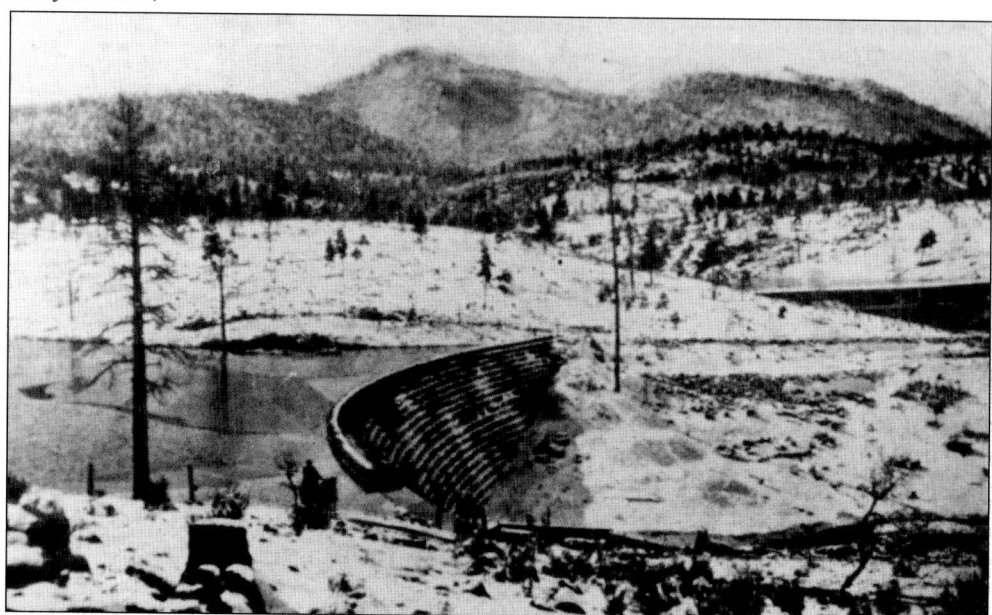

The Railroad and Saginaw Dam was one of many dams erected near the beginning of the 20th century in an effort to secure a sustainable water source for the Williams area. Water from the Railroad Dam was used primarily by the railroad, though it also provided an additional source for Williams residents, who were charged for the privilege. (Courtesy Williams Public Library.)

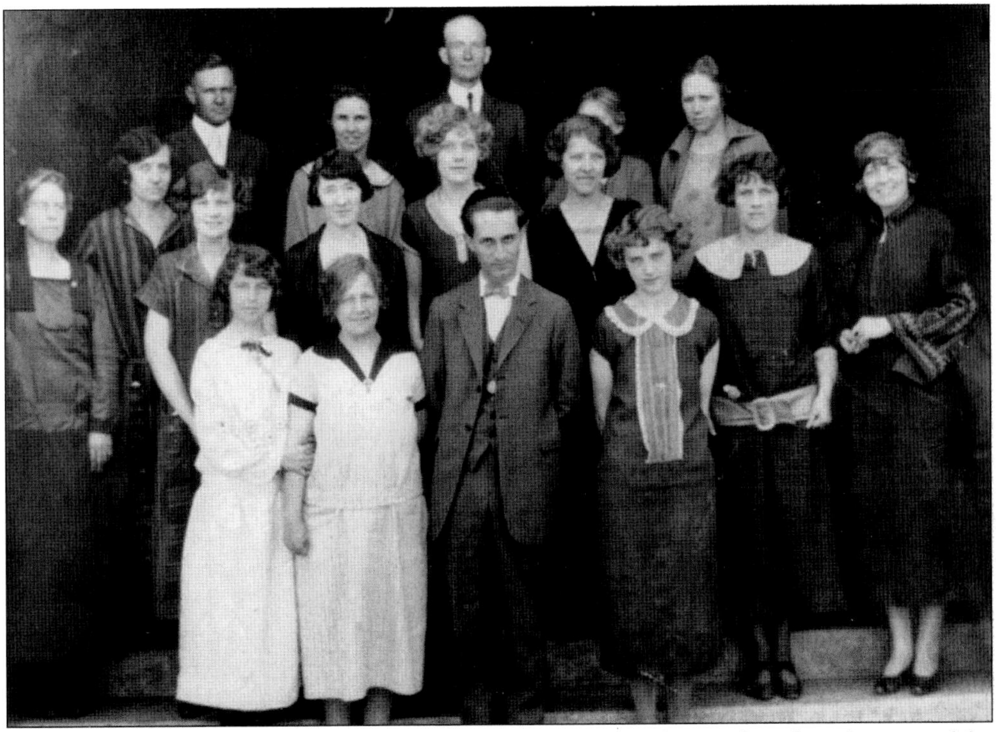

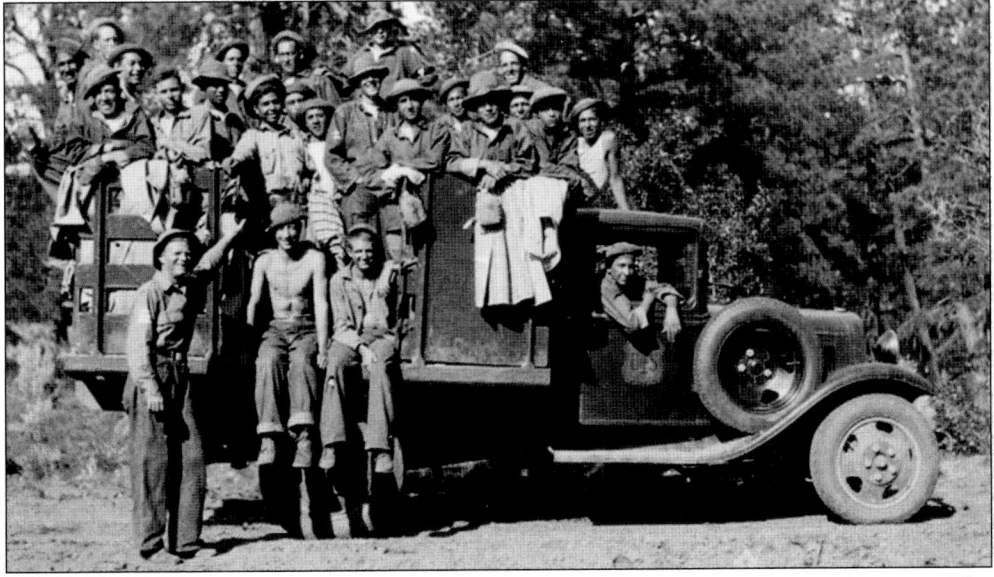

This 1920s photograph shows a number of Williams school teachers gathered on the steps of the new school, which was rebuilt after a fire in 1912. Enrollment in the school continued increasing steadily from 1915 to 1920. Construction of a separate school for high school students began in 1925. (Courtesy Williams Public Library.)

The Civilian Conservation Corps works in the Kaibab National Forest area in the 1940s. The corps was established in 1933 by Pres. Franklin D. Roosevelt as a work relief program for young men in Depression-era families. (Courtesy U.S. Forest Service, Southwestern Region, Kaibab National Forest.)

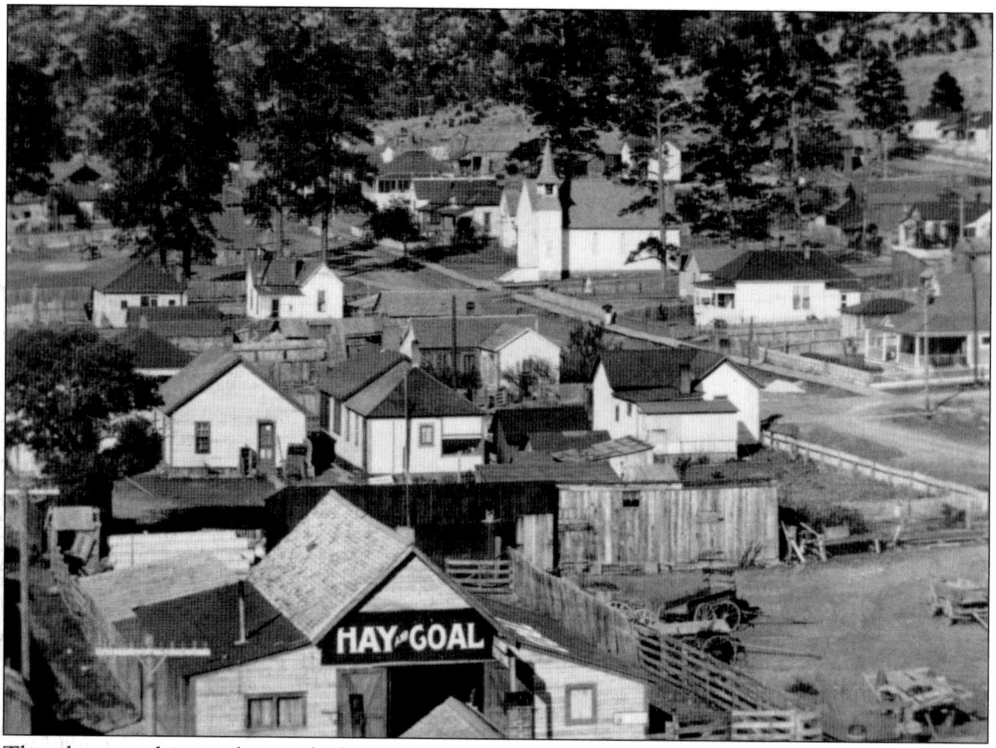

This photograph was taken at the height of the summer in 1915. Besides the city's popular Fourth of July activities each year, Williams's citizens also began to make a big deal out of the other holidays around this period. The citizens enjoyed their first community Christmas tree in 1914, donated by the U.S. Forest Service and lumber mill employees. (Courtesy Williams Public Library.)

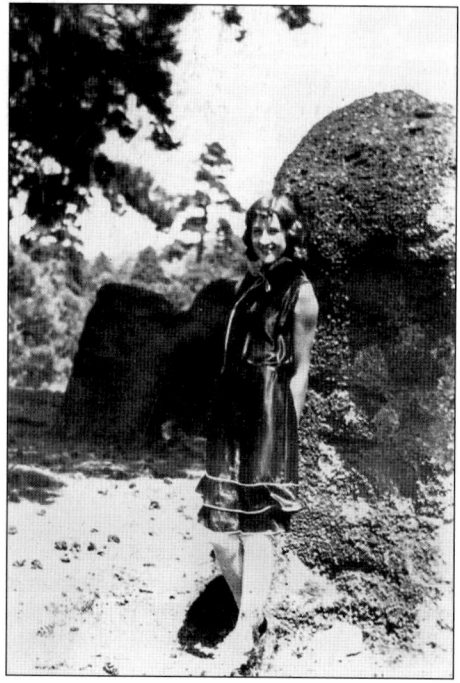

Local Williams resident Helen Roundsville takes in a little sun at Elephant Rocks in this late-1920s photograph. Named for their uncanny resemblance to elephants, Elephant Rocks became a popular attraction for residents and visitors to the area when a golf course was built on the site. The Williams Country Club, located at the nine-hole golf course, was built in 1932. (Courtesy Williams Public Library.)

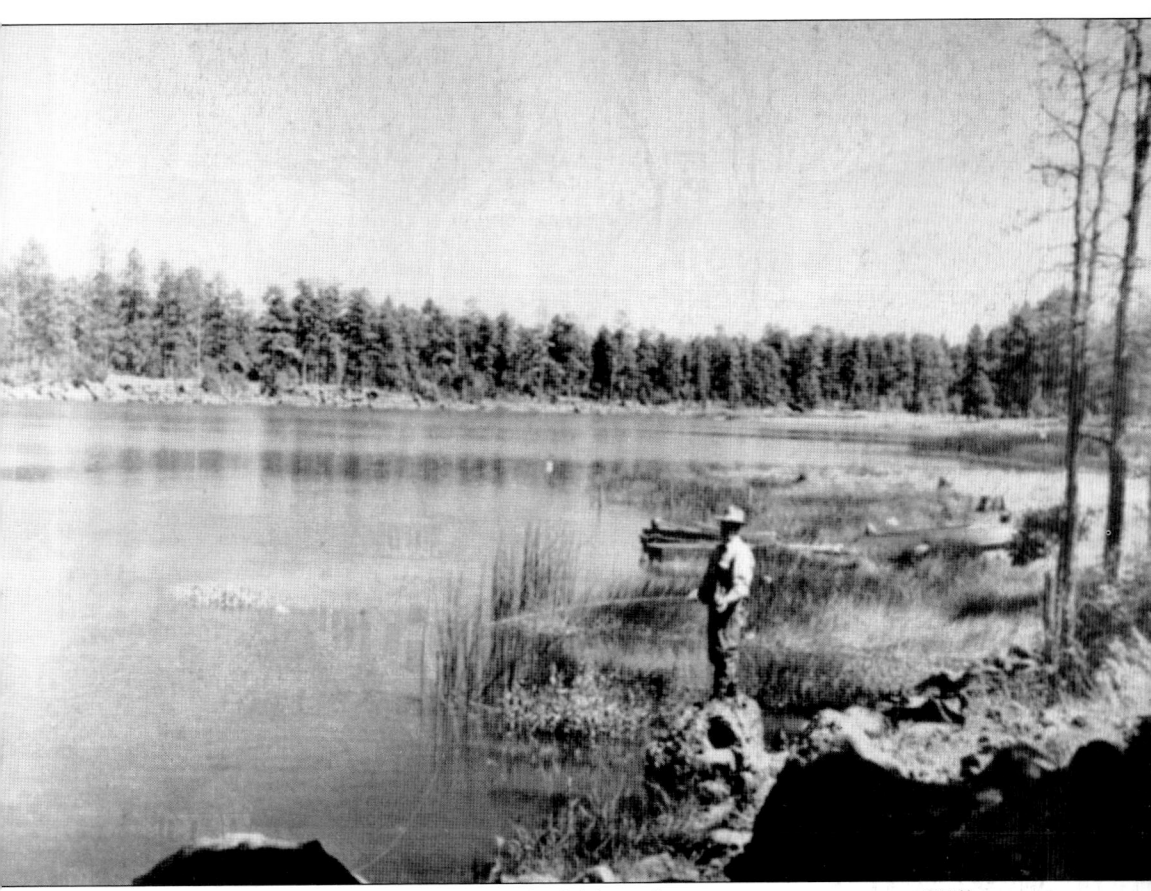

During the 1940s and 1950s, city officials worked diligently to promote visitation to Williams in the hopes that its many outdoor recreational activities would appeal to people traveling through the area. Local Ross Dykes does a little fishing at White Horse Lake in this 1950s photograph, one of the many areas that city officials hoped would help draw visitors to the area. (Courtesy Williams Public Library.)

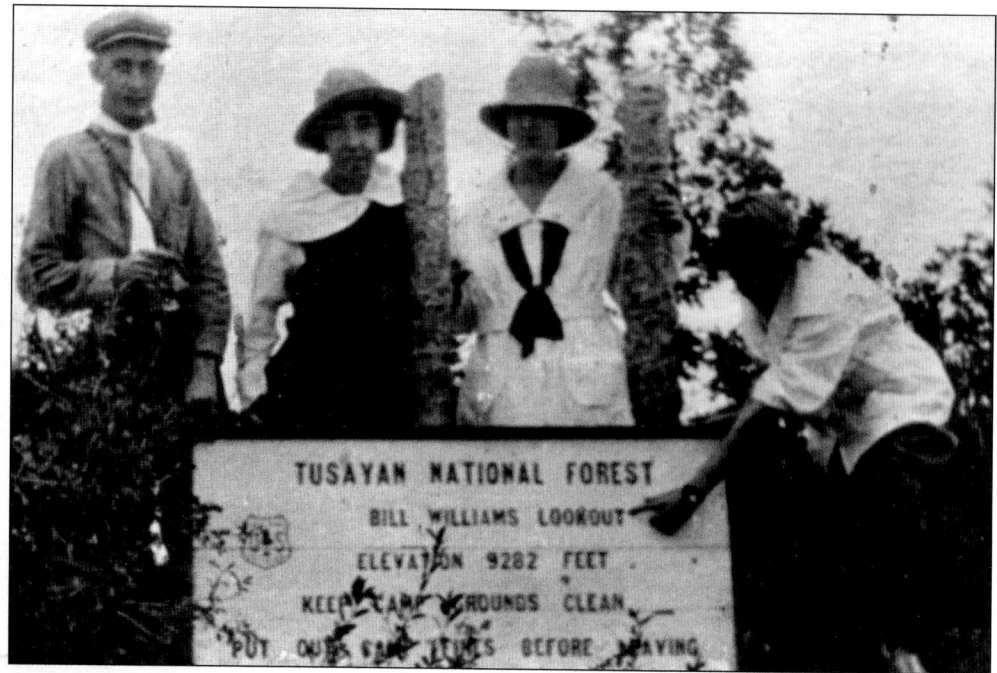

A group pauses for a photograph while visiting the top of Bill Williams Mountain. The Bill Williams Lookout was situated in part of the Tusayan National Forest in the early 1900s, though the area was designated as part of the Kaibab National Forest in later years. (Courtesy Williams Public Library.)

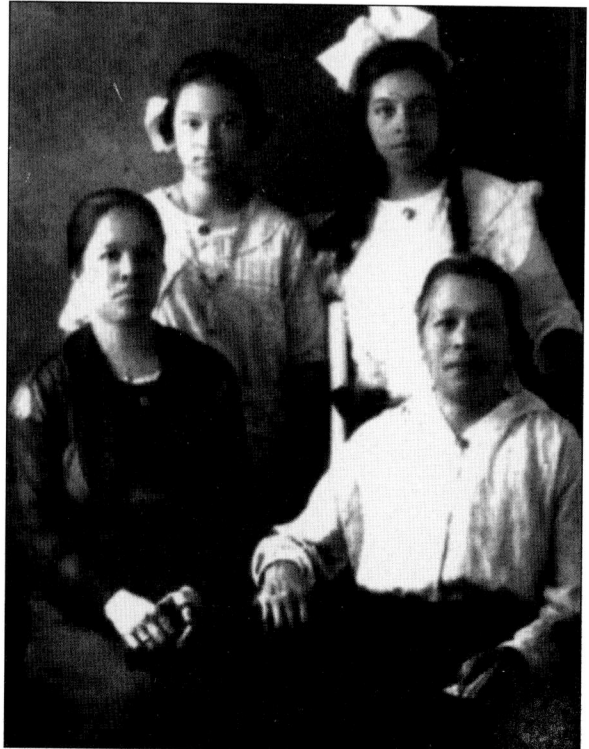

The Cardenas family, pictured here in the early 1900s, helped stimulate tourism in the Williams area when Lucy Cardenas, a graduate of Williams High School, married Sal Balderas. The Balderas family owned and operated a motel in the Williams area that they built cabin by cabin and owned a service station. (Courtesy author Frank Barrios and the Balderas family.)

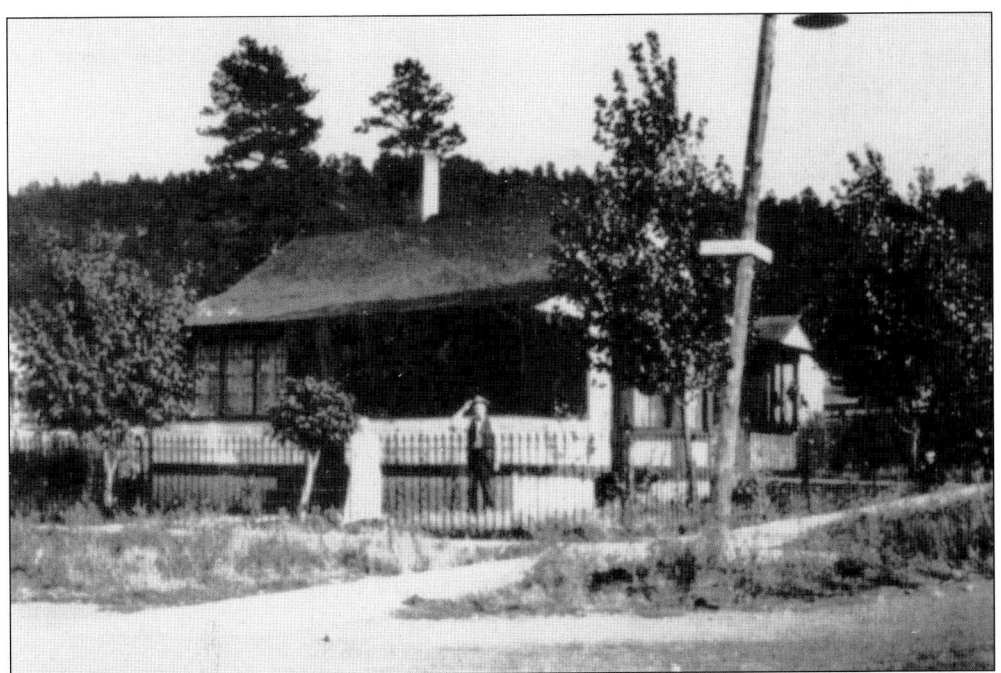

Williams resident Tom Lockett and his wife, Anna, stand in front of their house in 1930. Lockett, who served in the Civil War, lived at the corner of Second and Grant Streets. (Courtesy Williams Public Library.)

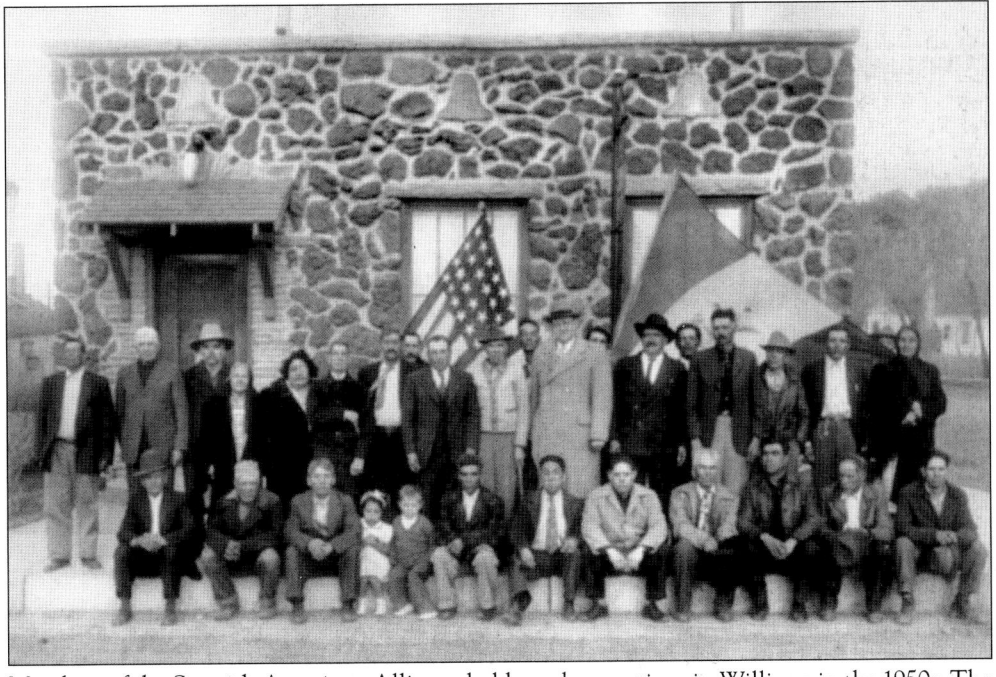

Members of the Spanish American Alliance held regular meetings in Williams in the 1950s. The group was quite influential and represented the Spanish population of Williams for a number of years. They held regular meetings from their business, which was located one block north of Bill Williams Avenue on Third Street. (Courtesy George Garcia.)

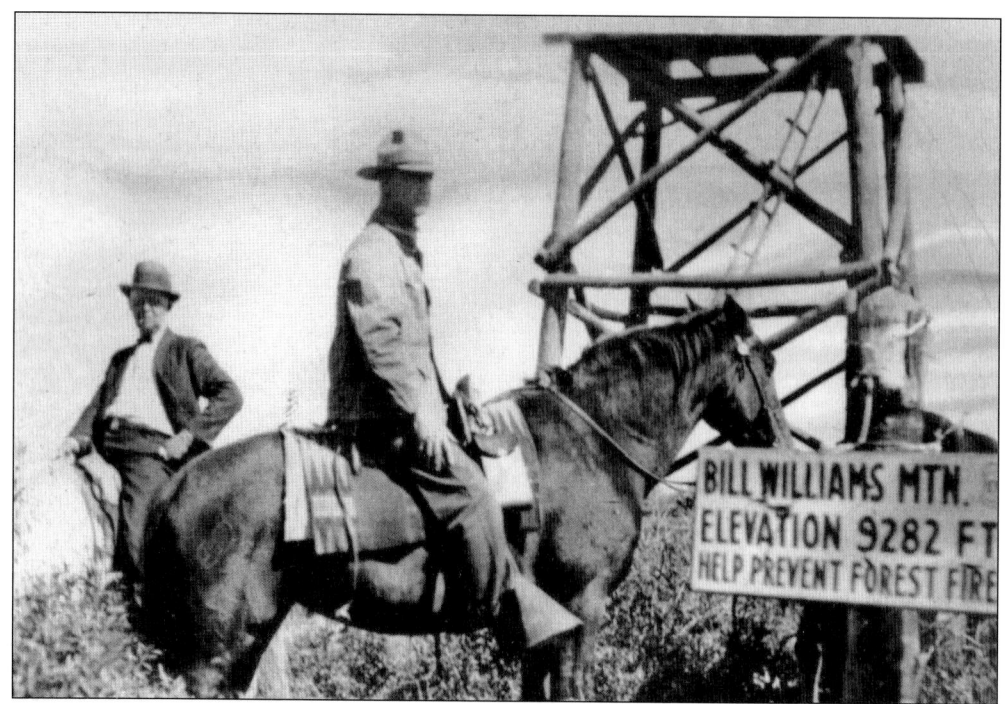

Two men travel the wilds of Bill Williams Mountain on horseback in this photograph, which also provides information on the height of the mountain itself, measured at 9,282 feet. The city of Williams can be found roughly 2,500 feet below the peak of Bill Williams Mountain. (Courtesy Williams Public Library.)

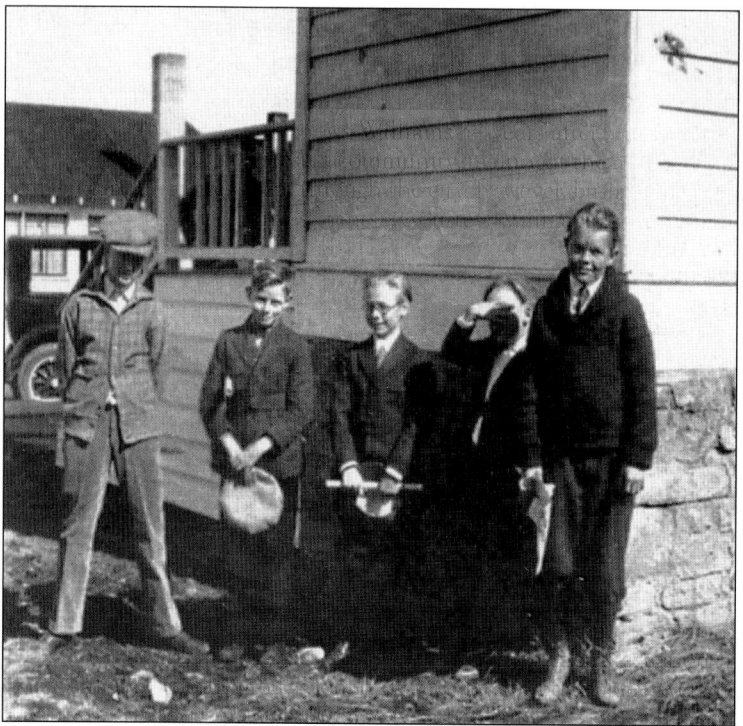

Five well-dressed young men stand outside the Williams Methodist Church at the corner of Second Street and Sherman Avenue in the 1920s. The church is commonly thought to be one of the oldest churches in the community, if not the oldest. Services are still held in the building to this day. (Courtesy Williams Public Library.)

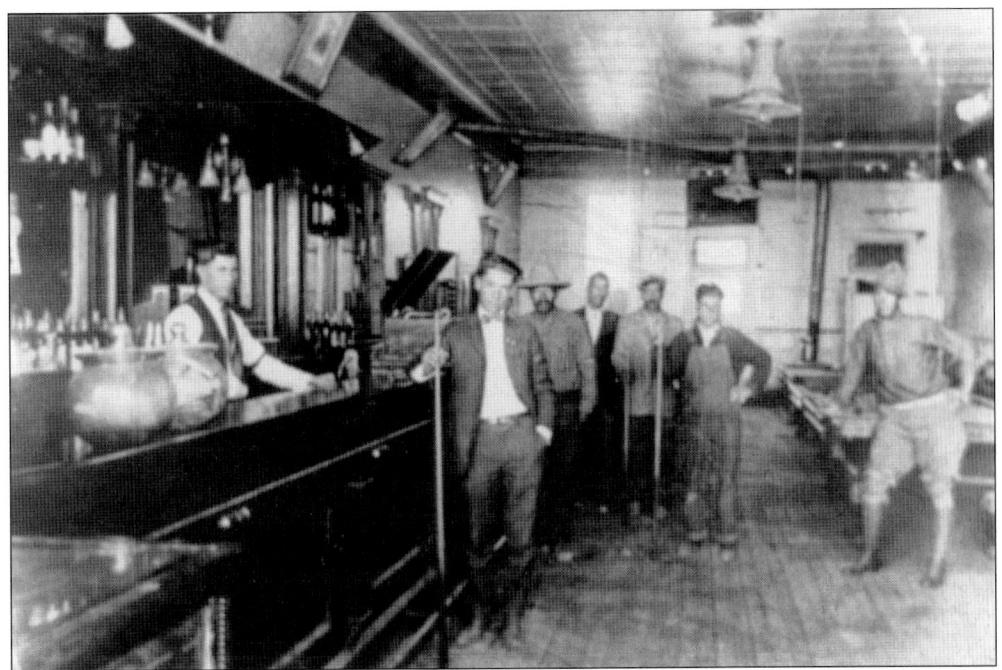

Customers of the Sultana Bar enjoy a little relaxation in 1921 thanks to bartender Frank Ornelas (far left), in this photograph taken by Felice Burghardt. The Sultana Bar is considered to be the oldest still-operating business in Williams. Ornelas also proved to be a sturdy soul; he lived to the ripe old age of 101. (Courtesy Williams Public Library.)

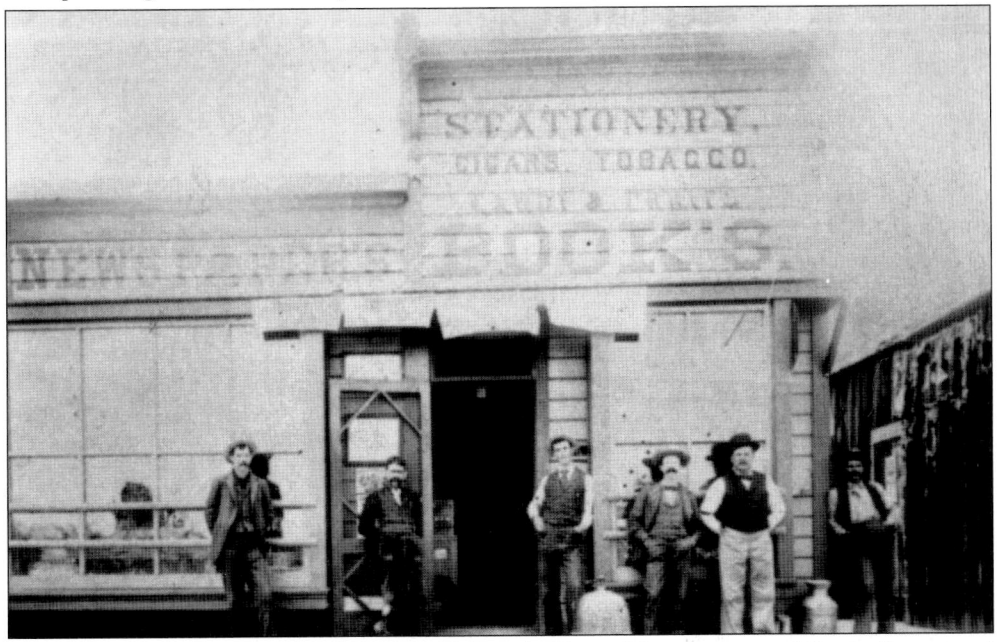

Patrons of Joe's Stationary, Cigars, Tobacco, Candy, Fruits, Newspapers, and Books Store stand outside the Williams business in this photograph, taken in the early 1900s. While tobacco and candy do not really mix in today's world, there seemed to be little distinction between the two when it came to business owners in the Wild West. (Courtesy Williams Public Library.)

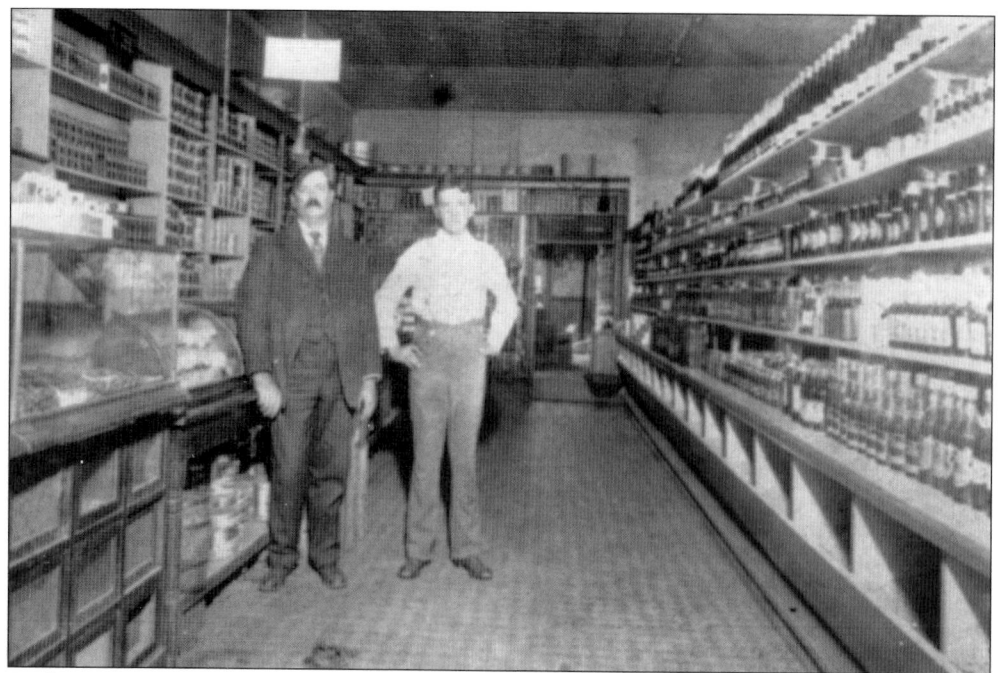

With a variety of customers from railroad workers, sawmill employees, ranch hands, and Chinese immigrants, all the way to Grand Canyon tourists, the need for supplies and goods was constant in Williams. Many businesses, such as the M. J. Kennedy General Store, pictured here in 1910, were readily available to fill that need. (Courtesy Williams Public Library.)

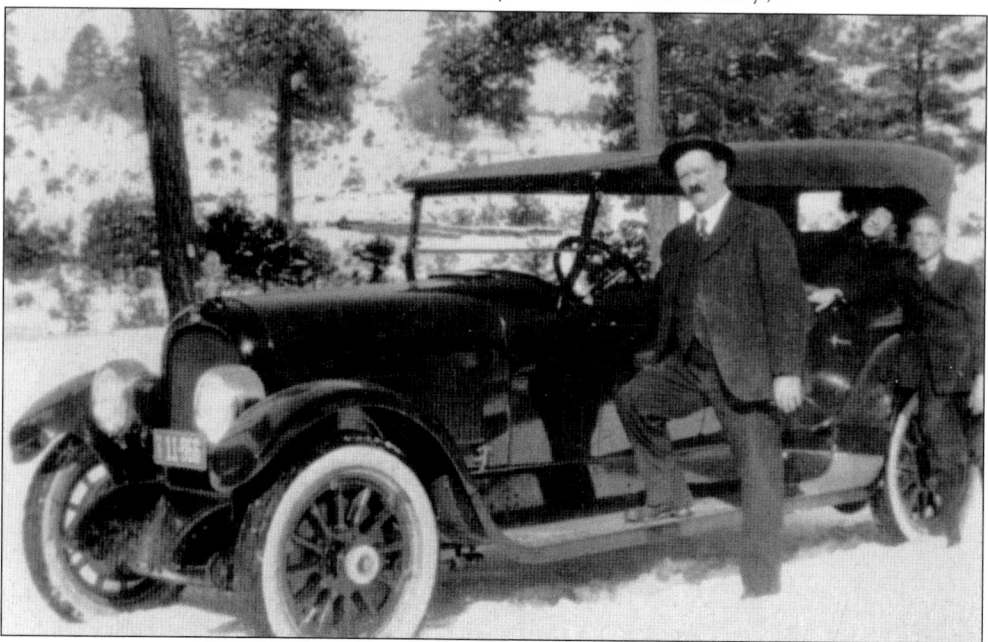

While business in Williams had its ups and downs, it proved substantial enough for M. J. Kennedy, seen in 1924 as he poses next to his new automobile. Kennedy undoubtedly saw his business increase in the 1920s, when the population of Williams grew by 60 percent between 1920 and 1930. (Courtesy Williams Public Library.)

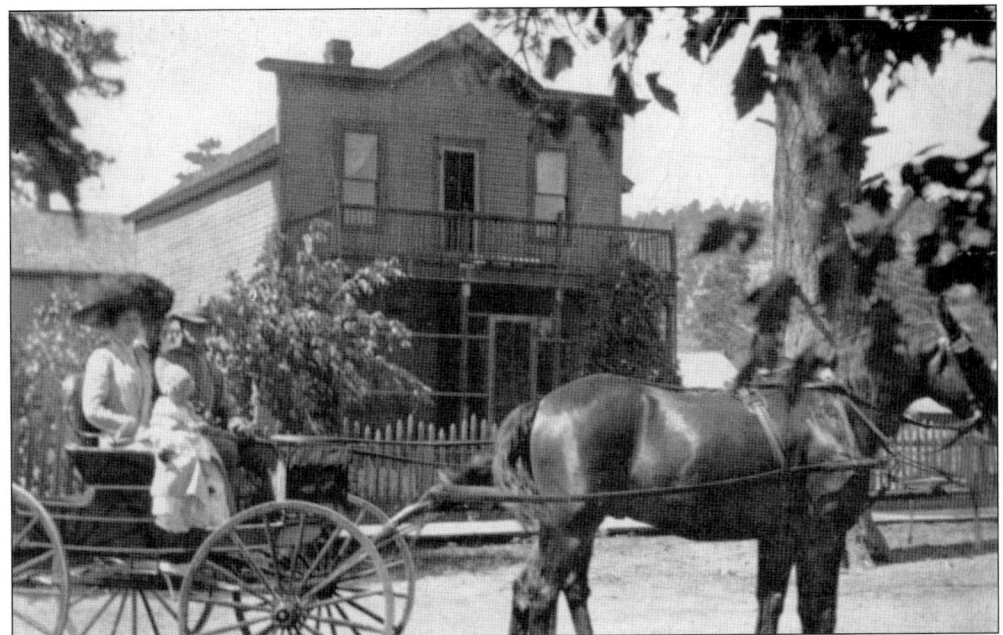

From left to right, Williams residents Root, Emma, and Nancy Miller pull up to the corner of Fifth Street and Sherman Avenue in 1909. While the city seemed serene, problems with prostitution and opium smokers persisted in the community, leading to the creation of a police court and police judge. (Courtesy Williams Public Library.)

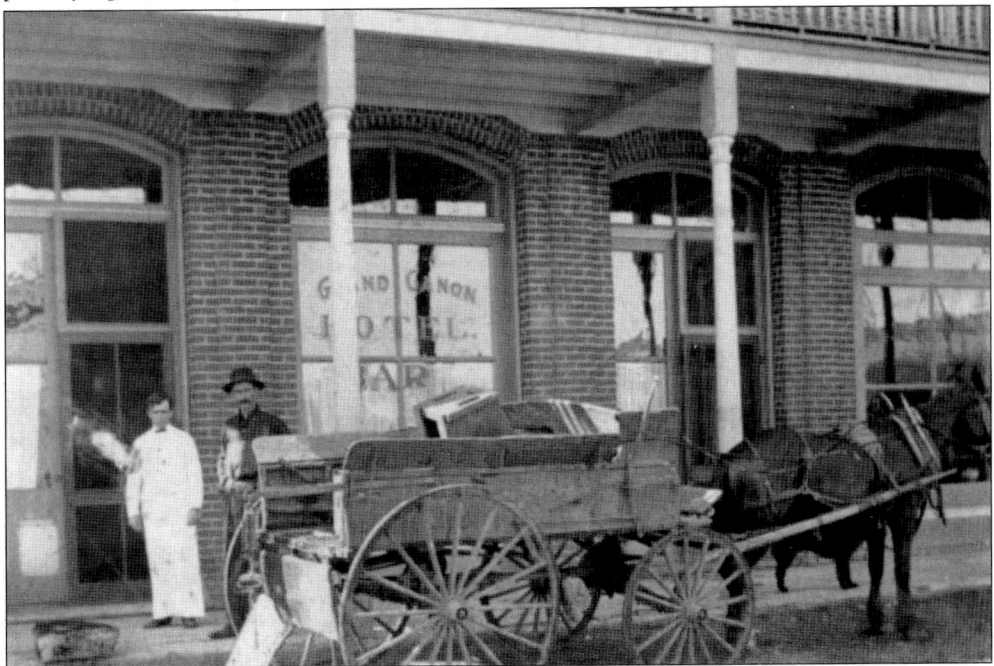

Jake Otter delivers a coveted load of ice to the Grand Canyon Hotel in this photograph, taken around 1909. Water, fire, and criminals remained problems for the city's inhabitants at the time. On a more positive note, the city was reported to have had some of the best wooden sidewalks in the territory. (Courtesy Williams Public Library.)

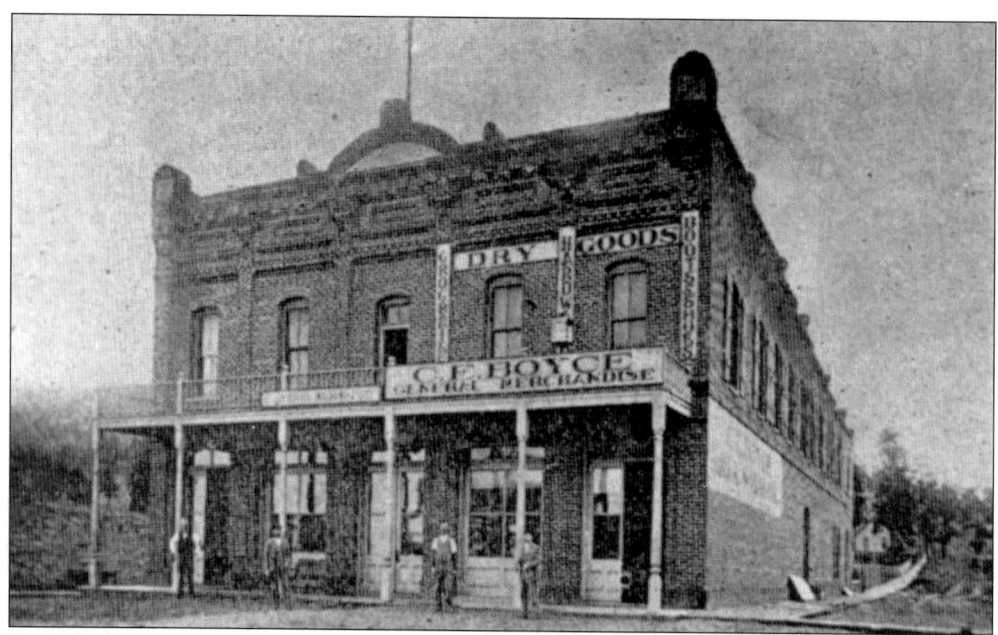

Prior to owning the Grand Canyon Hotel, shown here in 1898, Cormick Boyce was involved in a number of early Williams enterprises. His first unofficial business began while fixing his wagon while passing through the city. Boyce is said to have set up a tent in order to sell his goods to a needy population. (Courtesy Williams Public Library.)

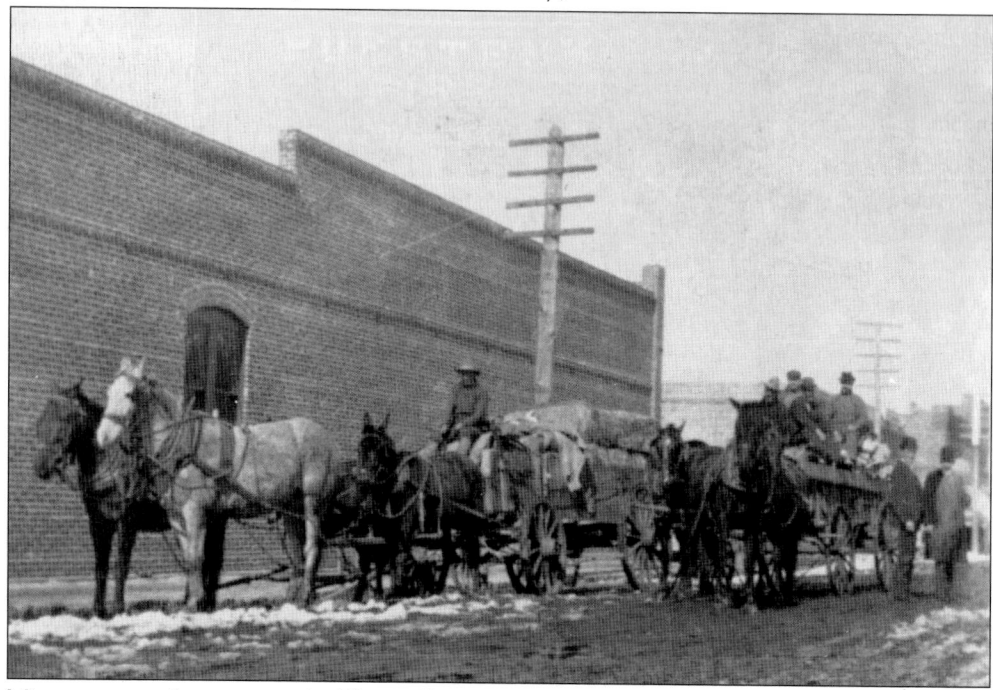

Miners prepare for a trip to the Plattaville Mines after loading their wagons full of supplies in Williams. The Plattaville Mines were located roughly 100 miles northwest of Williams. While speculation was plentiful in the Williams area when it came to mining, the idea rarely paid off for prospectors. (Courtesy Williams Public Library.)

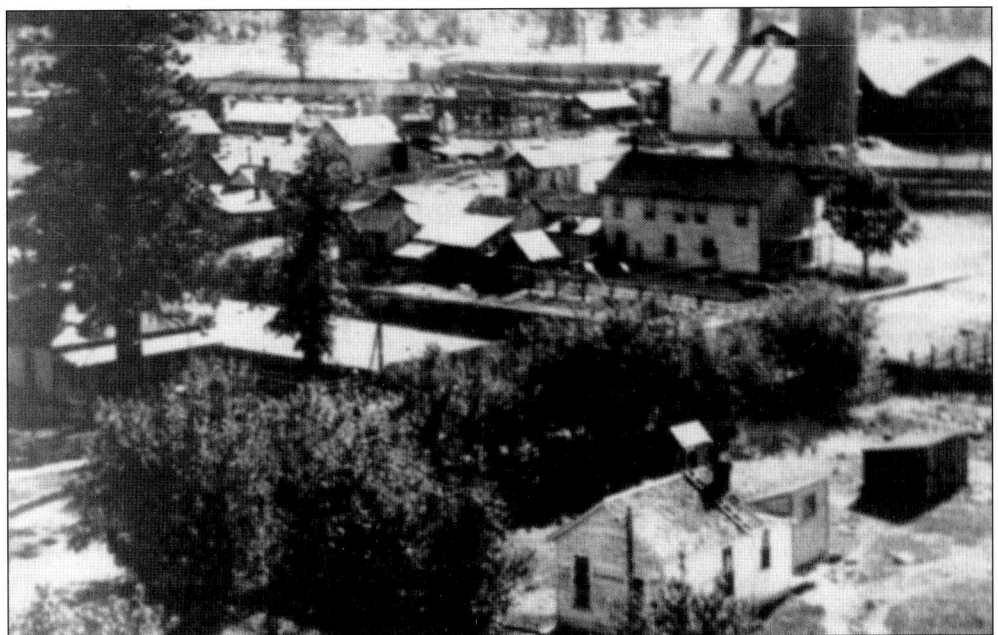

The Williams sawmill, shown in 1907, helped develop the principle industry in Williams during its formative years. The Saginaw mill, built in conjunction with a mill in nearby Chalender, cost the owners more than $100,000 to erect, which included a number of residences as well as buildings. (Courtesy Williams Public Library.)

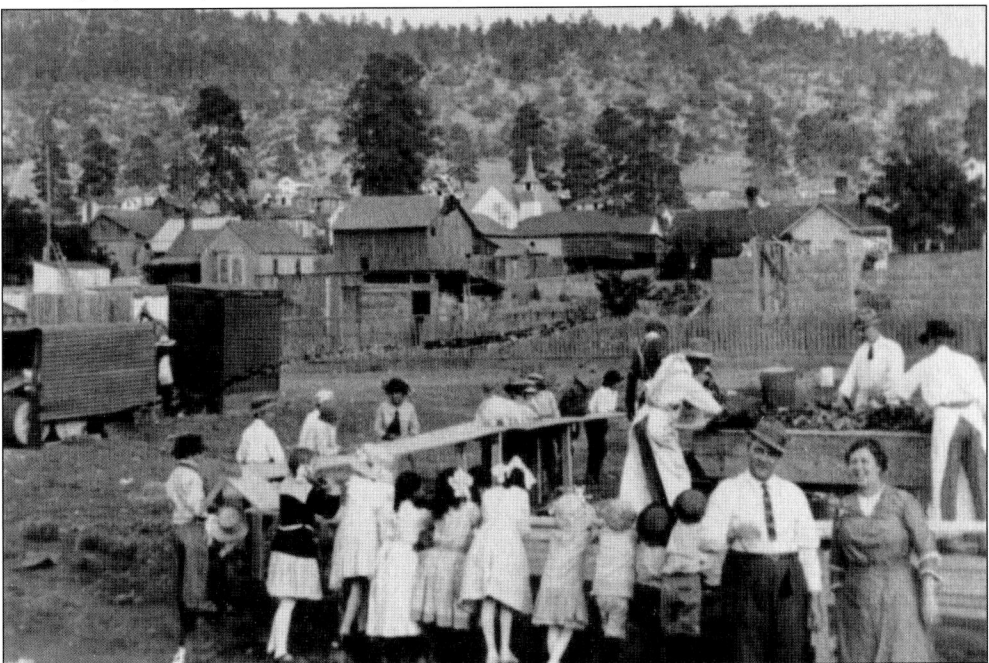

A large public celebration was held in Williams in 1913 to honor the nation's Independence Day. A large number of residents have turned out for a community barbecue in this photograph. Longtime Williams residents Chas Wade (right) and Claude Polson (left) can be seen cutting meat for the feast. (Courtesy Williams Public Library.)

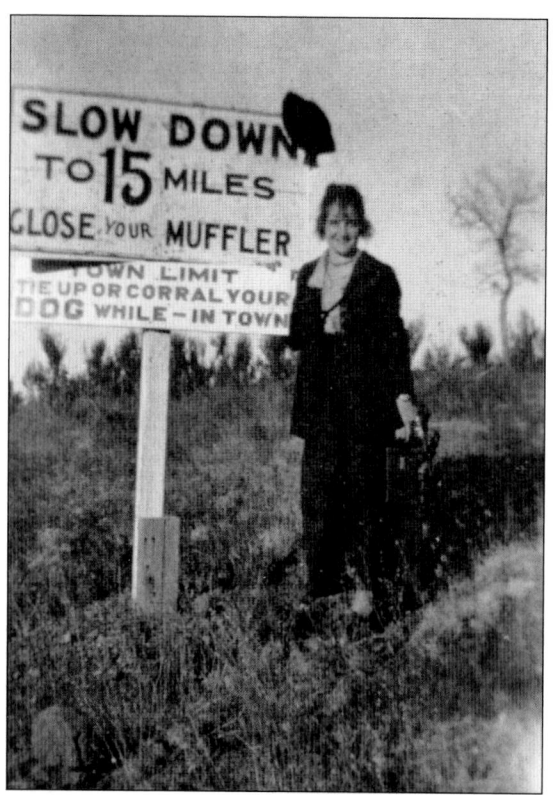

Nineteen-year-old Mildred Smith smiles for the camera as she poses by a Williams city limit sign in 1921. Street signs began to appear in Williams during this time, signifying the importance, as well as the popularity, of automobiles in the Williams community. (Courtesy Williams Public Library.)

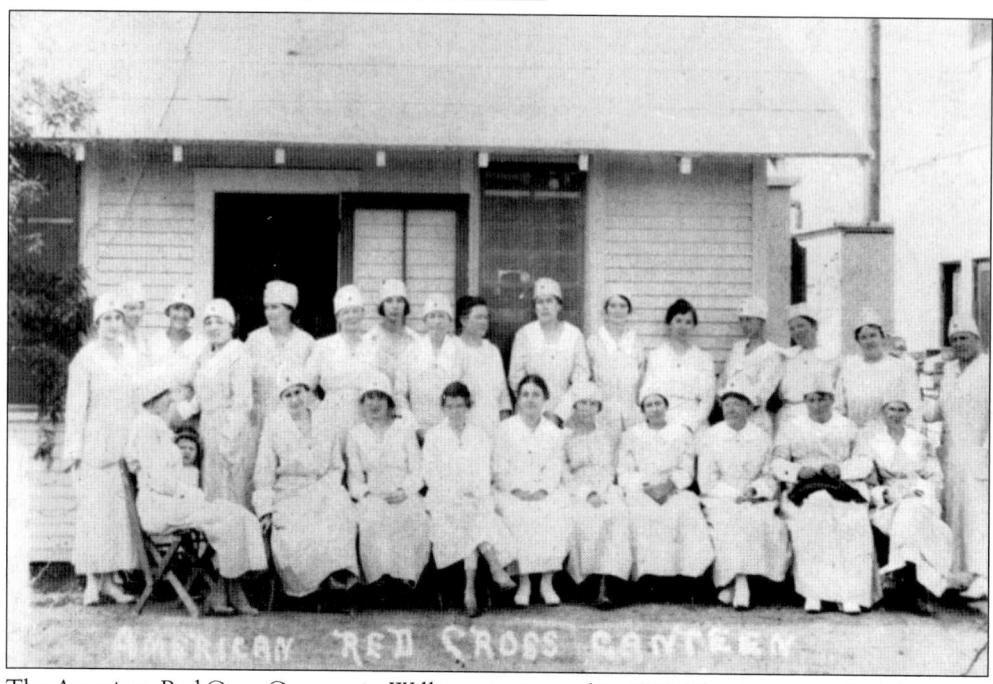

The American Red Cross Canteen in Williams is pictured in 1918. The American Red Cross was established in 1881 by Clara Barton, who was also the first president of the Washington, D.C., based organization. (Courtesy Williams Public Library.)

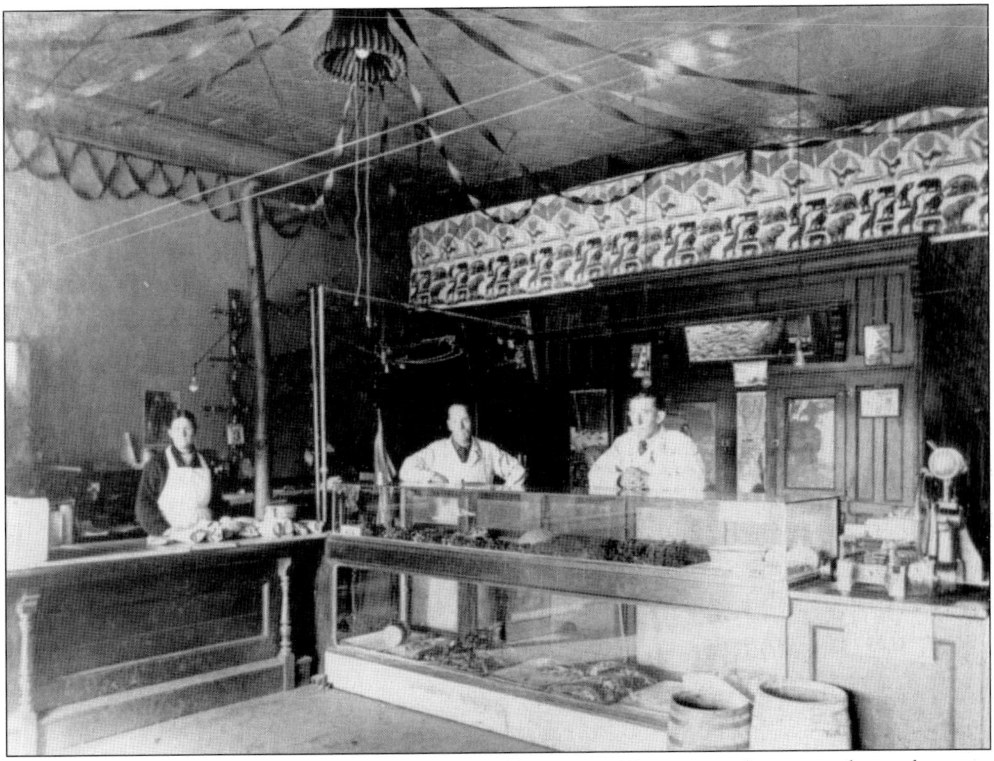

This photograph shows three employees of the Babbitt store. This particular image shows the meat department in the store, which was located in downtown Williams. Many of the businesses in the city would undergo numerous changes in ownership. The Babbitt brothers, however, remained a fixture in Williams for many years. (Courtesy Williams Public Library.)

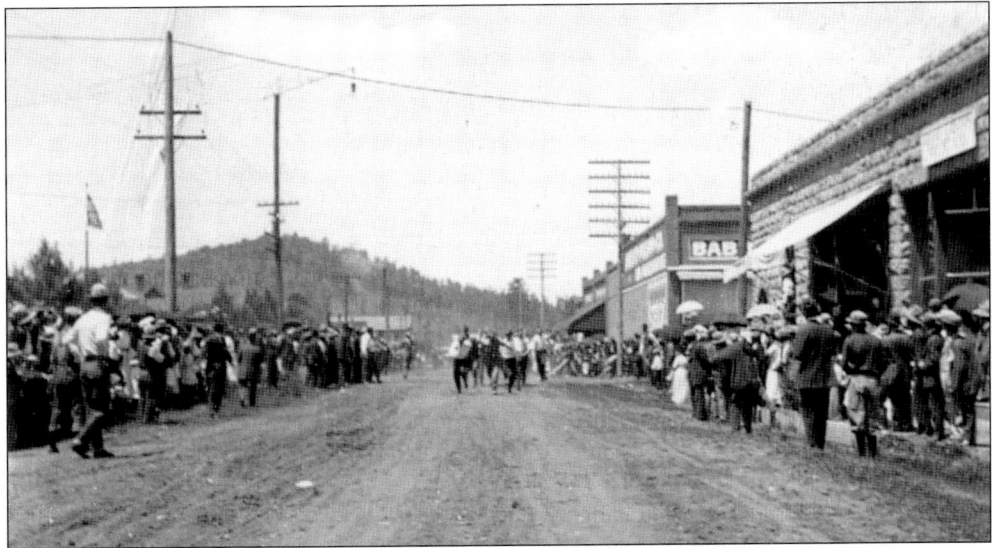

The Babbitt brothers' store is visible in this photograph, taken in the early 1900s, which shows the level of excitement Williams residents afforded to their cherished parades. In this photograph, a number of individuals charge down Bill Williams Avenue, then composed of dirt, while a large crowd cheers them. (Courtesy Williams Public Library.)

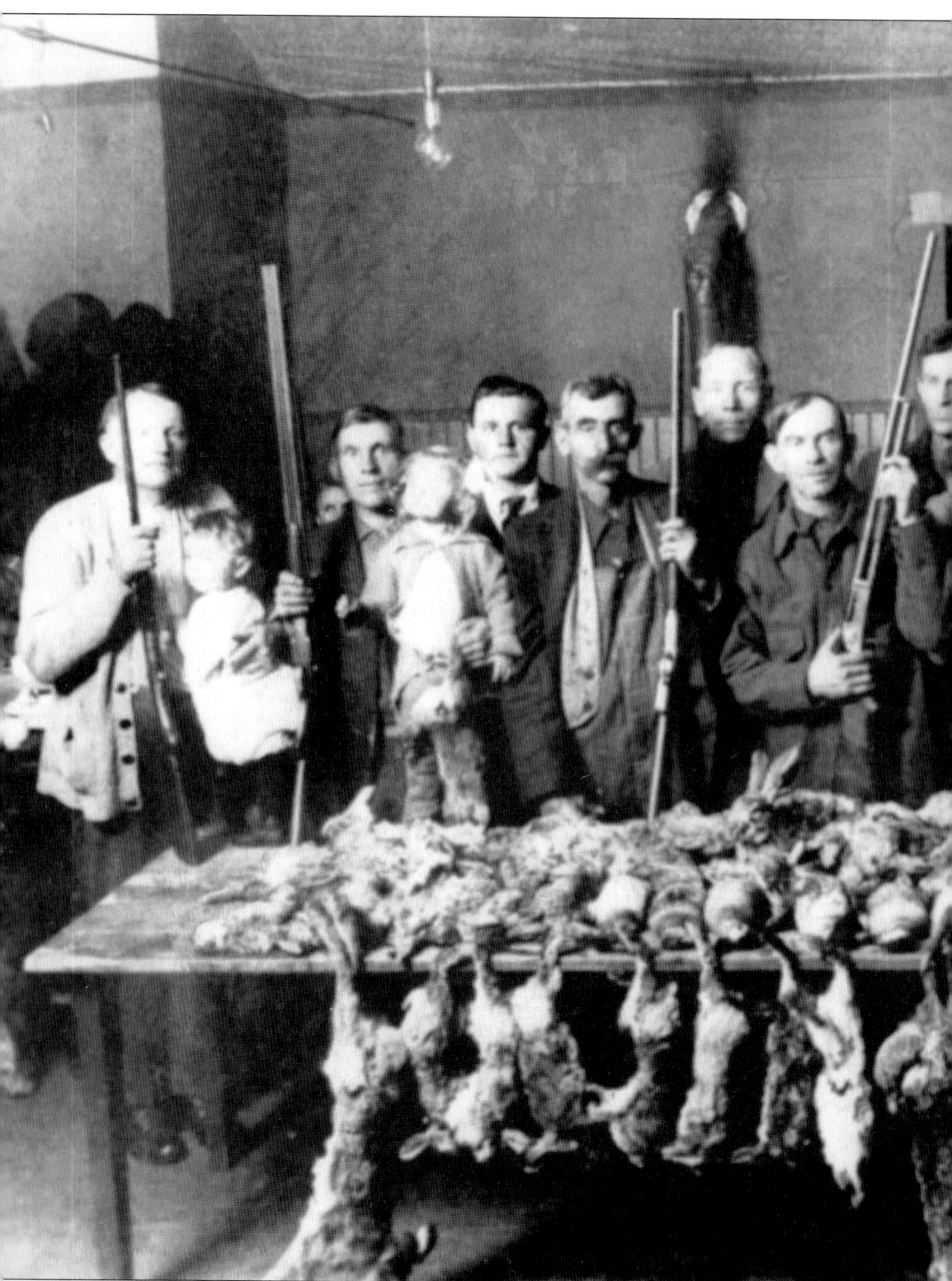

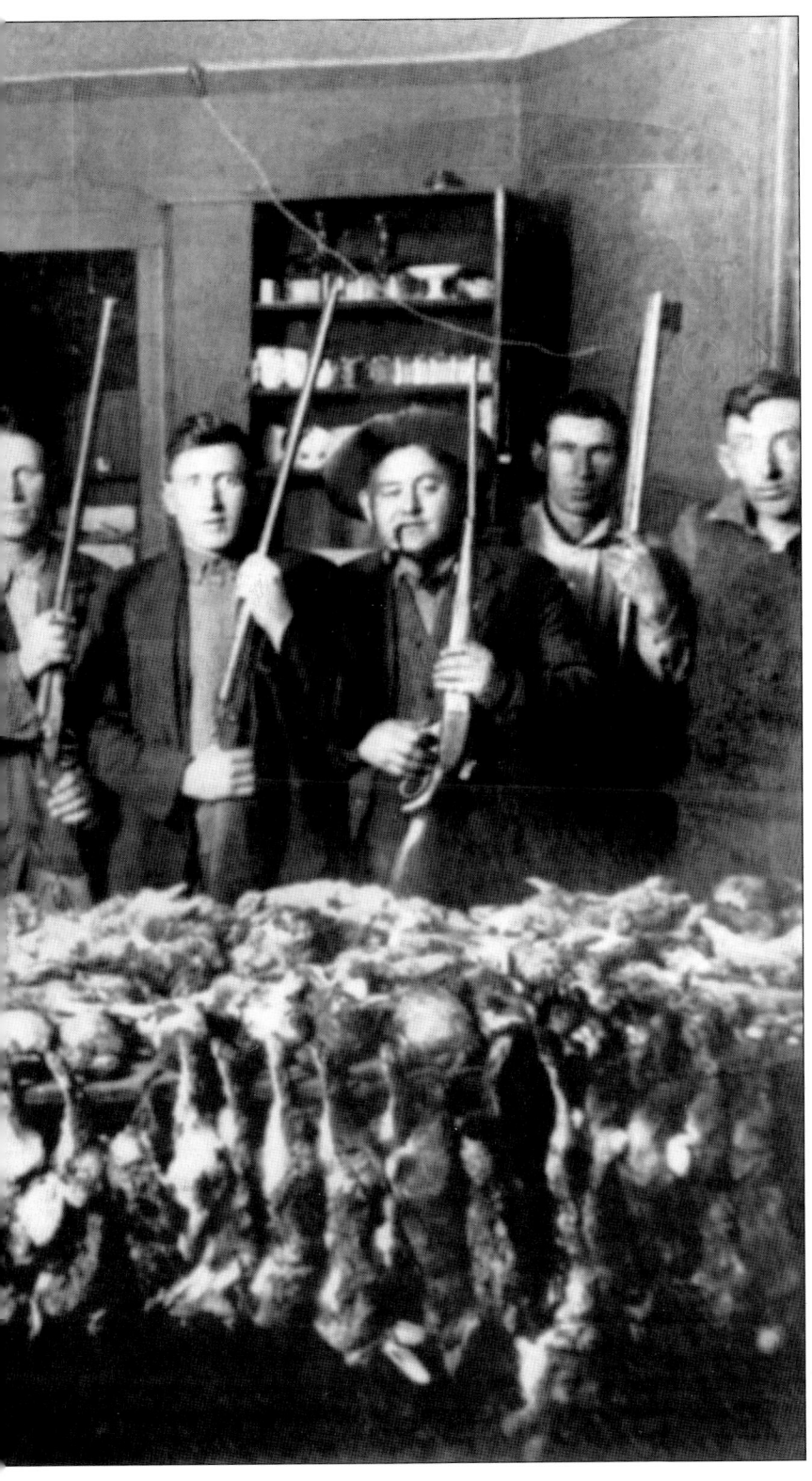

Fourteen Williams residents pose side by side with their guns, as well as one or two small children, in this 1935 photograph. The group of sturdy individuals, members of the Odd Fellows, would often hunt rabbit in the Williams area. The table in this photograph is filled, indicating a particularly successful hunt for the men. Hunting and fishing continue to be a draw for visitors to the area, as well as the reason why many of the residents around Williams originally moved to the city. (Courtesy Williams Public Library.)

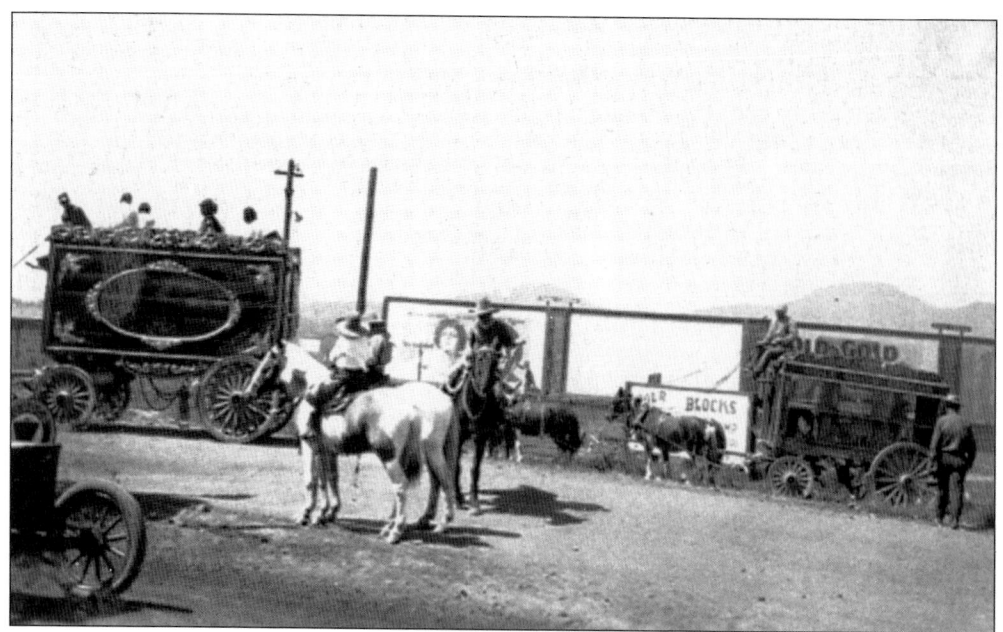

The Cole Brothers Circus pulls up to the Williams Rodeo Grounds in order to set up shop for their upcoming performance. The group visited Williams in the late 1920s. (Courtesy Williams Public Library.)

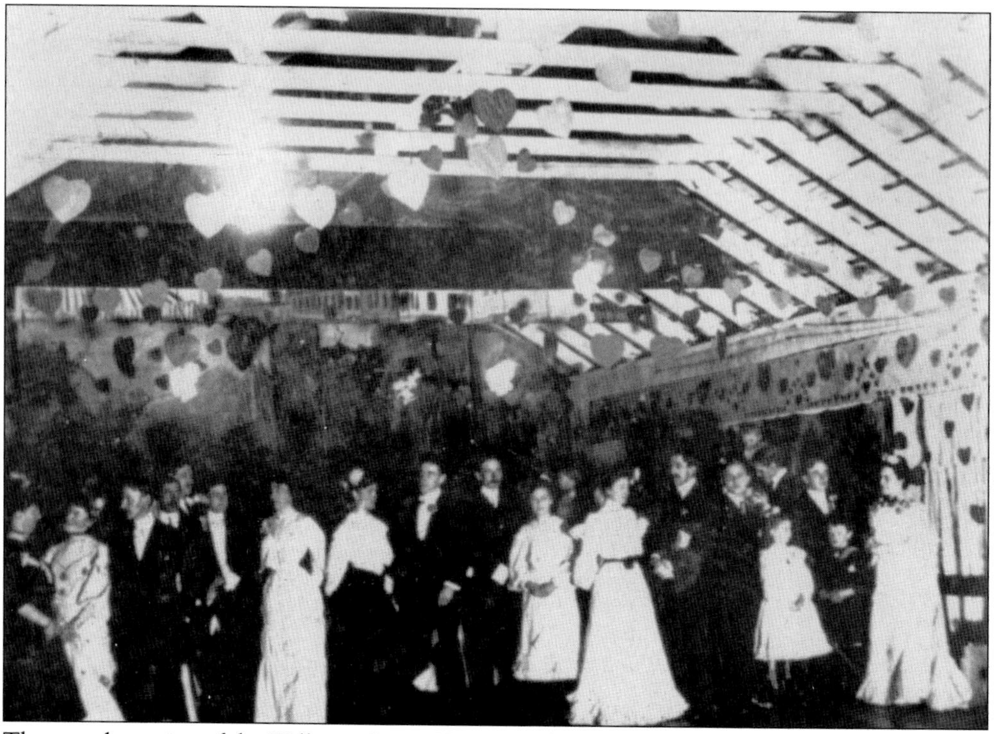

The grand opening of the Williams Opera House was held on Valentine's Day, February 14, 1912. Williams residents also celebrated Statehood Day at the same time in what became a double celebration. (Courtesy Williams Public Library.)

44

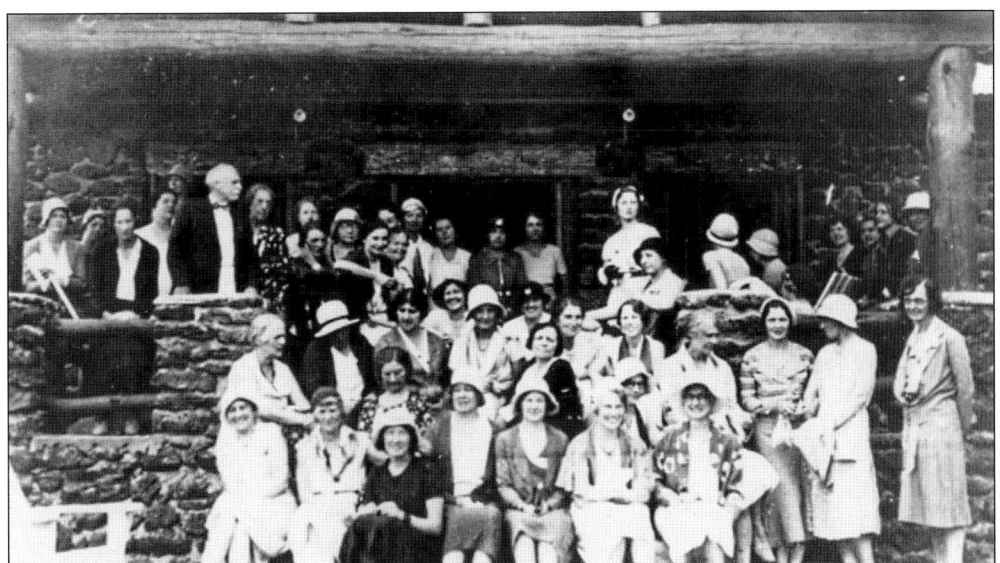

In 1915, a number of Williams women gather in front of the Williams Country Club, a popular recreation location for people in the community. Besides the country club, the Elephant Rocks Golf Course also grew in popularity. Many years later, the course underwent an upgrade, changing from 9 holes to 16. (Courtesy Williams Public Library.)

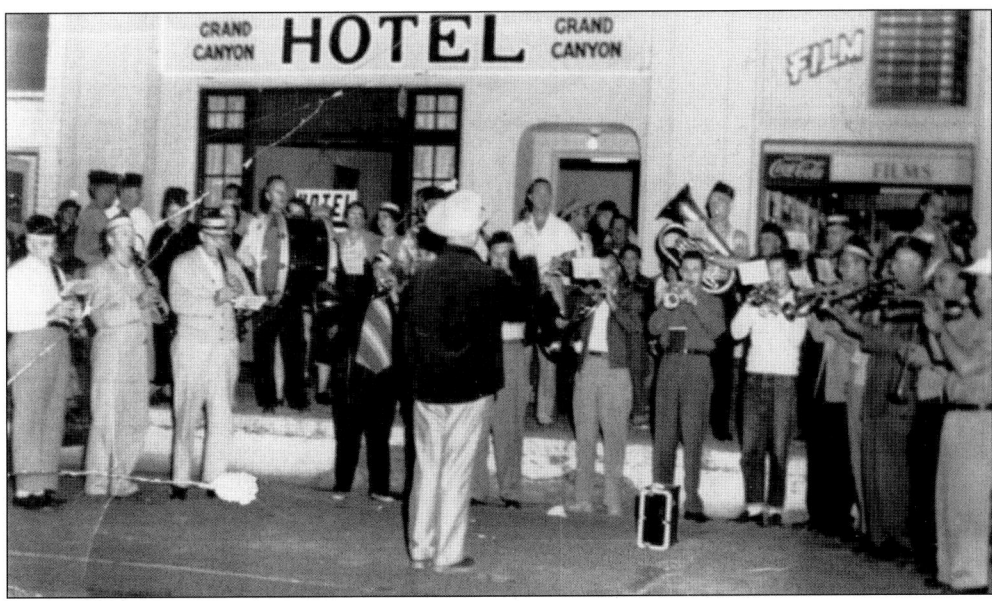

A band plays in front of the Grand Canyon Hotel as part of the Labor Day rodeo festivities in the 1950s. The Grand Canyon Hotel remains a fixture of the Williams community to this day. (Courtesy Williams Public Library.)

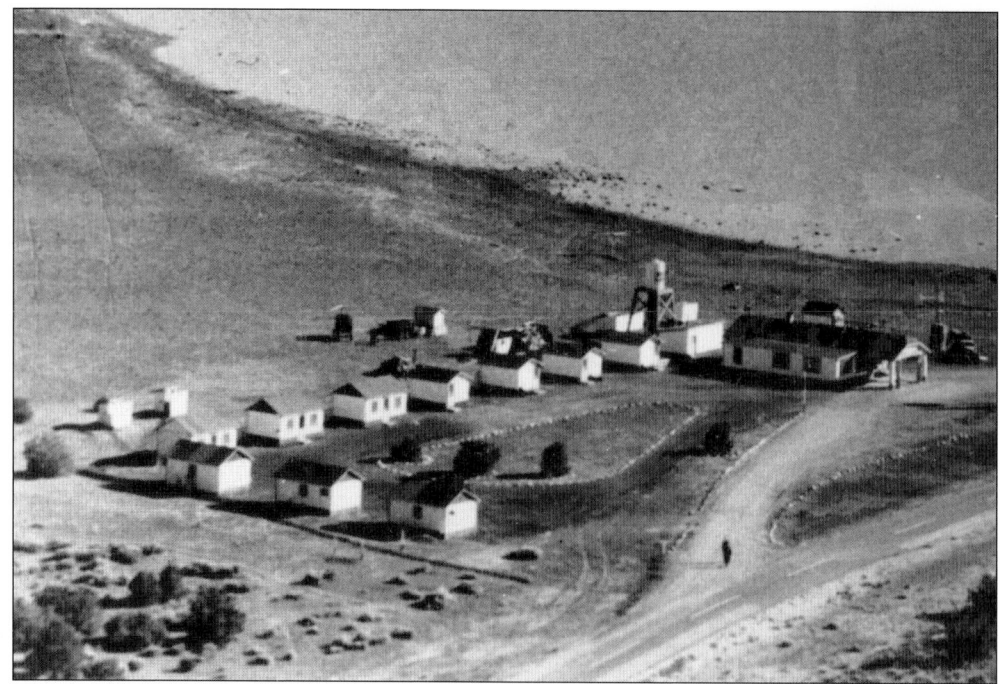

Communities began to spring up in the outlying area surrounding the city by the middle of the 1900s. Residents of these communities, such as the one that formed around Red Lake, pictured in the 1940s, frequented Williams's businesses and schools, though they were counted as county residents and not city residents. (Courtesy Williams Public Library.)

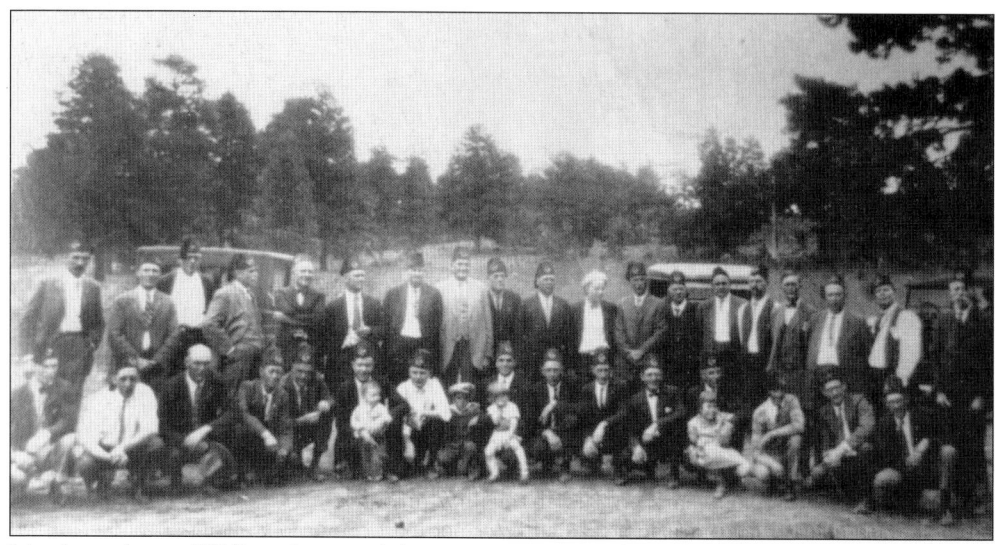

Members of one of Williams's many clubs enjoy a picnic in July in the forest surrounding Williams in 1925. (Courtesy Williams Public Library.)

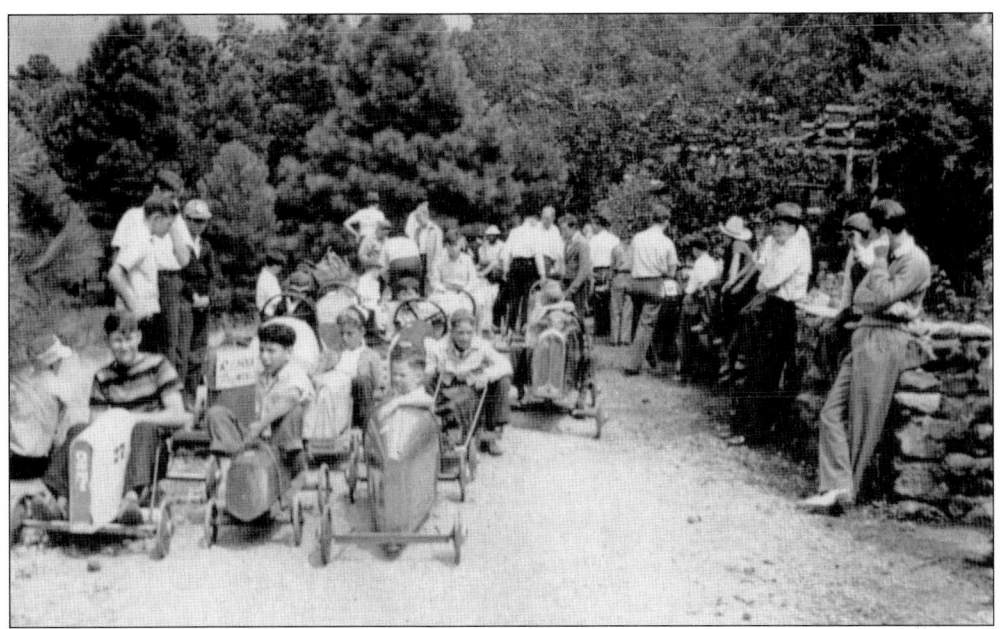

Children, as well adults, got into the competitive spirit in Williams. The youth in the community, assisted by a parent or two, race their soapbox cars in this 1940 derby. (Courtesy Williams Public Library.)

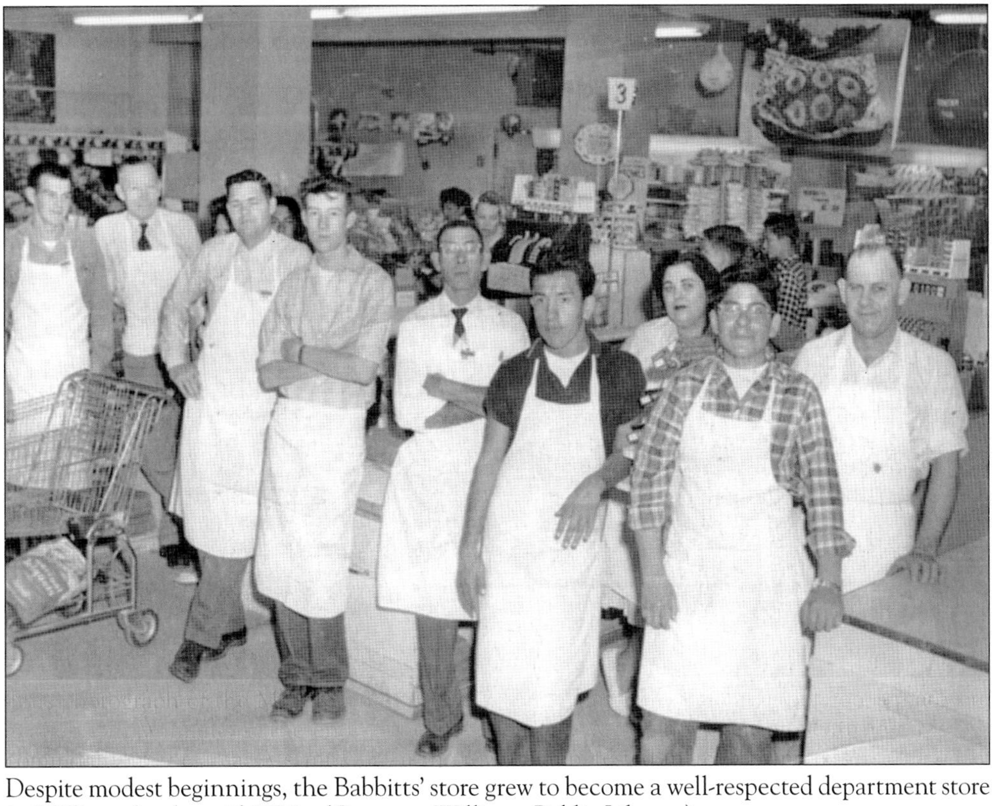

Despite modest beginnings, the Babbitts' store grew to become a well-respected department store in Williams by the mid-1900s. (Courtesy Williams Public Library.)

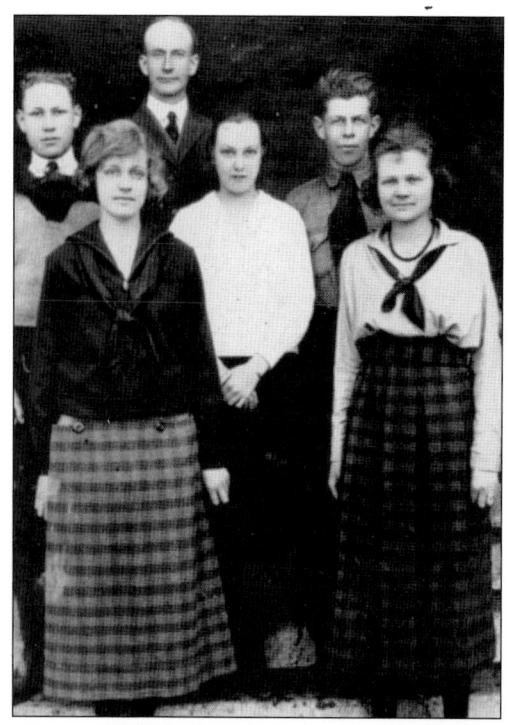

A collection of seniors in the class of 1921, where the girls outnumbered the boys, stands outside of the Williams Public School with their principal, T. H. Cureton. (Courtesy Williams Public Library.)

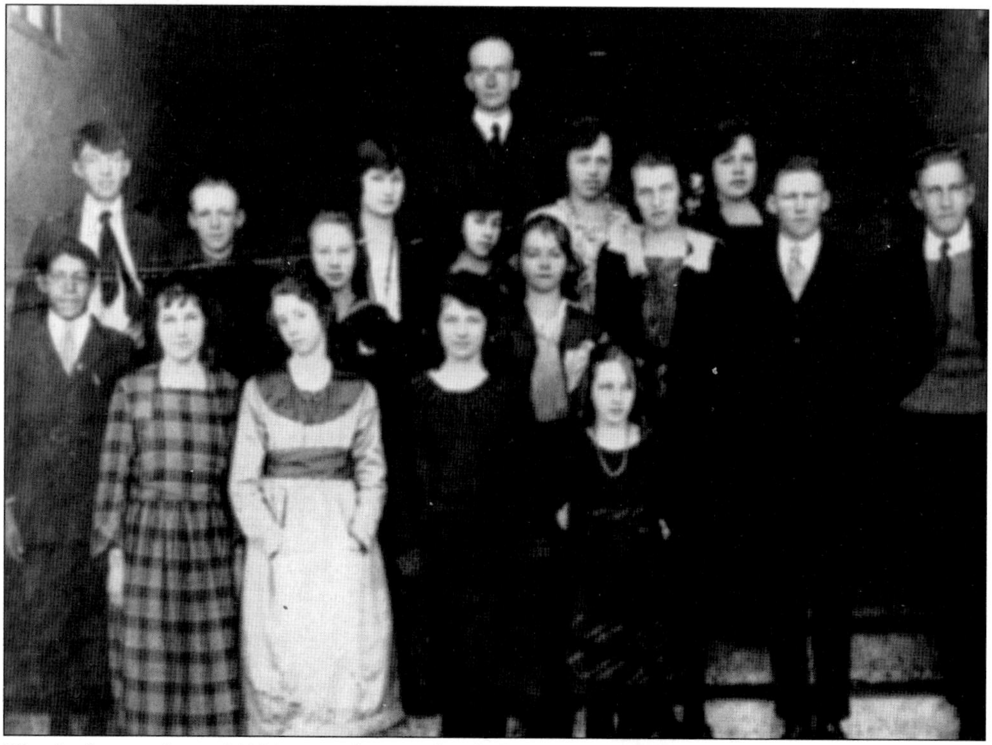

The freshman class of 1921 poses for its school photograph along with principal T. H. Cureton, who would remain in the Williams School District for a number of years. (Courtesy Williams Public Library.)

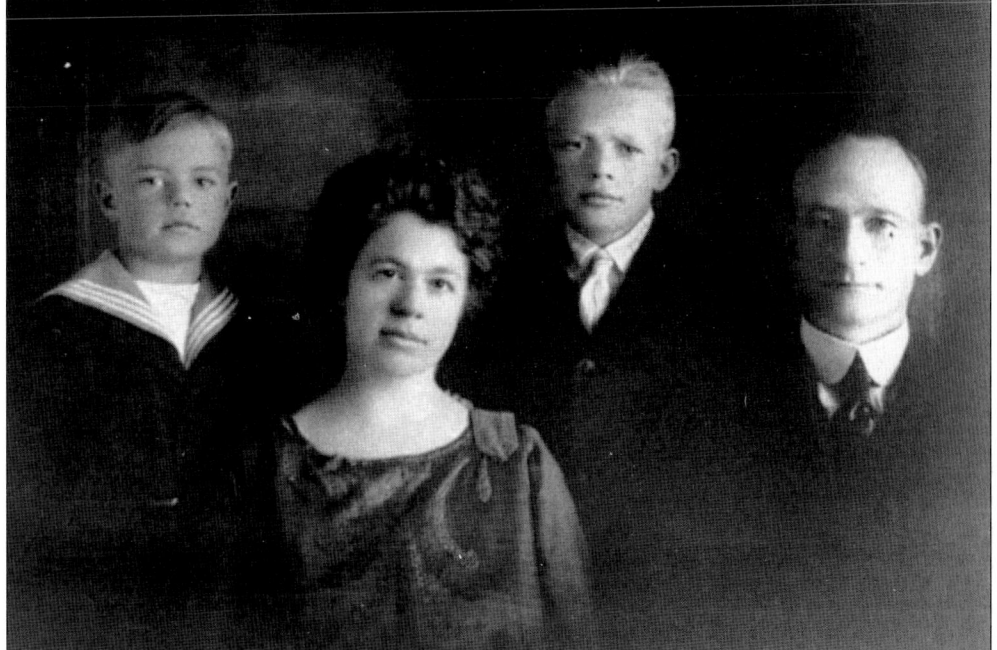

The family of Thomas H. Cureton is shown in 1919, including (from left to right) Miles, Nellie, Carl, and Thomas Cureton. By 1919, overcrowding issues were beginning to manifest themselves at the small Williams school, which led to the eventual construction of a new wing in 1920. (Courtesy Williams Public Library.)

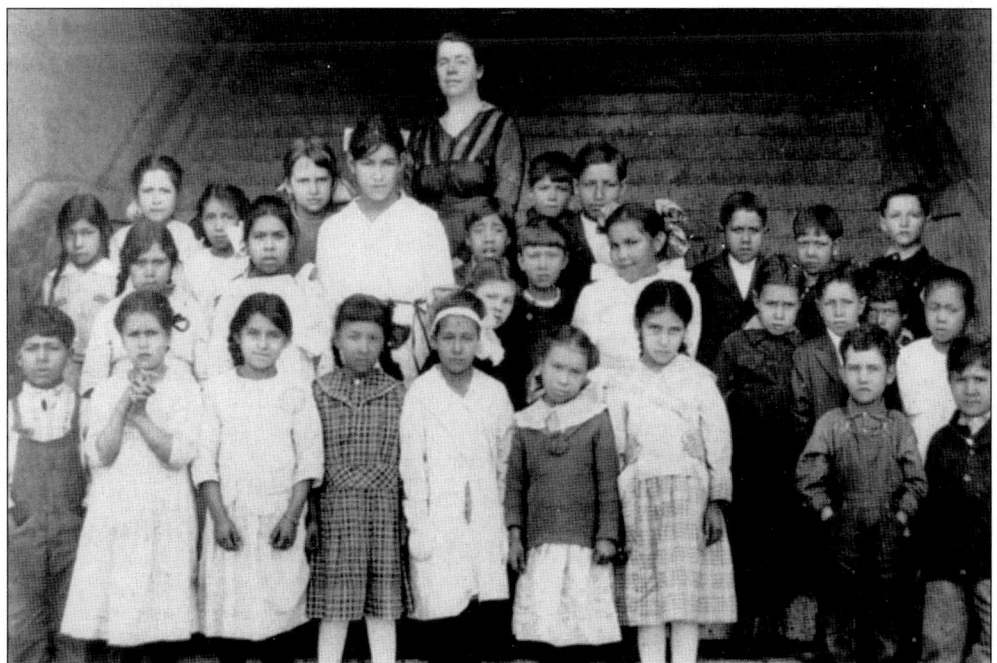

T. H. Cureton's wife, Nellie, also taught in the Williams School District. She is pictured in this 1921 photograph with her class of first-grade students in front of the school. (Courtesy Williams Public Library.)

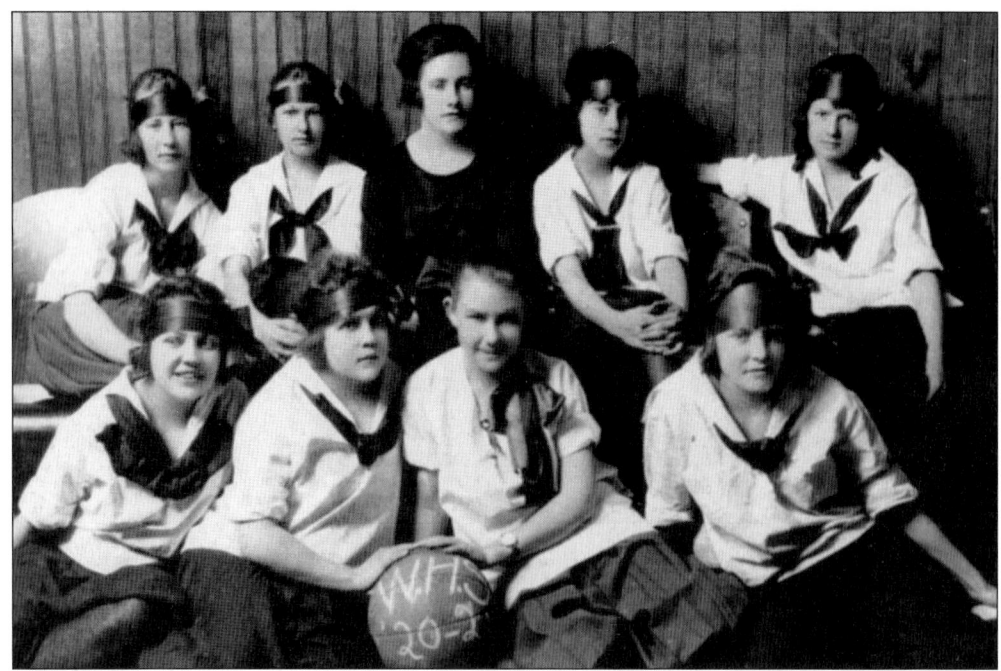

Under the tutelage of coach Marie Miller (second row, center), the 1921 girls' basketball team shows off their flashy uniforms. High school athletes in Williams later adopted the name "Vikings." Grade-school-aged athletes also picked a team name, the "Falcons." (Courtesy Williams Public Library.)

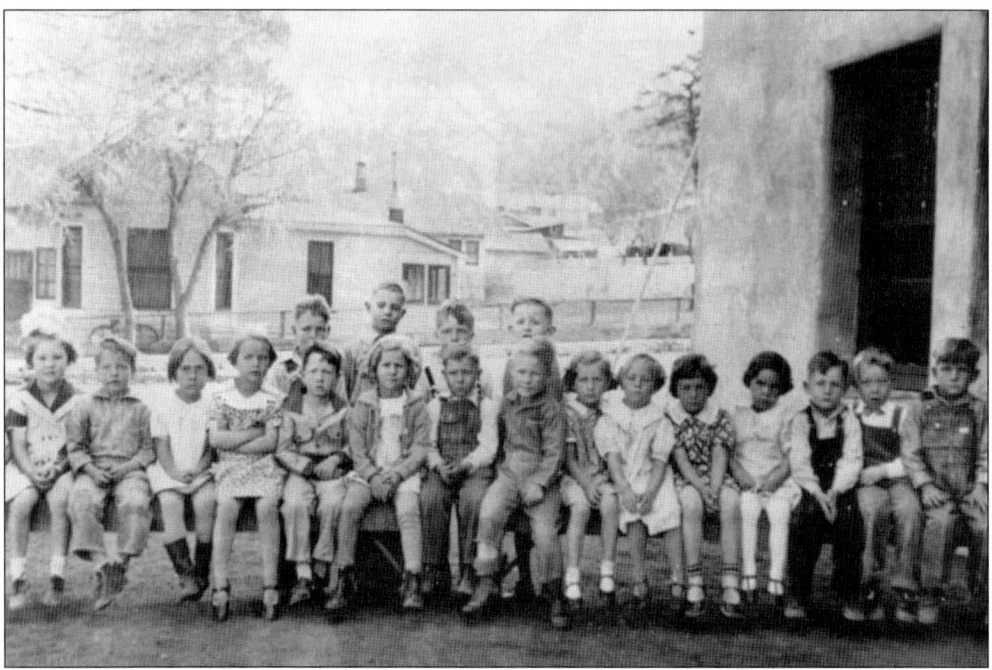

Nineteen students in the first grade class sit outside their school in this photograph, taken in 1938. More than 400 students were enrolled in the Williams School District by the 1930s. (Courtesy Williams Public Library.)

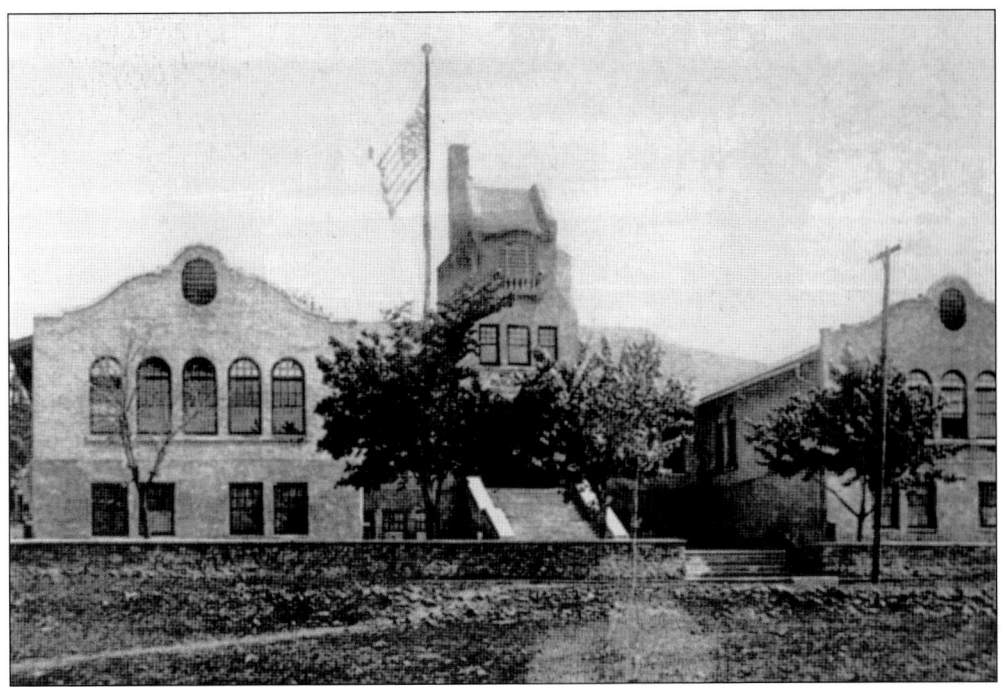

The old Williams grade school made for a striking addition to the Williams landscape, though it was not destined to last. The school burned to nothing more than a few scorched pieces of wall in 1912. (Courtesy Williams Public Library.)

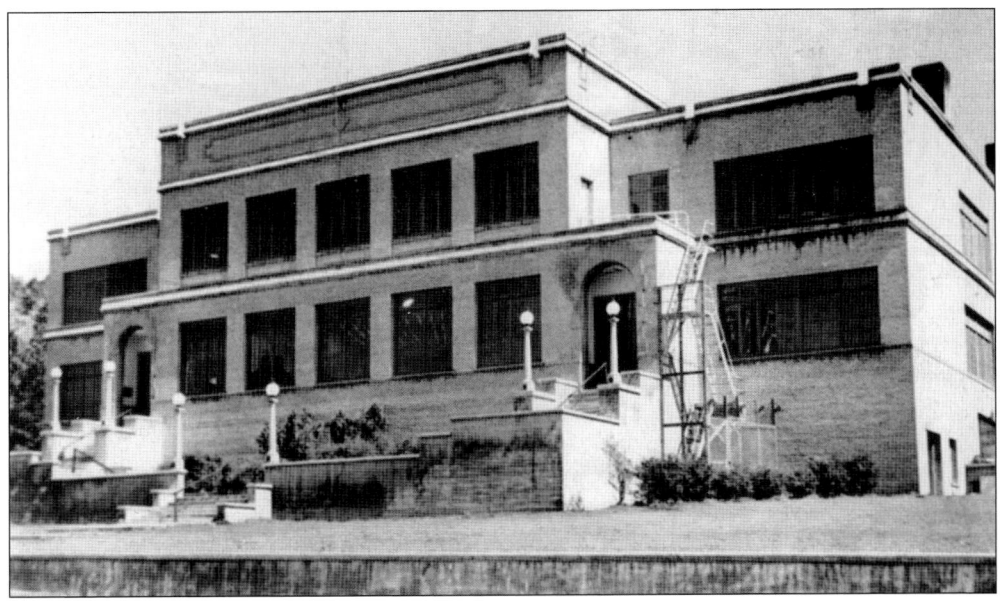

The old high school was built in 1944 in response to a growing student population in Williams. It sustained the needs of the community for many years. (Courtesy Williams Public Library.)

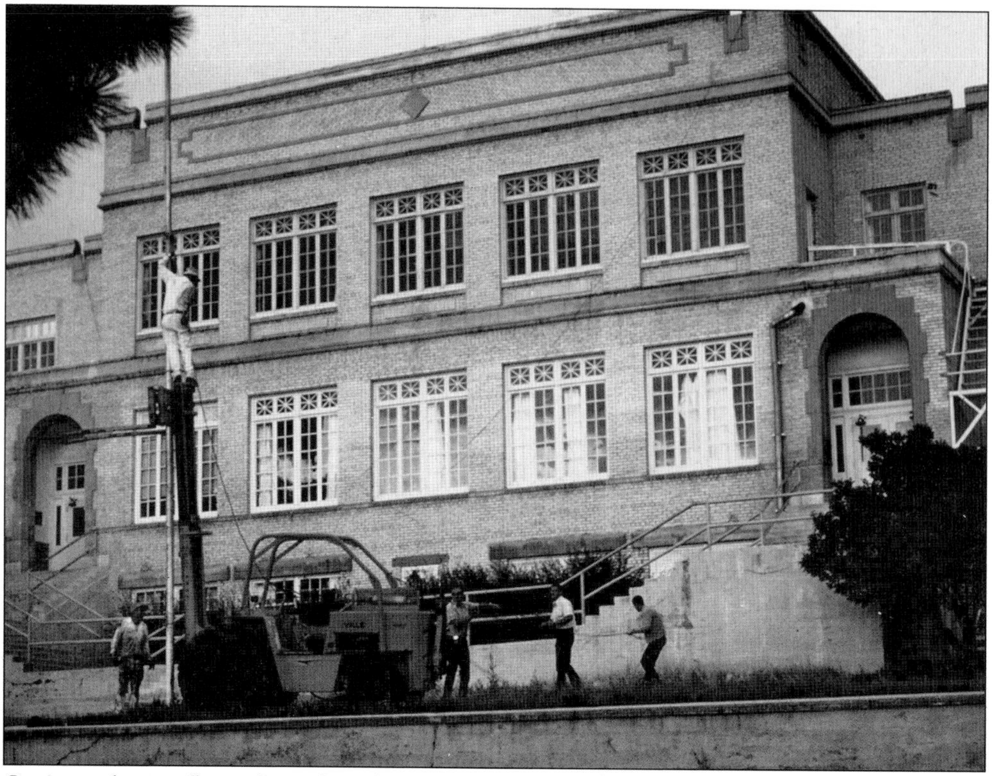

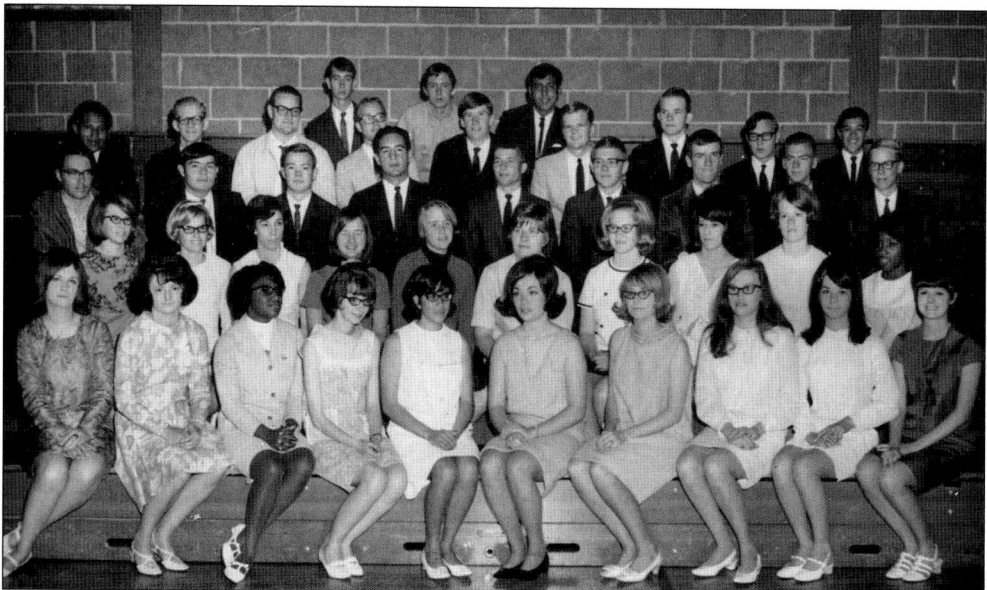

Crews work on a flag pole at the school in the 1960s. A number of changes are visible at the school since the 1940s, including a gutter system and safety handrails. A new high school was built in 1958 on Seventh Street. (Courtesy Williams Public Library.)

The graduating class of 1968 illustrates the rise in student numbers in Williams schools as compared to its prior numbers. Administrators at the school saw the first set of seniors graduate from the new high school in 1958. (Courtesy Williams Public Library.)

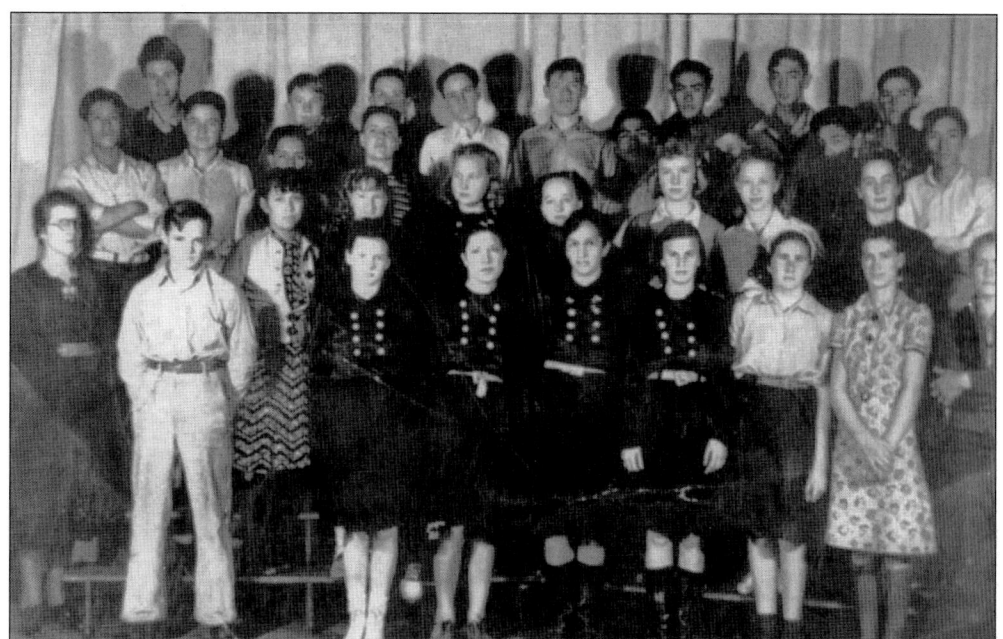

The Williams High School freshman class of 1940 shows how students in Williams, like anywhere else in the nation, would prefer to be outdoors rather than in class, if their sulking expressions are any indication. (Courtesy Williams Public Library.)

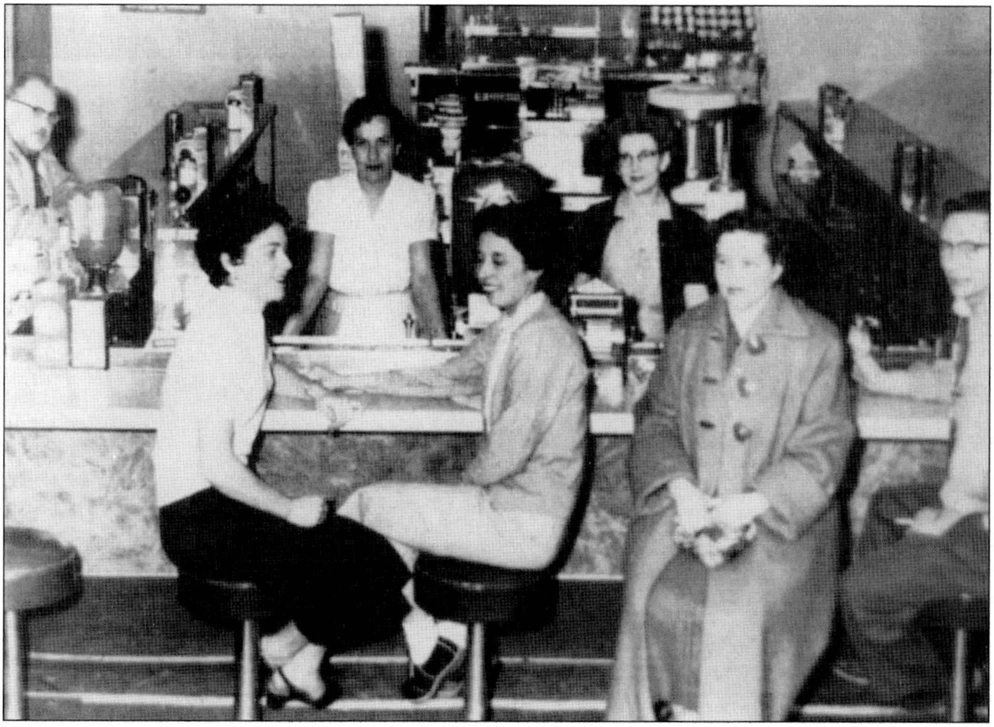

Fun and relaxation were never far for Williams students and adults. One particular hot spot in 1955 was the popular Fountain, located at Smith's Drug Store. (Courtesy Williams Public Library.)

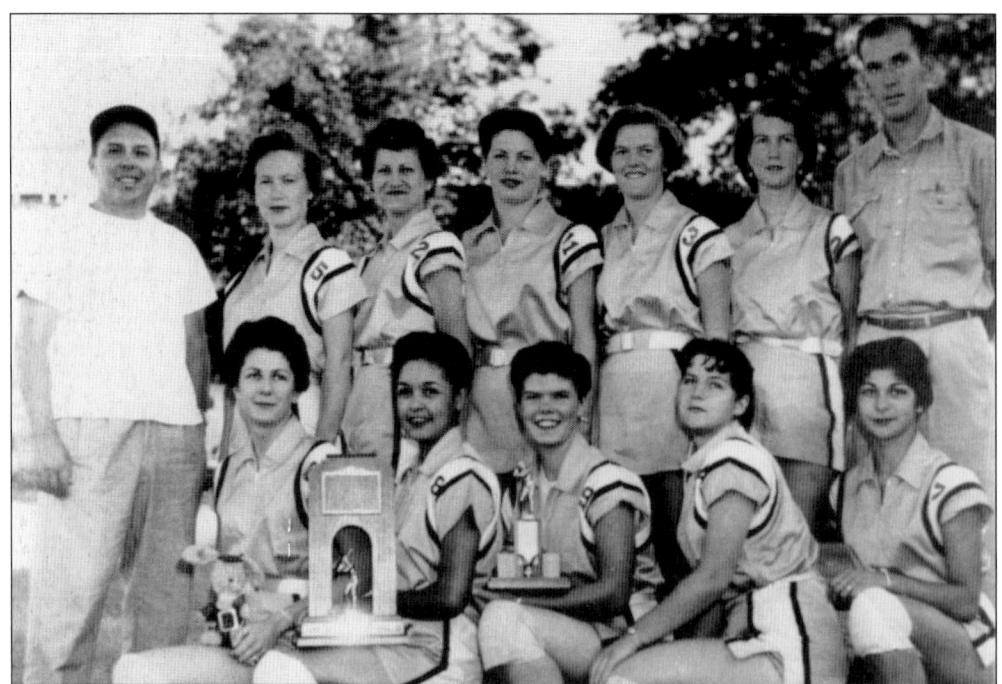

Longtime Williams resident Opal Means (first row, center) poses with her teammates from the Williams ladies' softball team in the 1950s. The girls' high school team came to be known as the "Lady Vikes." (Courtesy Williams Public Library.)

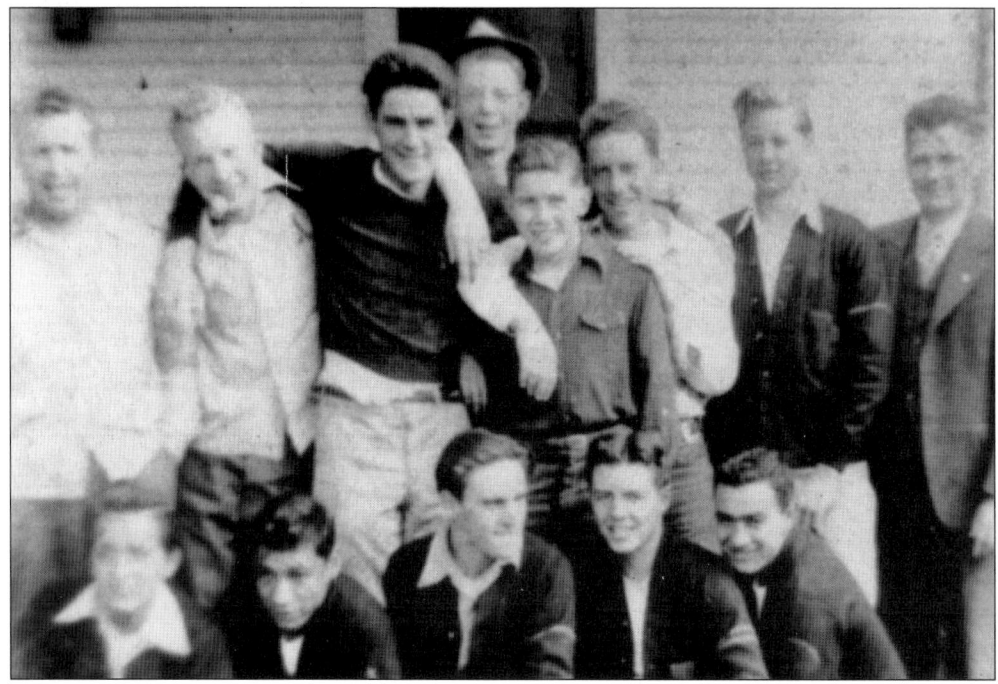

Students Tony L. Jubicich, Edward Gentsch, Hubert Clark, John Hock, Charles McCormack, Lynn Kirby, J. W. Duncan, Arthur Bowie, Raymond Corona, Joe Baca, Vance Brown, Martin Klass, and Henry Guiterrez participate in the 1944 Senior Ditch Day. (Courtesy Williams Public Library.)

Minnie Watson, pictured in 1943, was the school librarian at Williams High School for many years. (Courtesy Williams Public Library.)

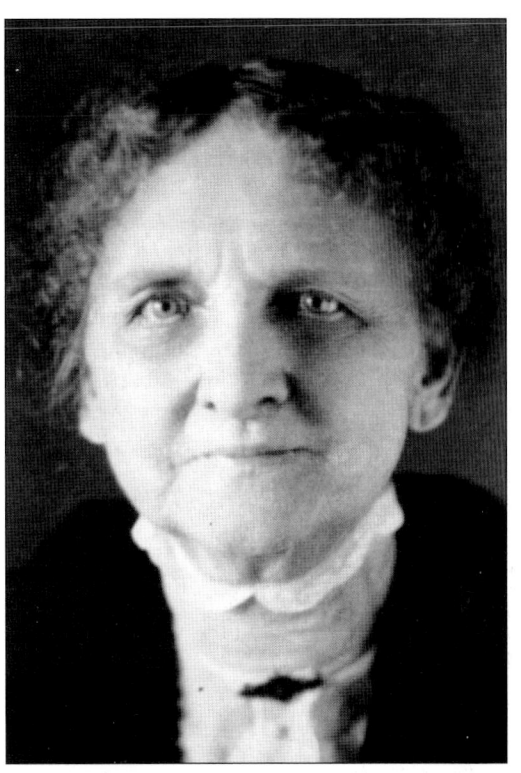

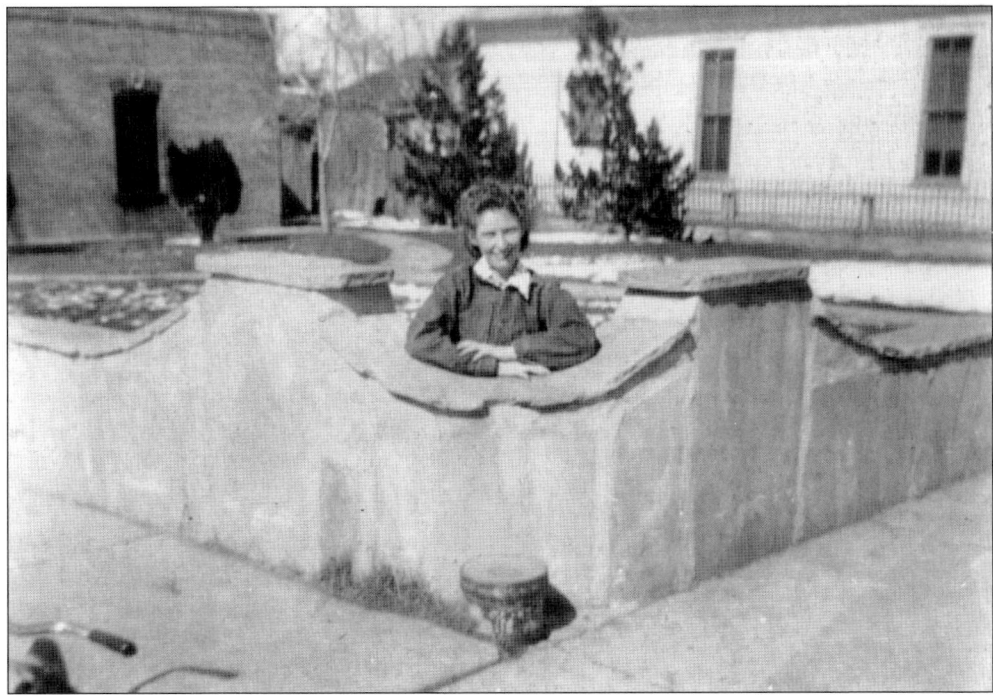

Anita Jarocho was the Williams public librarian in the 1940s. The first Williams Public Library was constructed in 1915. Donations supported the library until 1922, when the city took control of the building. (Courtesy Williams Public Library.)

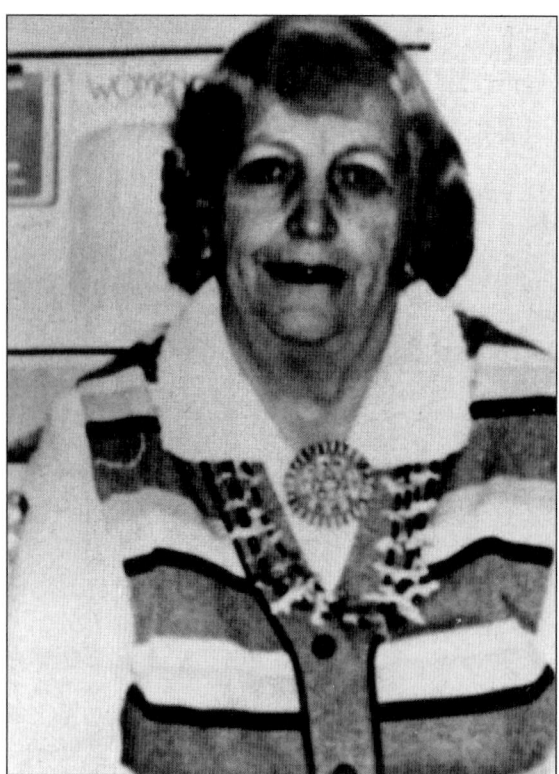

Marjorie Pouquette taught in the Williams School District from 1934 until her retirement in 1978. (Courtesy Williams Public Library.)

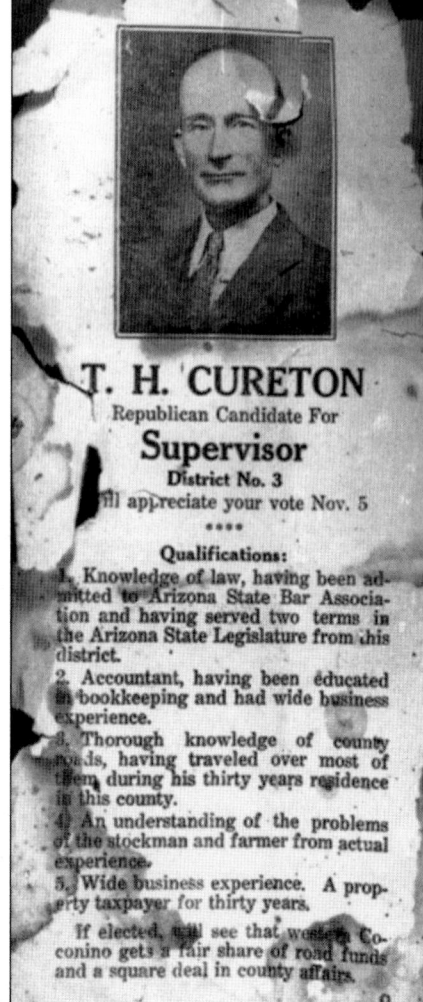

T. H. CURETON

Republican Candidate For

Supervisor

District No. 3

ill appreciate your vote Nov. 5

* * * *

Qualifications:

1. Knowledge of law, having been admitted to Arizona State Bar Association and having served two terms in the Arizona State Legislature from this district.
2. Accountant, having been educated in bookkeeping and had wide business experience.
3. Thorough knowledge of county roads, having traveled over most of them during his thirty years residence in this county.
4. An understanding of the problems of the stockman and farmer from actual experience.
5. Wide business experience. A property taxpayer for thirty years.

If elected, will see that western Coconino gets a fair share of road funds and a square deal in county affairs.

Thomas H. Cureton ran as a Republican candidate for the District 3 Supervisor position in 1940, when he promised to improve road conditions in the Williams area. (Courtesy Williams Public Library.)

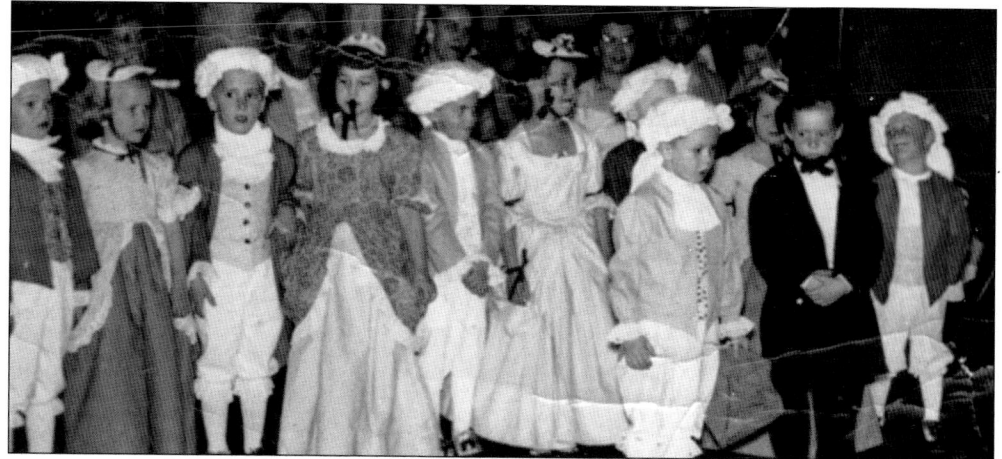

Students in Williams participated each year in a well-dressed school play to the delight of parents and Williams residents alike, who looked forward to the event each year. (Courtesy Williams Public Library.)

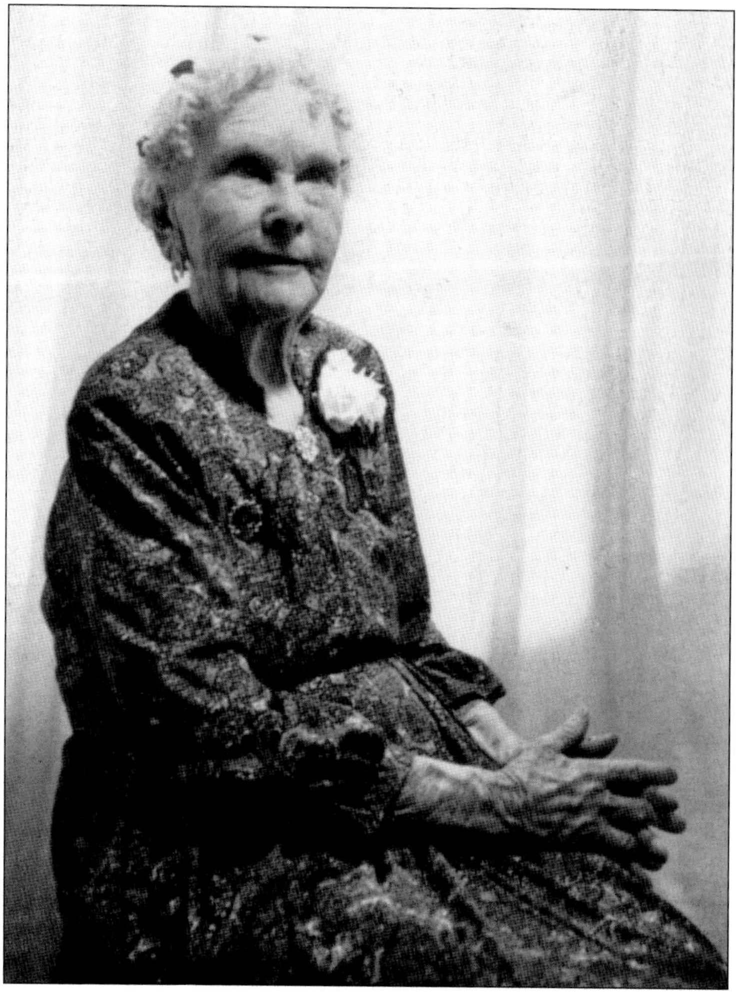

Mary Ford Platten, pictured in 1951, was a popular member of the Williams community. She was the first Caucasian child to be born in Alaska after it became a part of the United States and lived to be 96 years old. Known by the nickname of "Aunt Mary," Platten passed away in 1966. (Courtesy Williams Public Library.)

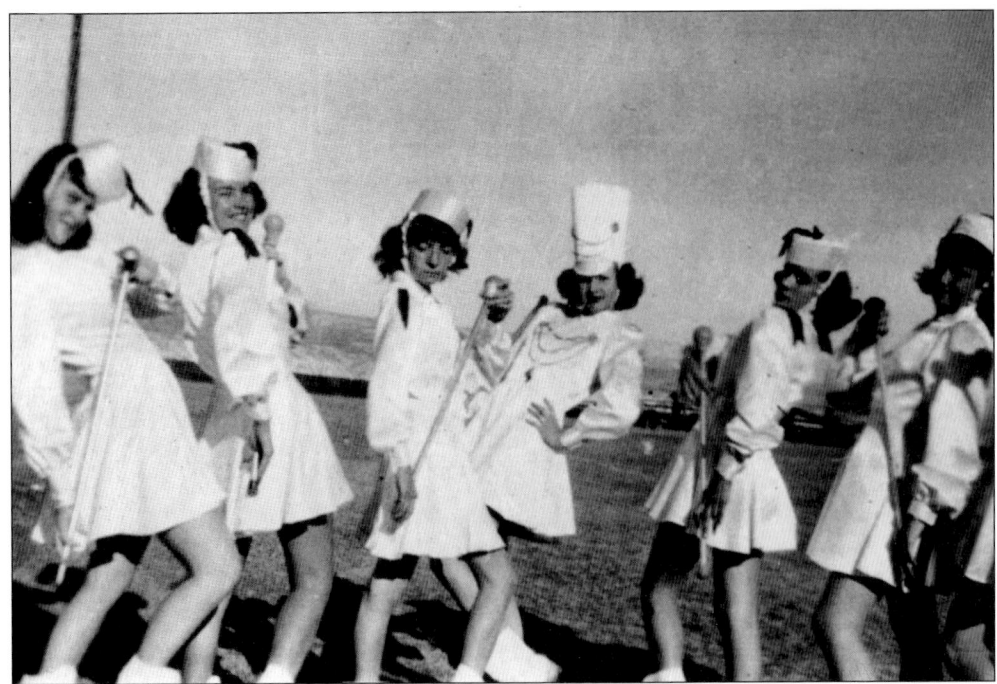

A group of Williams High School baton twirlers, including students Jeanne Vick, Ann Mowry, Bryce Bowden, and Retta Lee Melick, practice their art in the 1950s. (Courtesy Williams Public Library.)

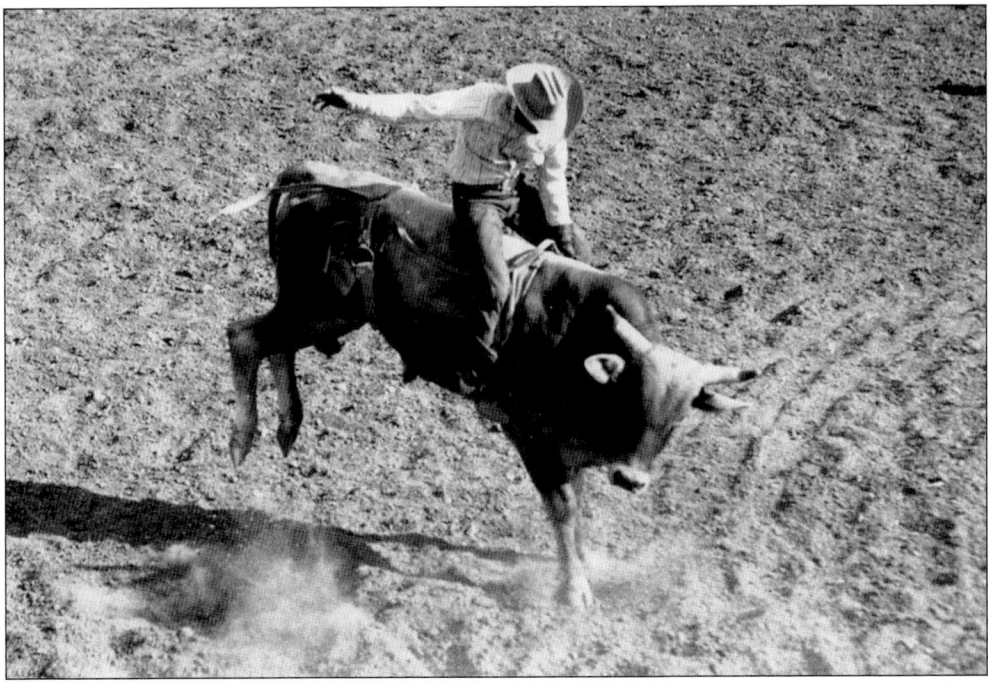

Eddie January competes in the Williams Rodeo in 1950. His brother Jake January was one of the founding members of the area's popular Bill Williams Mountain Men organization. (Courtesy Eddie Sandoval.)

A bronco buster gets thrown from his horse in this 1955 photograph. Rodeos have been a mainstay and a serious sport in Williams since the early 1900s. (Courtesy Williams Public Library.)

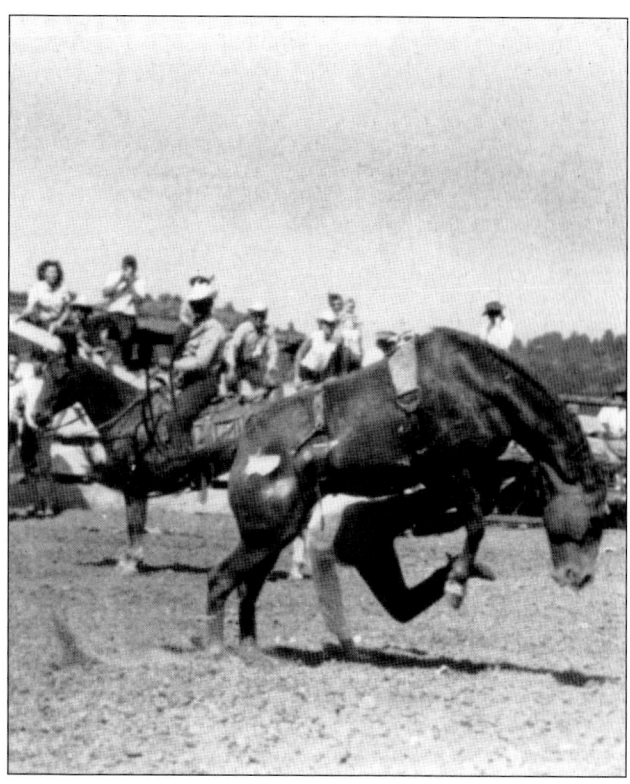

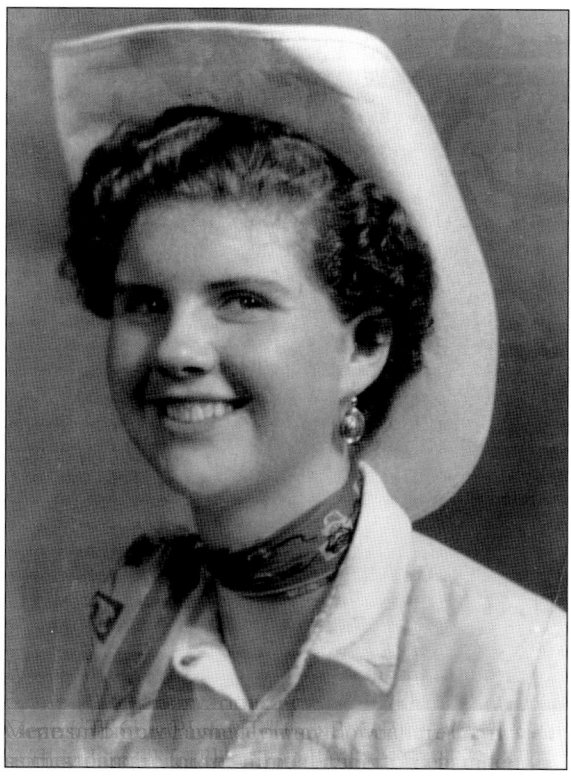

Earlene Kennedy, a 1950s rodeo queen, was the granddaughter of Williams rancher Roy Nagler. Rodeos in Williams, known for being a large ranching community, seemed a natural fit. (Courtesy Eddie Sandoval.)

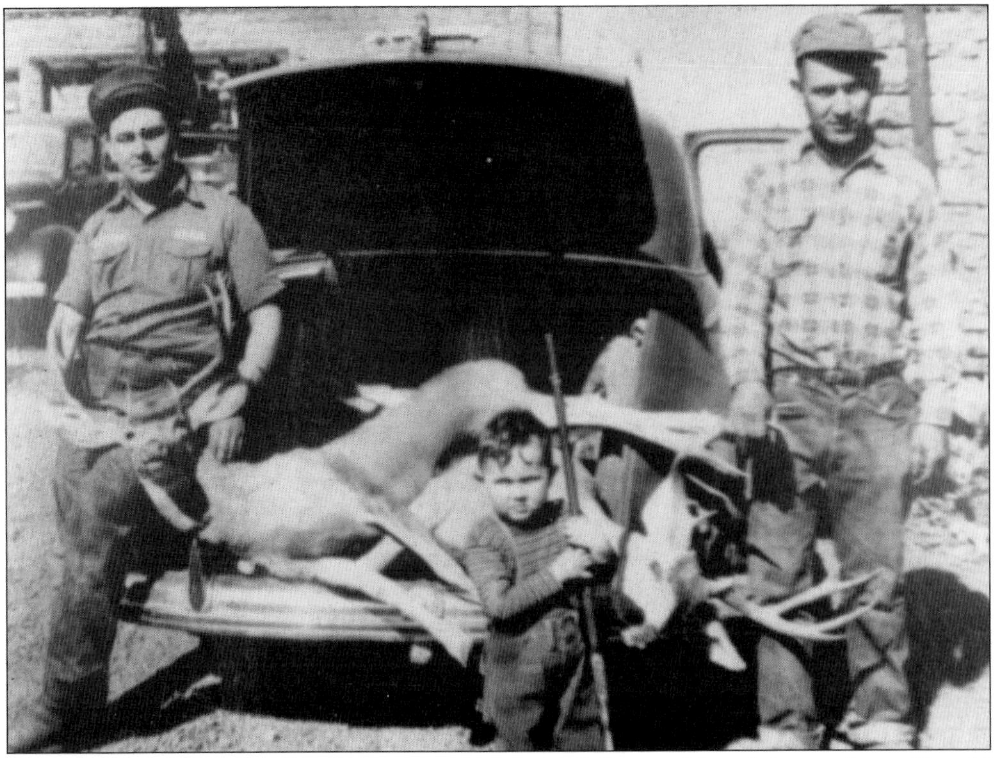

Deer hunters in Williams show off their trophies in 1943. Pictured from left to right are Donald Ziriax, young Eddie Sandoval, and Gene Sandoval. (Courtesy Eddie Sandoval.)

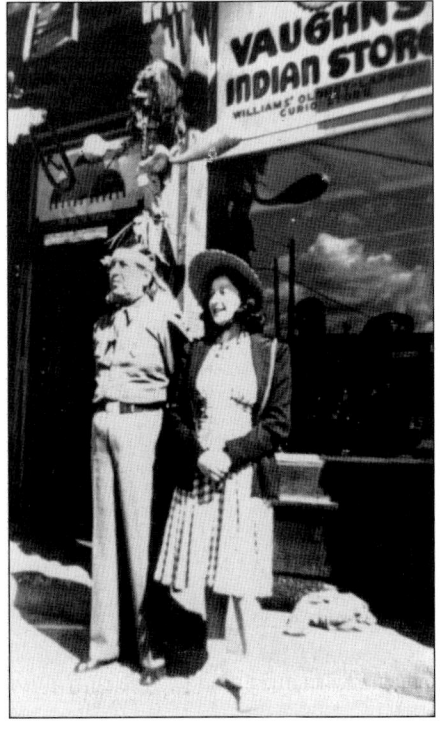

Hopi silversmith Randall Honwesima and an unidentified friend stand in front of Vaughn's Indian Store in 1937. Native American treasures, including jewelry, became favorite collectibles for tourists passing through Williams. (Courtesy Williams Public Library.)

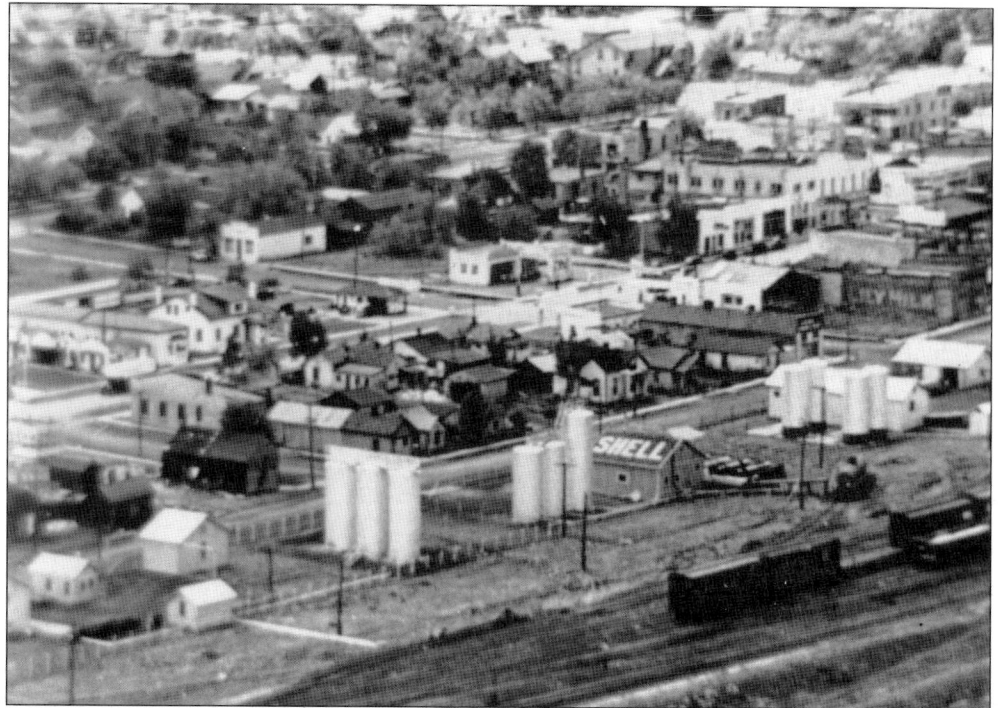

This 1939 photograph offers a glimpse of Bill Williams Avenue and First Street. The landscape of the downtown area, while it underwent some changes, remained largely the same over the years. (Courtesy Williams Public Library.)

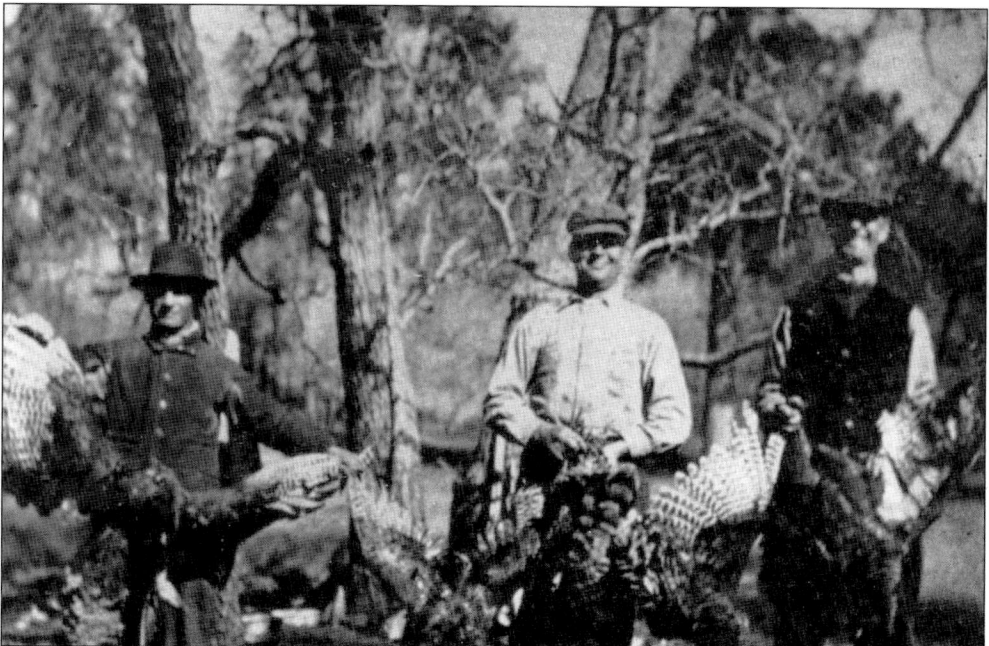

From left to right, Williams residents Geo Barns, P. A. Melick, and Bobbie Way have been hunting for turkeys and caught more than a few of the wily birds during a hunting trip in 1921. (Courtesy Williams Public Library.)

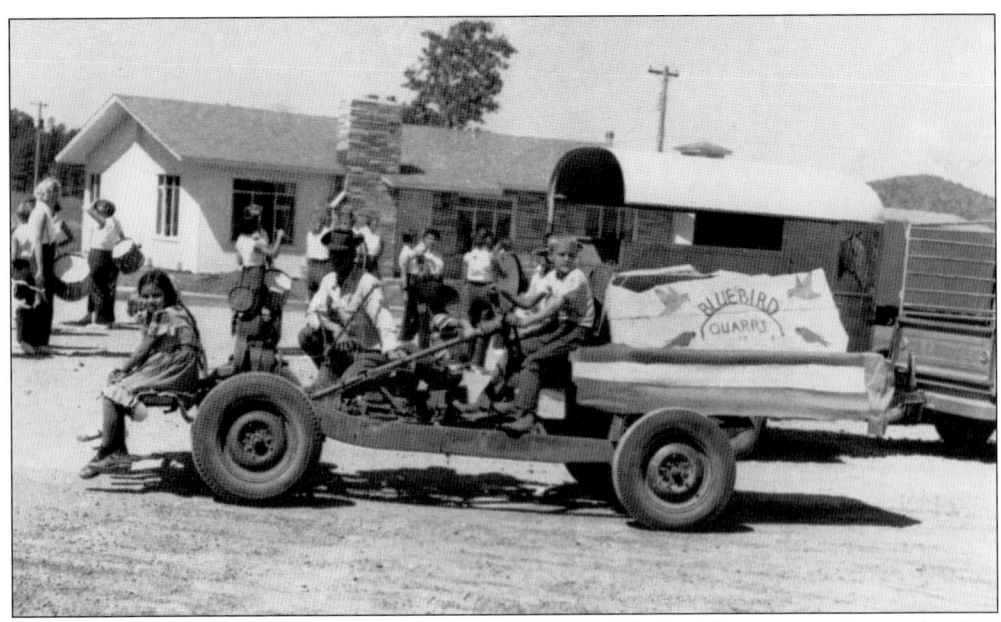

A number of Williams schoolchildren, including a young Bluebird (a group similar to the Girl Scouts), enter the Williams 1950 Labor Day parade. (Courtesy Williams Public Library.)

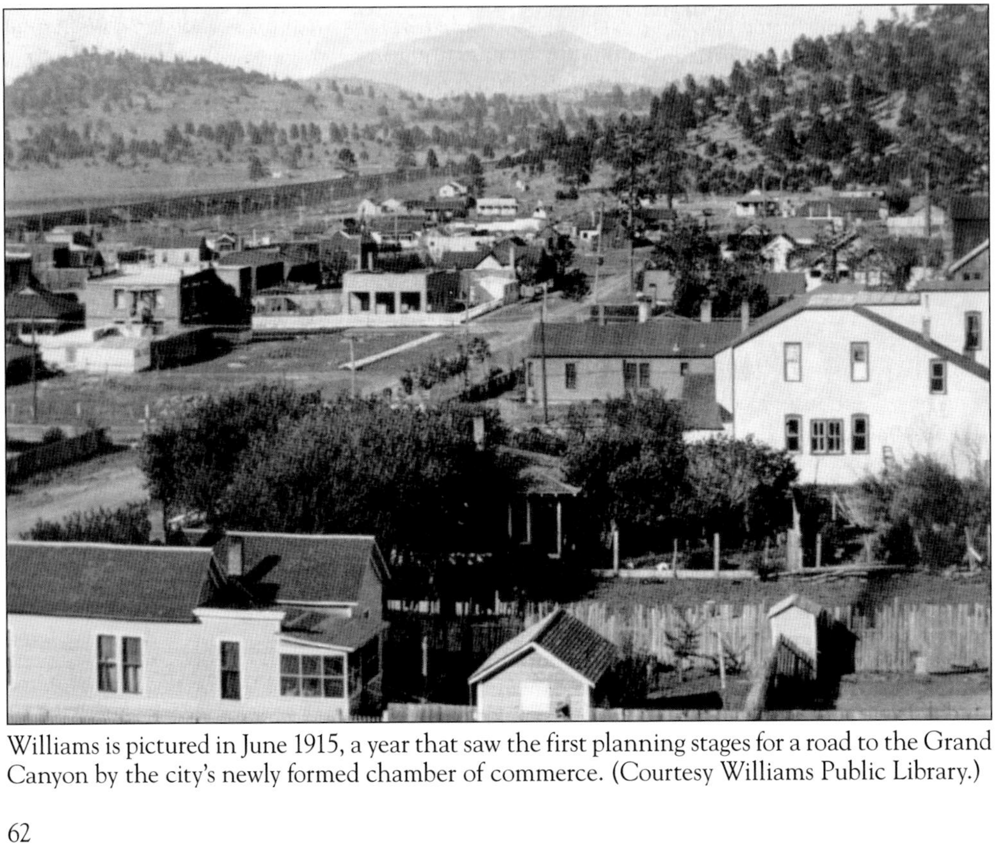

Williams is pictured in June 1915, a year that saw the first planning stages for a road to the Grand Canyon by the city's newly formed chamber of commerce. (Courtesy Williams Public Library.)

Three

THE RAILROAD STEAMS IN
PROFITABLE TIMES FOR THE CITY

Prior to 1882, travelers in northern Arizona and the Williams area in particular made their way across the wooded high country in wagons and on horseback. While some small-scale logging operations had already moved into the area, the arrival of the Atlantic and Pacific Railroad freight line created a surge in Williams's meager population. The track, having arrived in the Arizona Territory from New Mexico, eventually connected Chicago to Los Angeles.

By 1901, crews with the Santa Fe Railroad completed a spur line from Williams to the Grand Canyon. Visitors from all over the world flocked to northern Arizona in order to visit the now accessible wonder of the world. Prior to the completion of the spur line, travelers in stagecoaches and other conveyances visited the famed South Rim. Pres. Theodore Roosevelt even made his way to the Grand Canyon aboard one of the Santa Fe's comfortable Pullman cars for a special visit in 1903.

It did not take long for Williams to become a division point for travelers going both east and west. A Harvey House was soon opened, along with the Fray Marcos Hotel, in 1908. Built under the direction of manager J. B. Canfield and the Los Angeles–based firm Leonhart Contracting, the Harvey-owned hotel boasted 33 luxurious rooms for travelers riding the rails through the area.

The popularity of the automobile caused the Santa Fe Railroad to discontinue its services to the Grand Canyon in 1968. Three passengers rode the final train back from the Grand Canyon that year. The line sat untouched for more than 20 years.

When Max and Thelma Biegert became owners of the property years later, they reinstated passenger service to the canyon. Called the Grand Canyon Railway, the daily train service transports hundreds of visitors to the Grand Canyon each day via a vintage steam engine, much to the delight of rail enthusiasts, many of whom have come to be known as "foamers," or die-hard fans of steam engines.

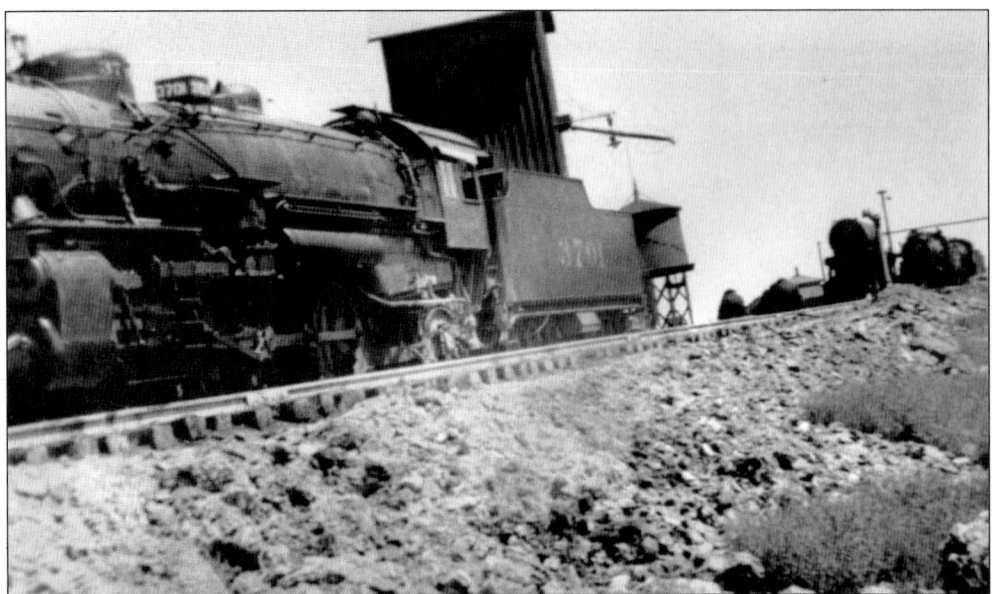

The arrival of the Atlantic and Pacific Railroad freight line stimulated an economic boom in Williams when the tracks were finally laid in 1882. The line eventually connected Chicago to Los Angeles. (Courtesy Williams Public Library.)

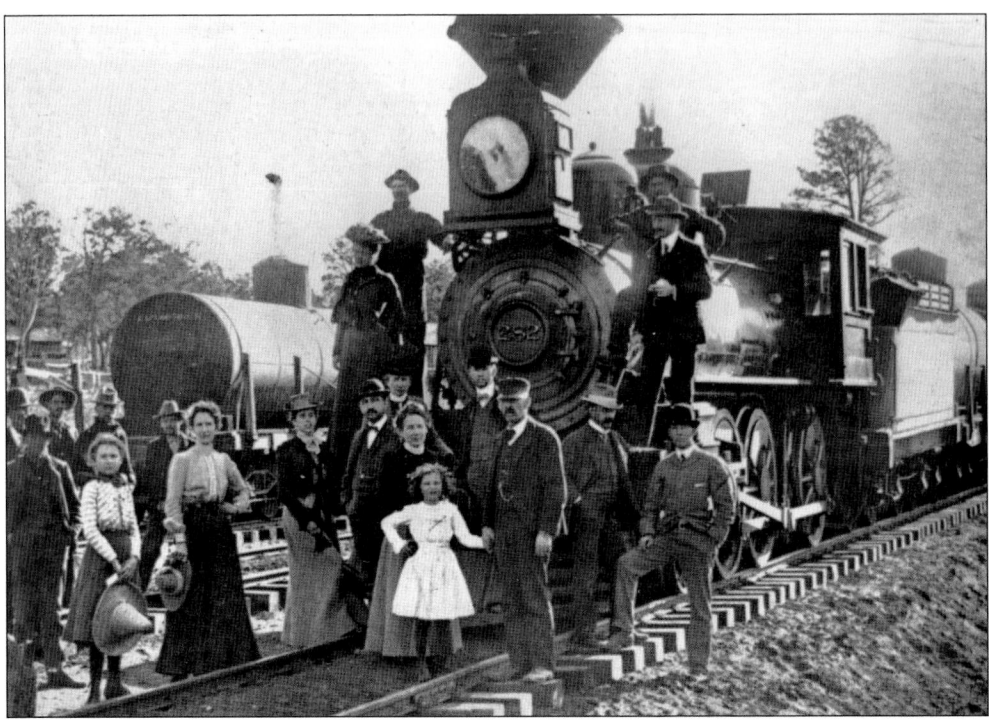

The first passengers arrived at the South Rim of the Grand Canyon on board a steam engine on September 17, 1901. The trip was made possible via a spur line created by the Santa Fe Railroad that same year. (Courtesy *Williams–Grand Canyon News*.)

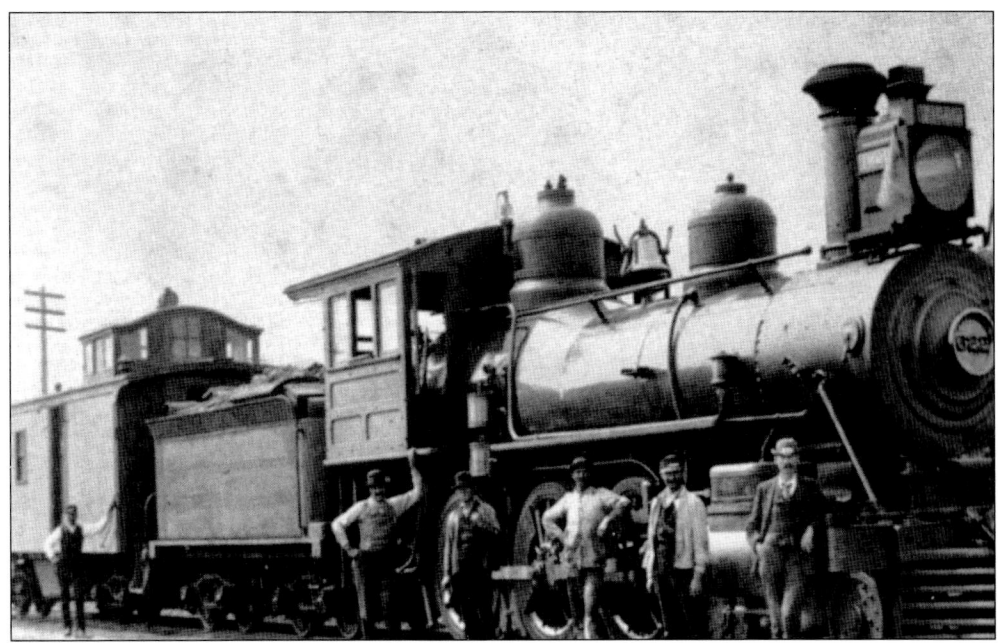

Early steam travelers that rode the rails from Williams to the Grand Canyon included Pres. Theodore Roosevelt, royalty, political dignitaries, and even the cast from the popular television show *Lassie*. (Courtesy Williams Public Library.)

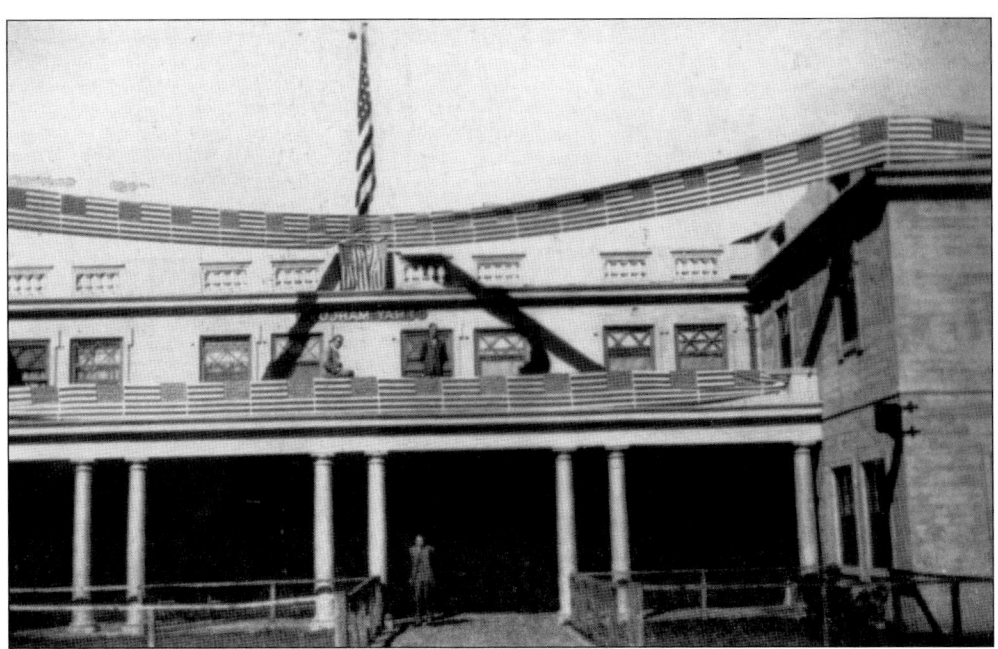

Construction on the grand Fray Marcos Hotel was completed in 1908. The elegant structure quickly became a hub for social activity in the city of Williams. (Courtesy Williams Public Library.)

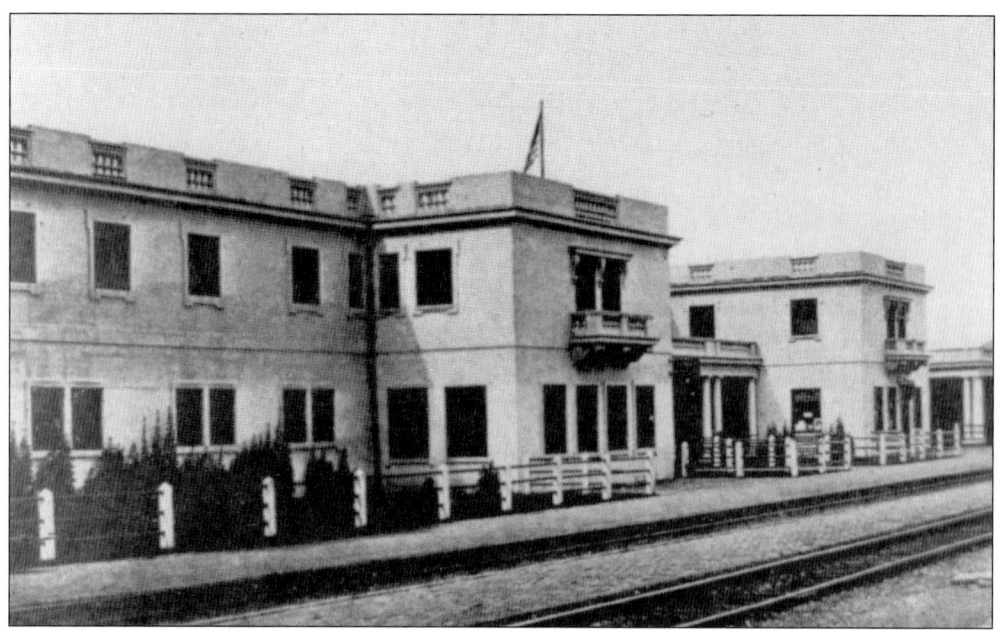

The railway depot building and the Fred Harvey House are pictured in 1917. Built almost 10 years prior to this photograph, the 33-room Harvey-owned hotel would soon begin work on an addition to the large complex. (Courtesy Williams Public Library.)

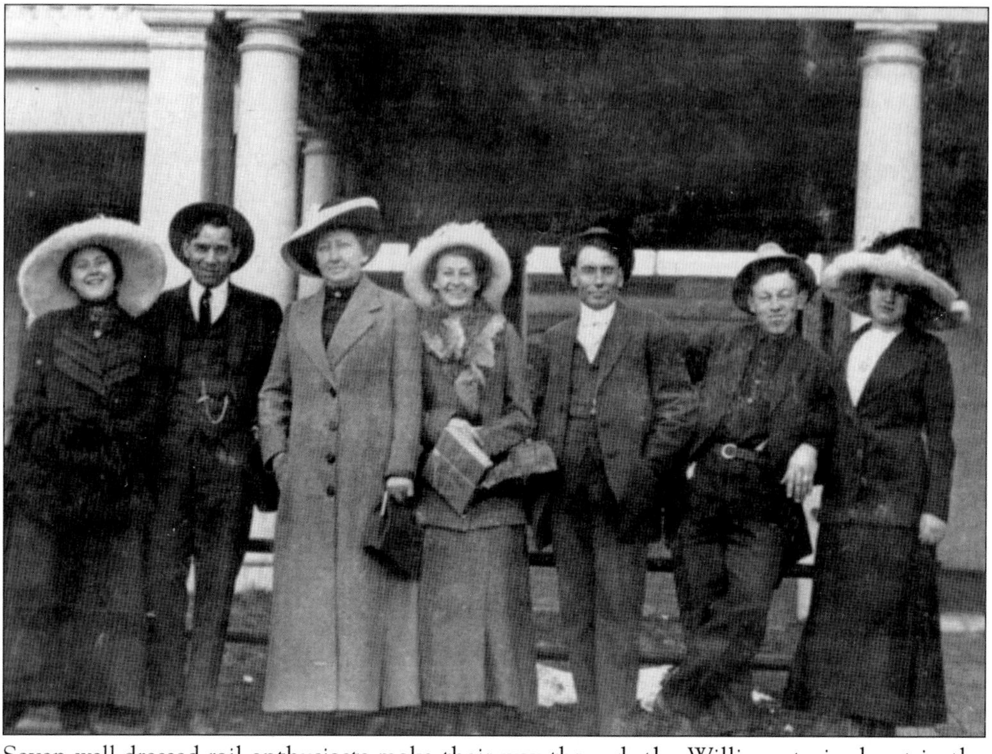

Seven well-dressed rail enthusiasts make their way through the Williams train depot in the 1920s. The depot was generally referred to as the Williams Harvey House. (Courtesy Williams Public Library.)

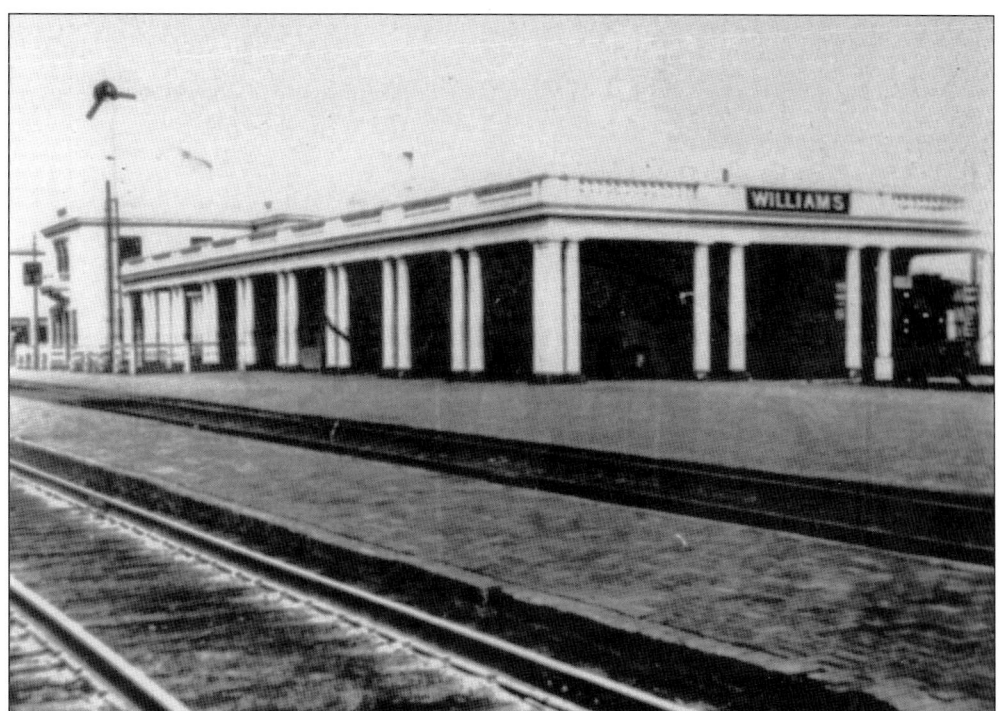

The view of the Fray Marcos Fred Harvey Depot in Williams would change little over the years. Shown here in 1930, the depot looks similar to when it was first built, though new buildings have popped up since then. (Courtesy Williams Public Library.)

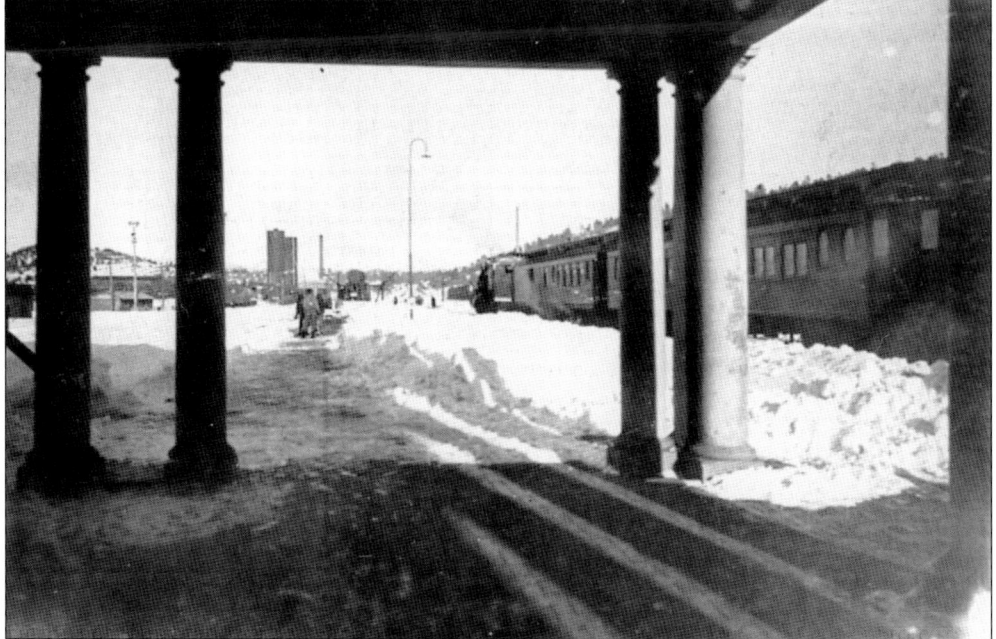

A snowstorm blanketed the depot in the 1920s, giving station personnel the tasking job of clearing a path for travelers to embark and debark from the comfort of their Pullman passenger cars. (Courtesy Williams Public Library.)

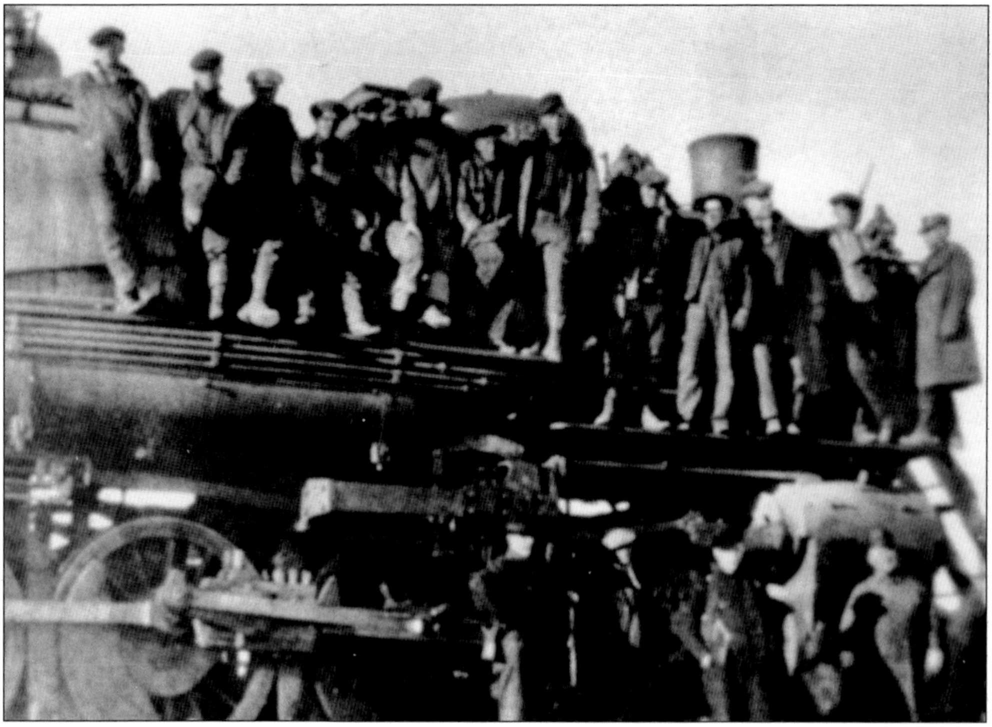

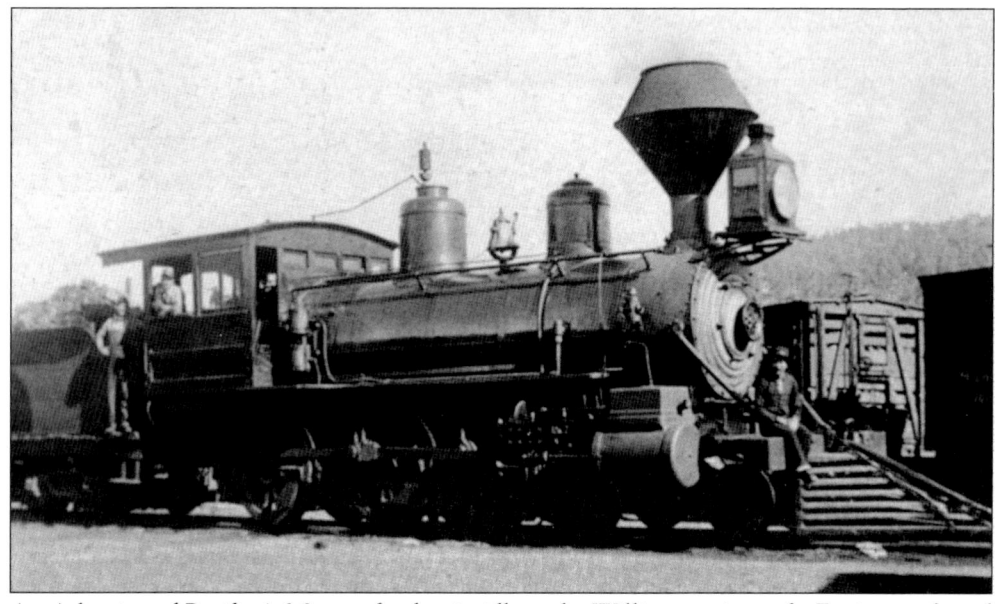

The W. V. Tie Gang, like many of the tie gangs employed by the railway, tackled large-scale and smaller rail construction work, including the creation of bridges and fast repair work. (Courtesy Williams Public Library.)

An Atlantic and Pacific 4-6-0 ten-wheeler sits idle at the Williams train yards. Engineers aboard the train used coal to fuel the large engine. (Courtesy Williams Public Library.)

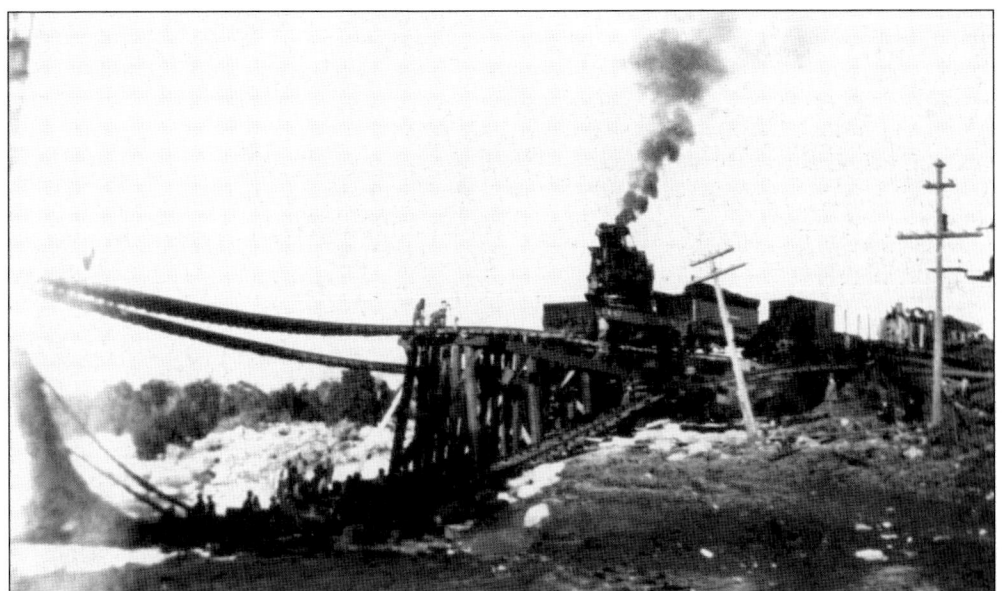

A washed-out bridge was to blame for destroying a large portion of the rail structure between Williams and the Grand Canyon. Wrecking crews and construction crews often worked elbow to elbow in order to implement timely cleanup and repair work. (Courtesy Williams Public Library.)

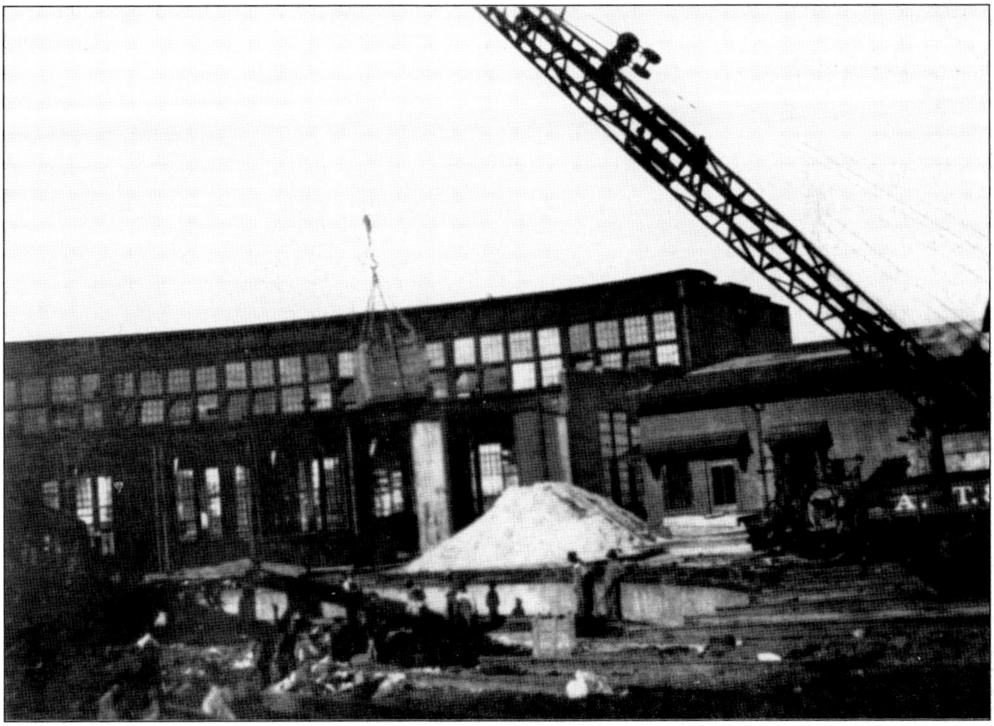

Construction gets underway on the Williams roundhouse during the early 1900s. Engines would wait at the roundhouse until they were needed for trips to the Grand Canyon. (Courtesy Williams Public Library.)

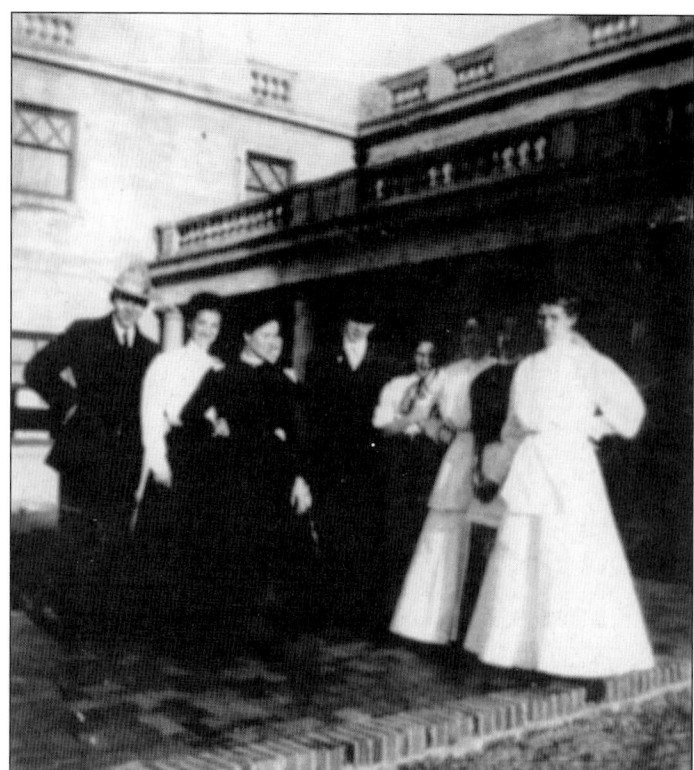

Dressing up for exciting excursions seemed to be the norm at the beginning of the 20th century when it came to travel on the Atlantic and Pacific Railroad. Visitors to the depot in Williams were no exception. (Courtesy Williams Public Library.)

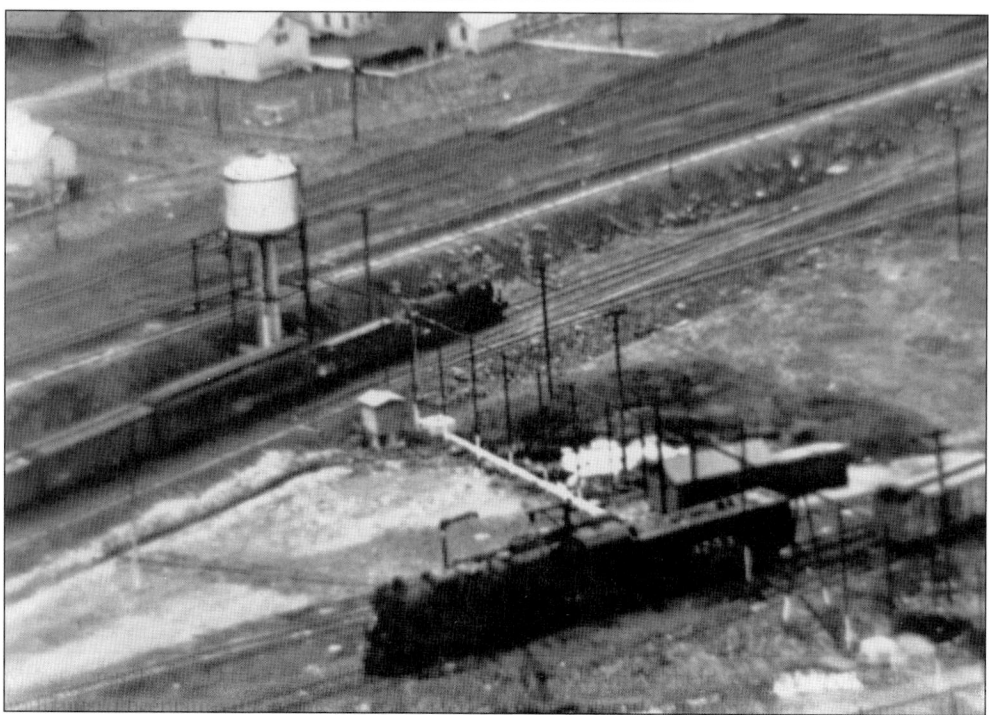

Rail activity stayed quite busy in Williams in 1939. Engines came and went through the railroad yard, located on the north side of the city. (Courtesy Williams Public Library.)

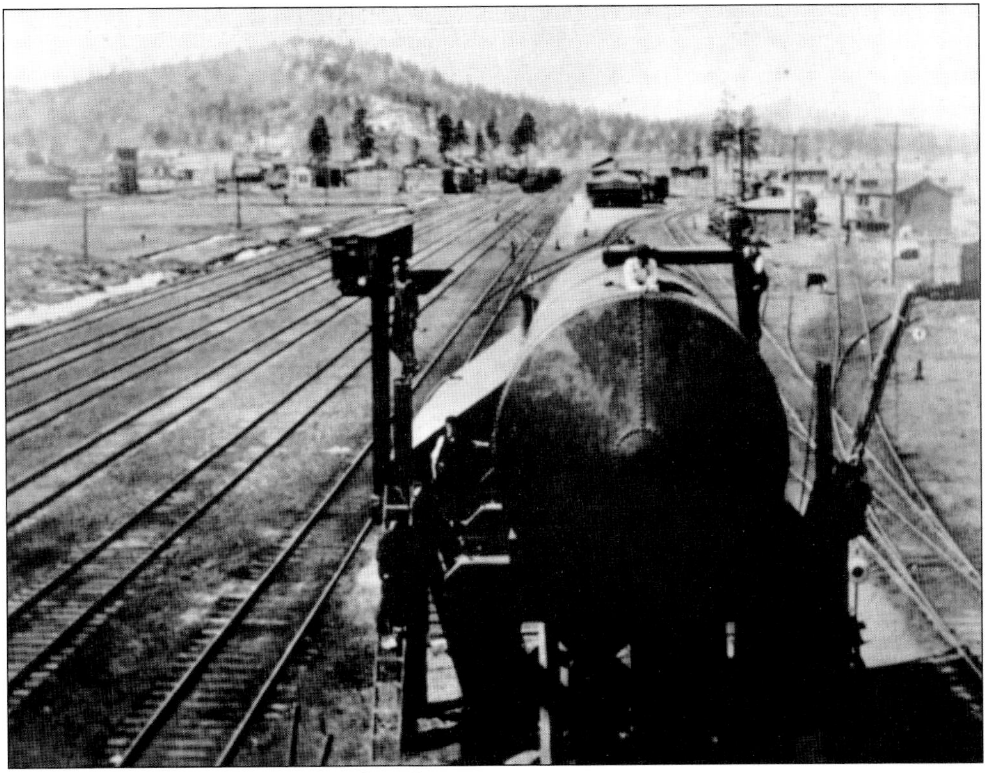

An early-1900s view of the railroad track looks west. The arrival of the rail lines in Williams allowed far better access for ranchers to ship livestock from one location to another. (Courtesy Williams Public Library.)

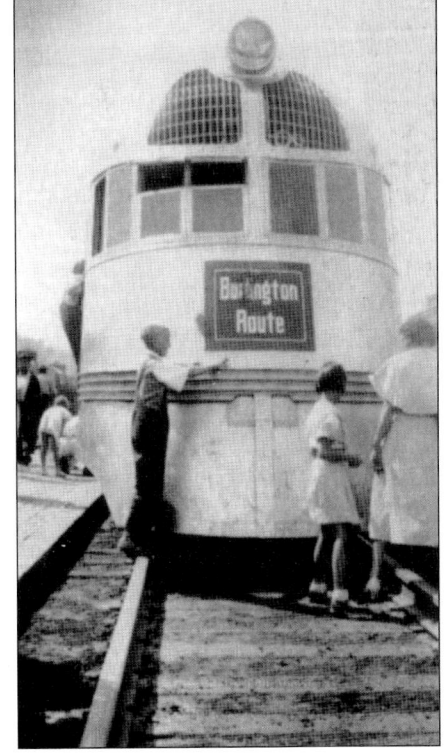

A Burlington Zephyr arrives in Williams in 1945 during its initial pass through the city. Children got a chance to marvel at the engine as it stopped in front of the Fray Marcos. (Courtesy *Williams–Grand Canyon News*.)

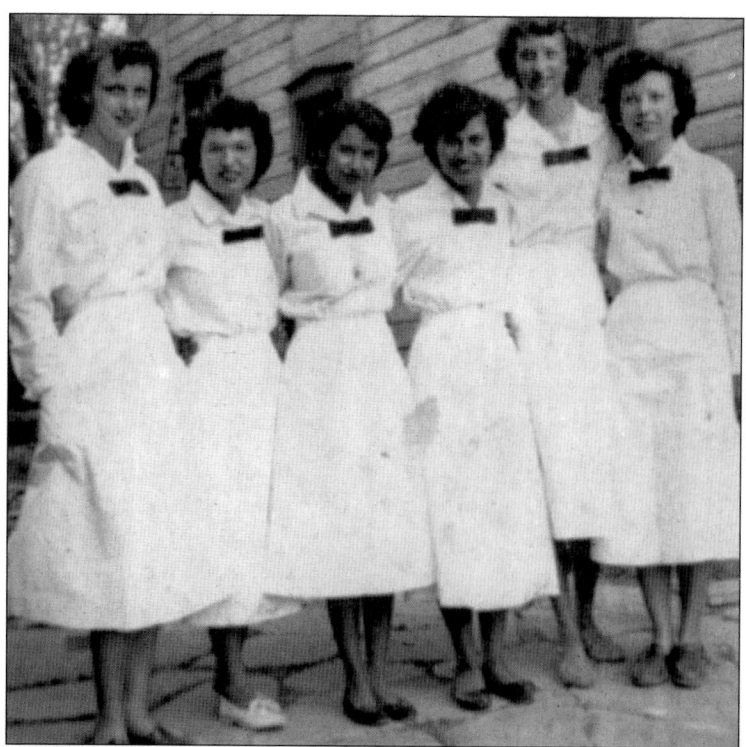

Fred Harvey Girls in the 1950s included Barbara Miller, Frances Dickerson, Carolyn Rincon, Dora DeAlva, Stella Baca, and "Dottie." (Courtesy *Williams–Grand Canyon News*.)

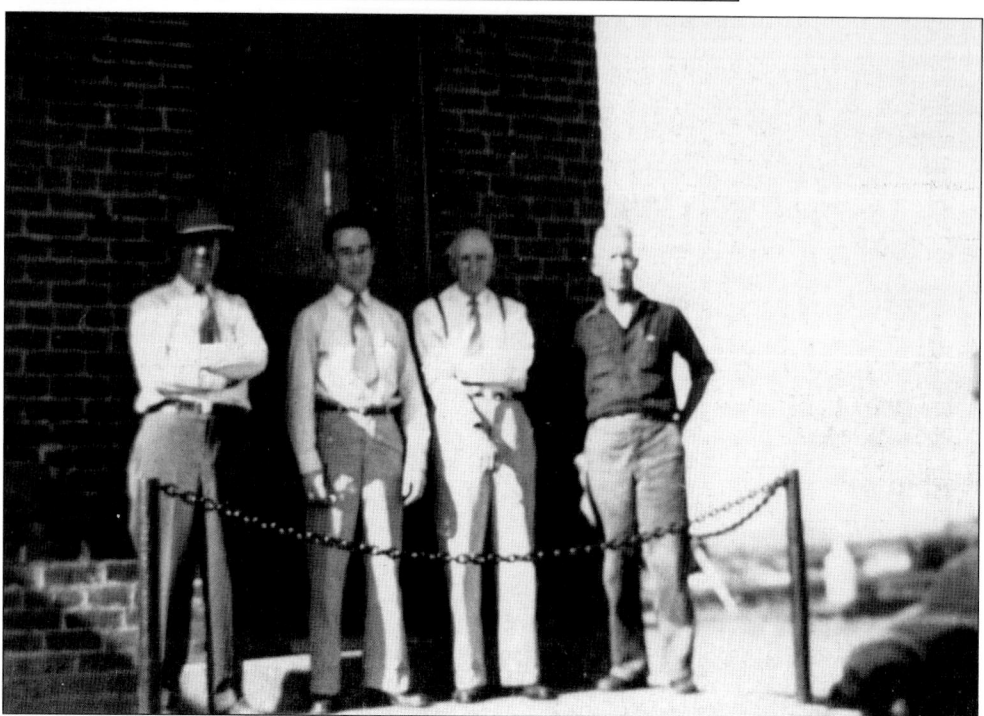

Williams Freight Depot employees in September 1945 included (from left to right) agent E. J. Nordyke, ticket cashier Robert Brinias, freight cashier H. L. Benham, and yard foreman Charlie Gunther, among others. (Courtesy Williams Public Library.)

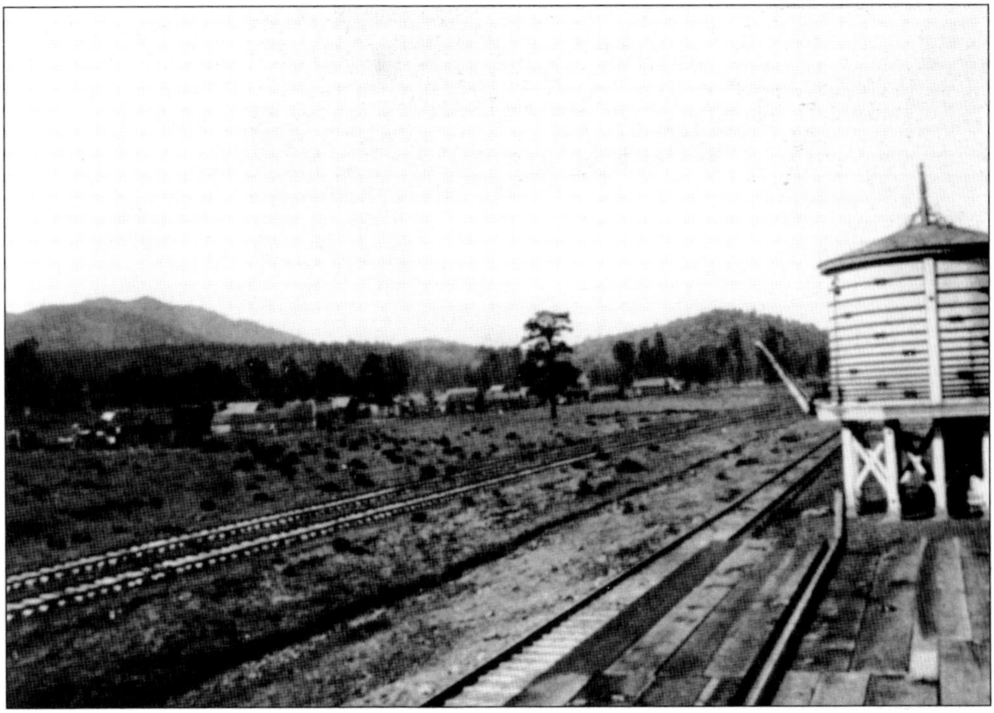

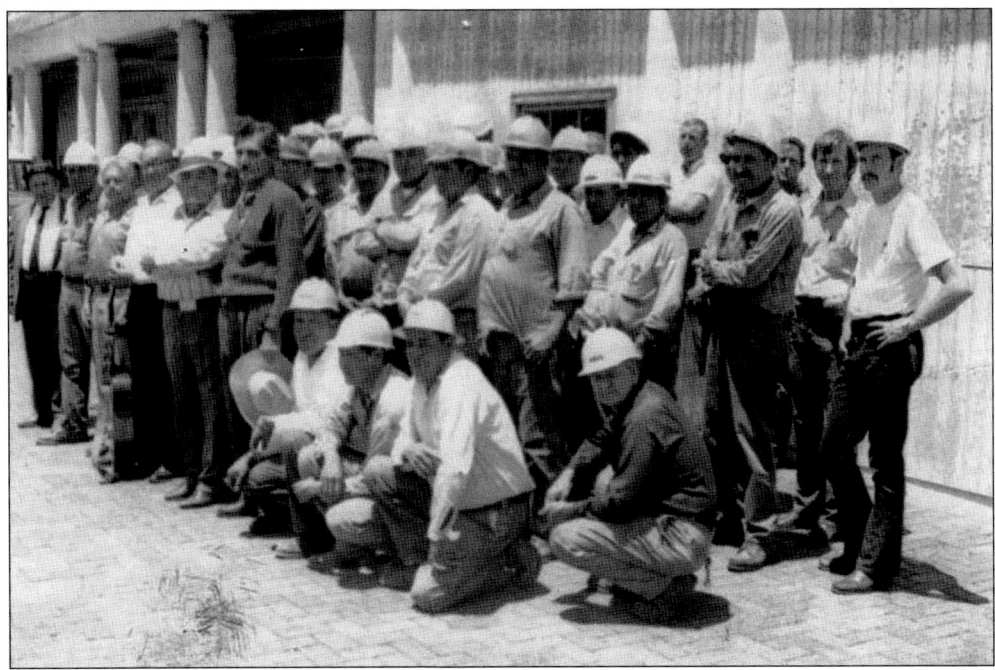

Prior to the arrival of the railroad in Williams, travelers in northern Arizona were faced with riding by stagecoach, on the back of an animal, or by foot. (Courtesy Williams Public Library.)

Even after the rail line to the Grand Canyon from Williams was discontinued in 1968, Atchison, Topeka, and Santa Fe section crews continued to congregate at the Fray Marcos in the 1970s. (Courtesy Williams Public Library.)

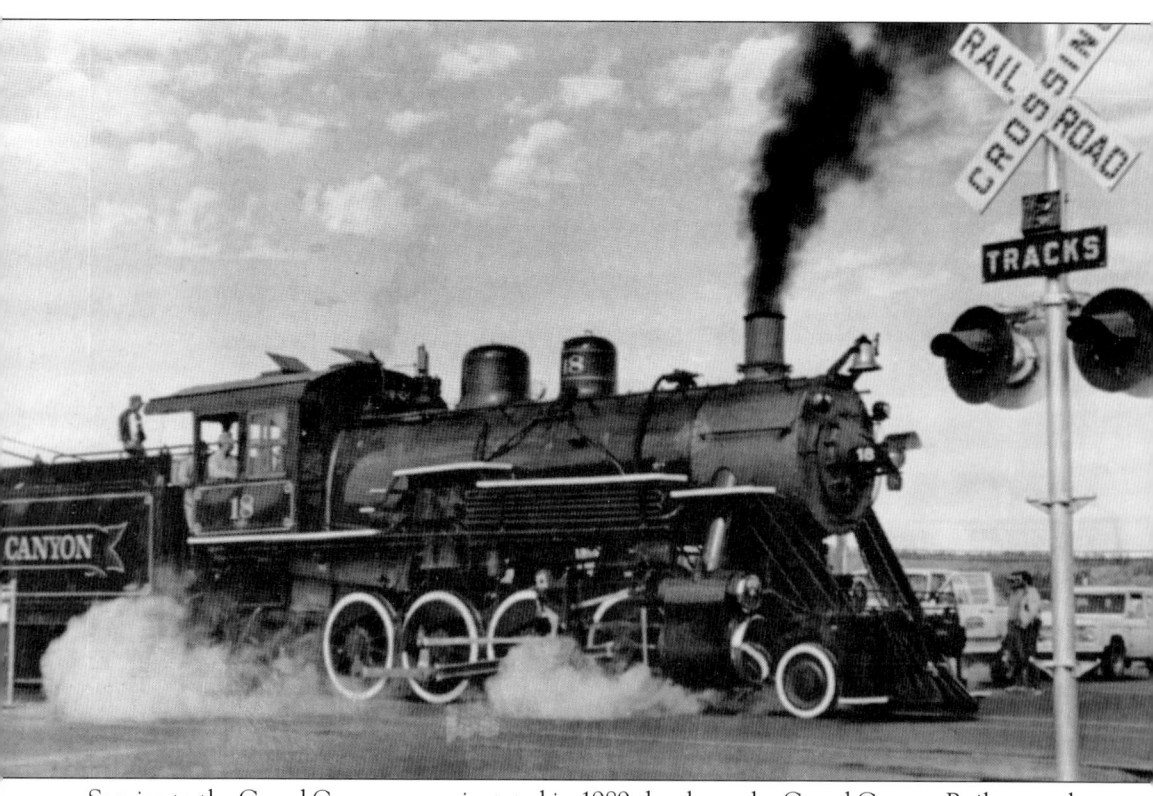

Service to the Grand Canyon was reinstated in 1989 thanks to the Grand Canyon Railway and founders Max and Thelma Biegert. The beloved steam engine to the canyon could once again be heard tooting its horn in the Williams community. (Courtesy *Williams–Grand Canyon News.*)

Four

THE SAGINAW LUMBER COMPANY
LOGGING BECOMES
BIG BUSINESS

The first large-scale sawmill in Williams opened for business around 1894, when employees with the Saginaw Lumber Company built a mill capable of producing 30,000 to 35,000 feet per day. The new mill was destined for a short lifespan, however, as a fire destroyed the operation in 1897. A box factory and planing mill, recently added to the lumber plant, were also destroyed in the blaze. Roughly eight million feet of lumber was lost. Work quickly began on a new lumber plant, located near the old plant's remains in an area of Williams where the high school and health care center now stand.

Logs arrived at the mill on skids and were pulled into the plant via a bull wheel assembly after they were placed on loading cars. They were then dropped on the deck, loaded, and turned onto carriages by cant hooks. The lumber was typically hauled to the yard by mule-powered carts.

The new mill was capable of producing far more than the previous one, with a capacity of 45,000 to 55,000 feet per day. The planing mill and box factory were also rebuilt and brought up to date. Three years after it was rebuilt, the mill once again underwent a change. The company was reorganized to become the Saginaw and Manistee Lumber Company in 1900. A number of changes were made in line with the company's reorganization, including two band mills, a resaw, a double edger, a small lath mill, and a big burner.

The Saginaw and Manistee Lumber Mill stimulated the economic boom in the area, as it allowed entrepreneurial business owners to set up shop. Businesses included brothels, saloons, and opium dens, among more standard fare. Railroad construction workers also contributed to the abundance of offerings that sprang up in the area at the time. The lumber mill continued its operations in Williams until 1941, when Saginaw and Manistee officials decided to move the entire operation to Flagstaff, 35 miles away.

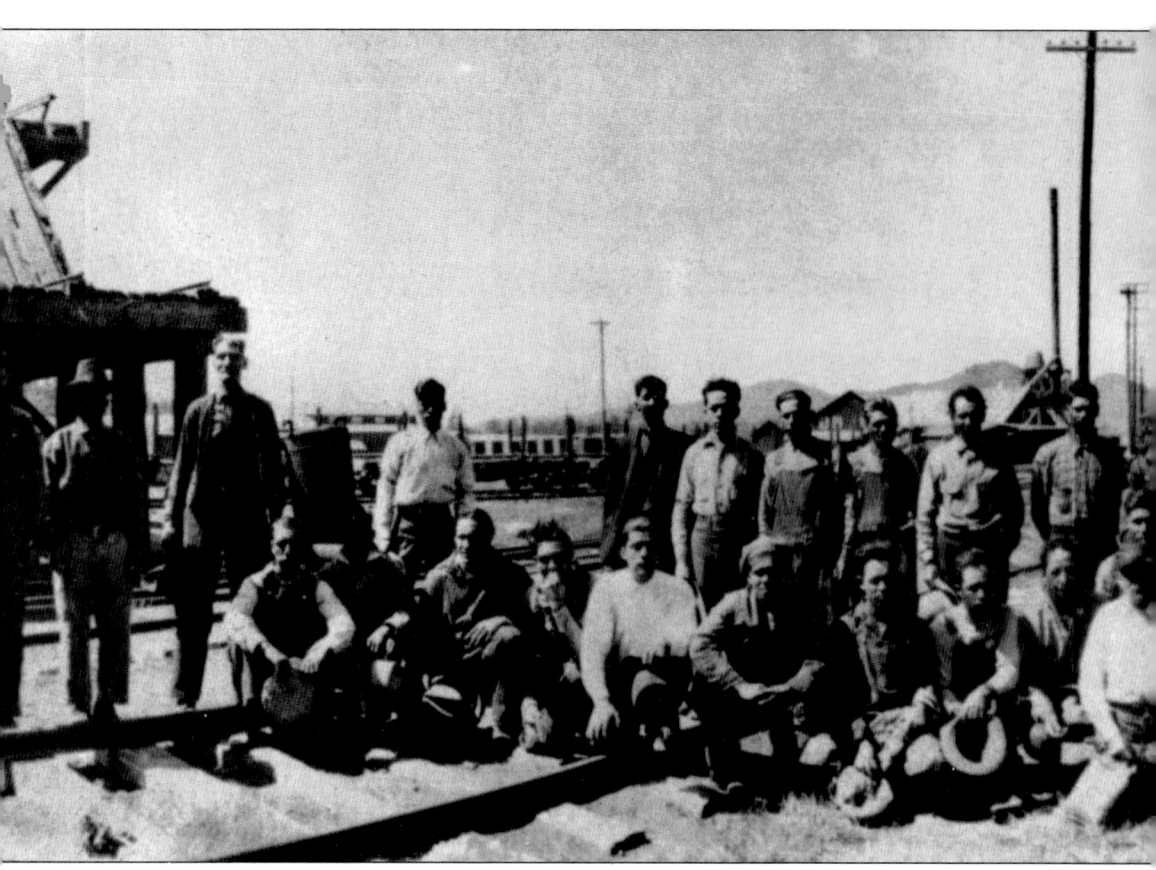

Employees with the Saginaw and Manistee Lumber Mill stand near the large-scale lumber operation based out of Williams. By 1920, the company had been operating in northern Arizona for more than 20 years. Originally under the sole proprietorship of the Saginaw Company,

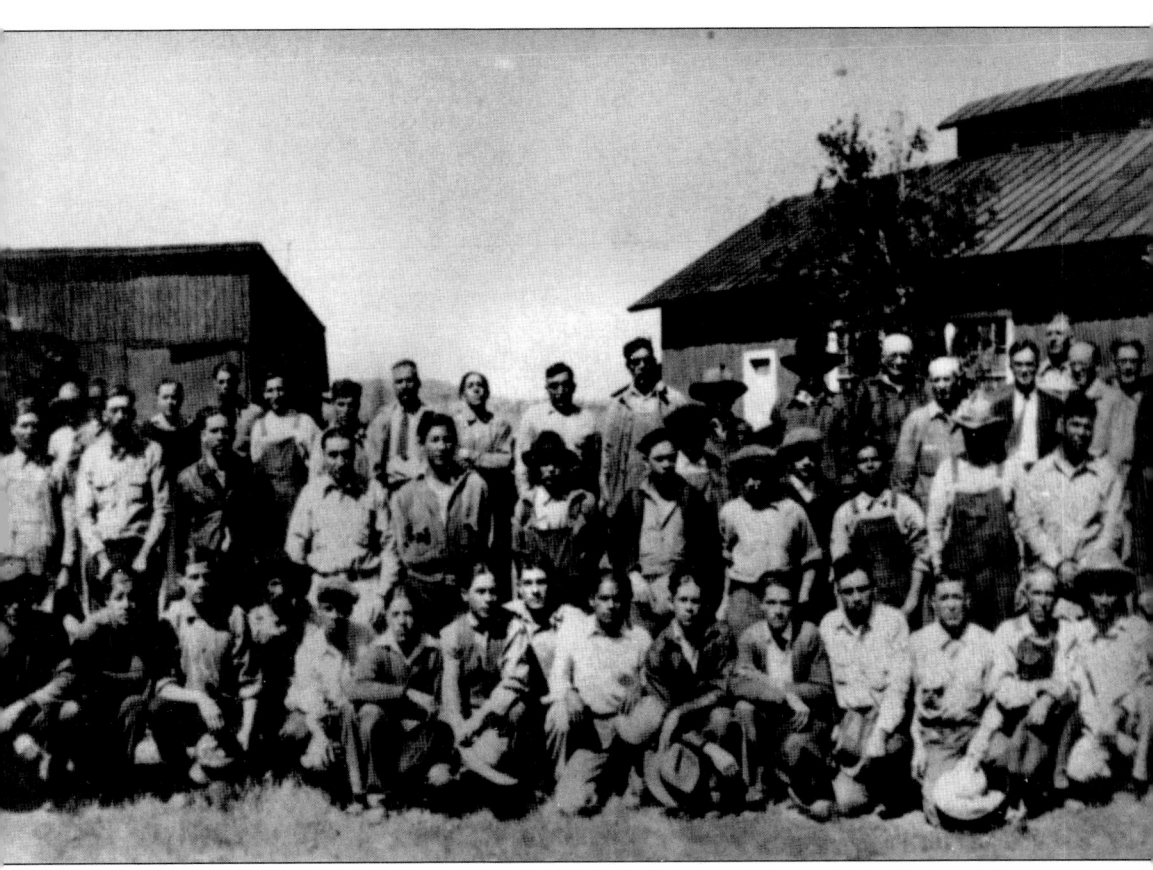

it joined with the Manistee Company in 1900 to become one of northern Arizona's largest industries. (Courtesy Williams Public Library.)

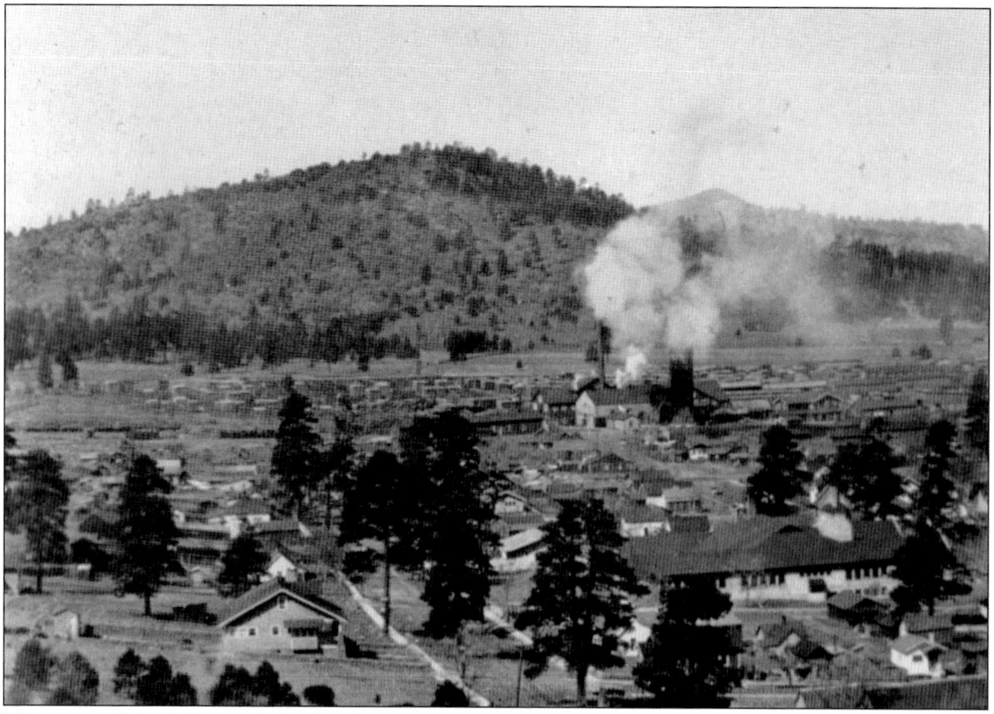

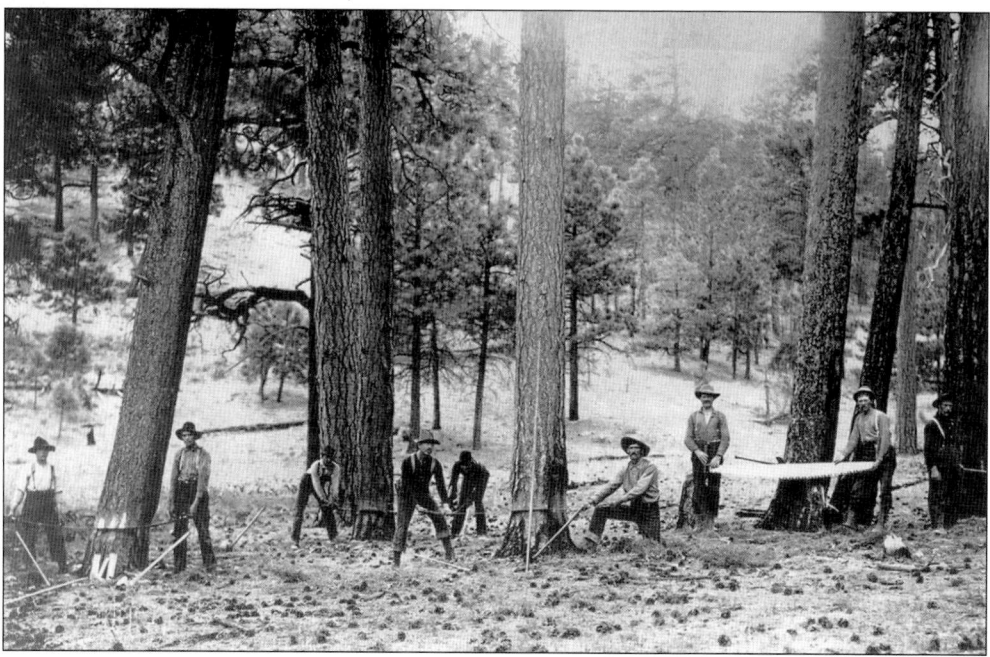

The sawmill had changed the landscape of Williams considerably by 1925. Both the community and the surrounding forest underwent a major change thanks to the large-scale operation. (Courtesy Williams Public Library.)

Nine lumberjacks set to work on a clutch of tall pine trees near Williams with their large two-man saws. Lumber operations began in northern Arizona around 1892. (Courtesy U.S. Forest Service, Southwestern Region, Kaibab National Forest.)

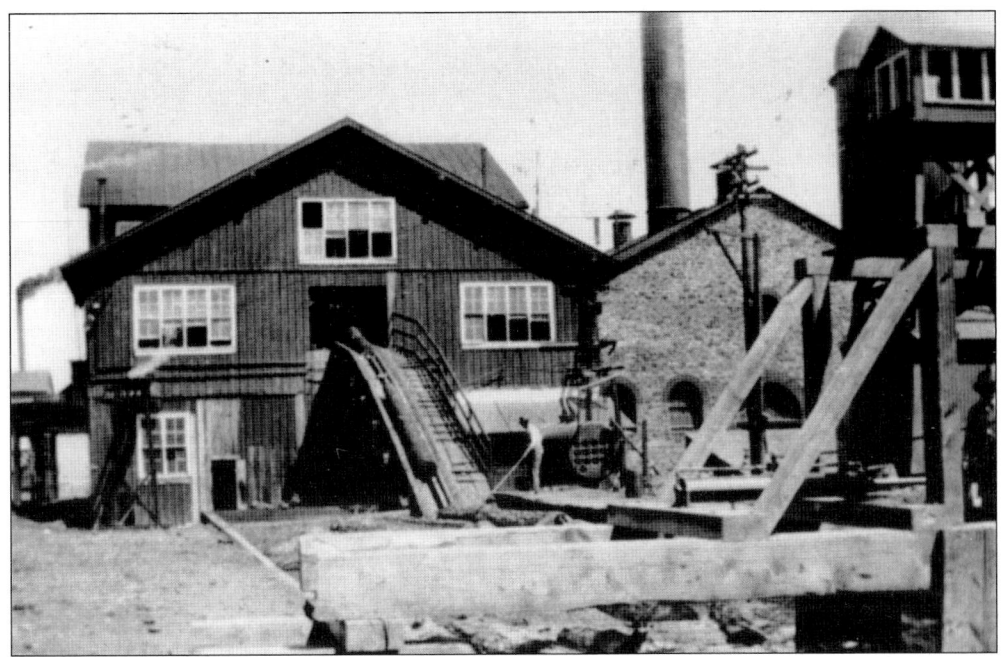

Logs were transported in the Saginaw and Manistee Lumber Mill from skids. They were pulled into the mill from loading cars via a bull wheel. (Courtesy Williams Public Library.)

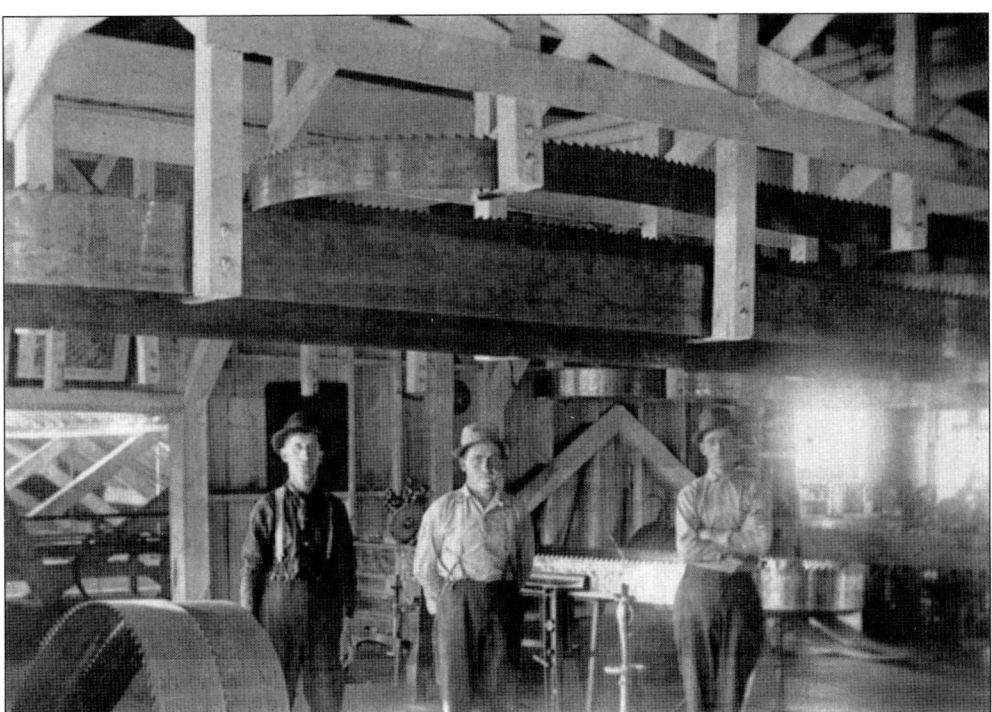

Saginaw and Manistee employees, including Williams resident Will Miller (center), stand inside the mill's saw filing room. Logs were typically brought to the plant for processing by mule-powered carts. (Courtesy Williams Public Library.)

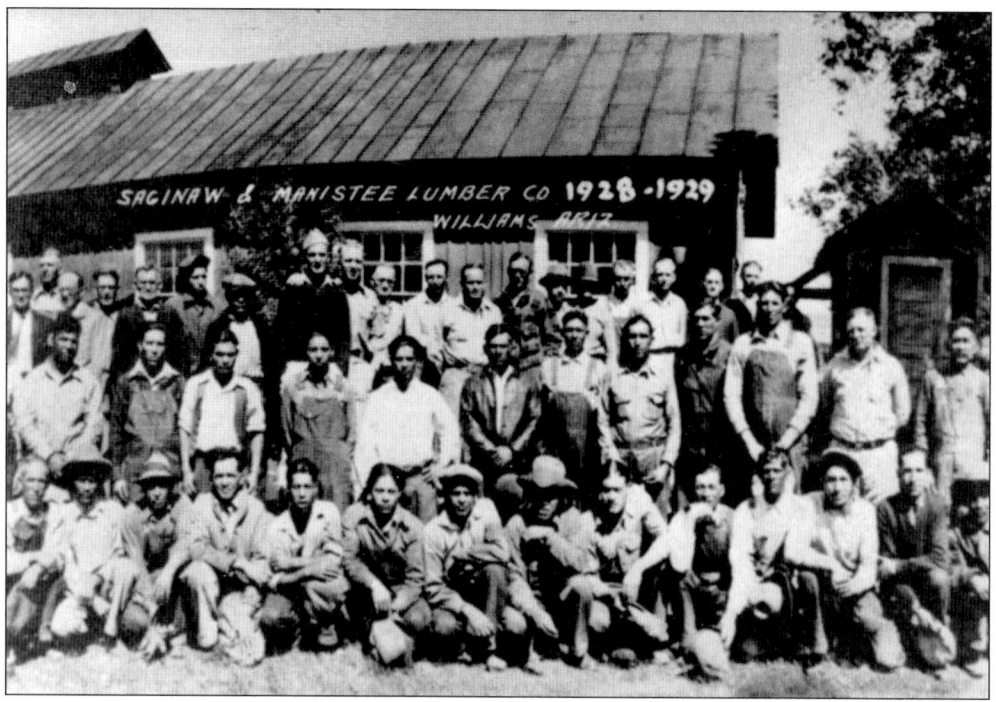

Employees of the Saginaw and Manistee Lumber Mill gather outside the mill in 1928. The Saginaw Company, hailing from Saginaw, Michigan, obtained lumber rights to a large portion of what is now the Kaibab National Forest in 1893. The company supplied lumber not only to Williams businesses, but also to ranchers and railroad workers in the area. (Both, courtesy Williams Public Library.)

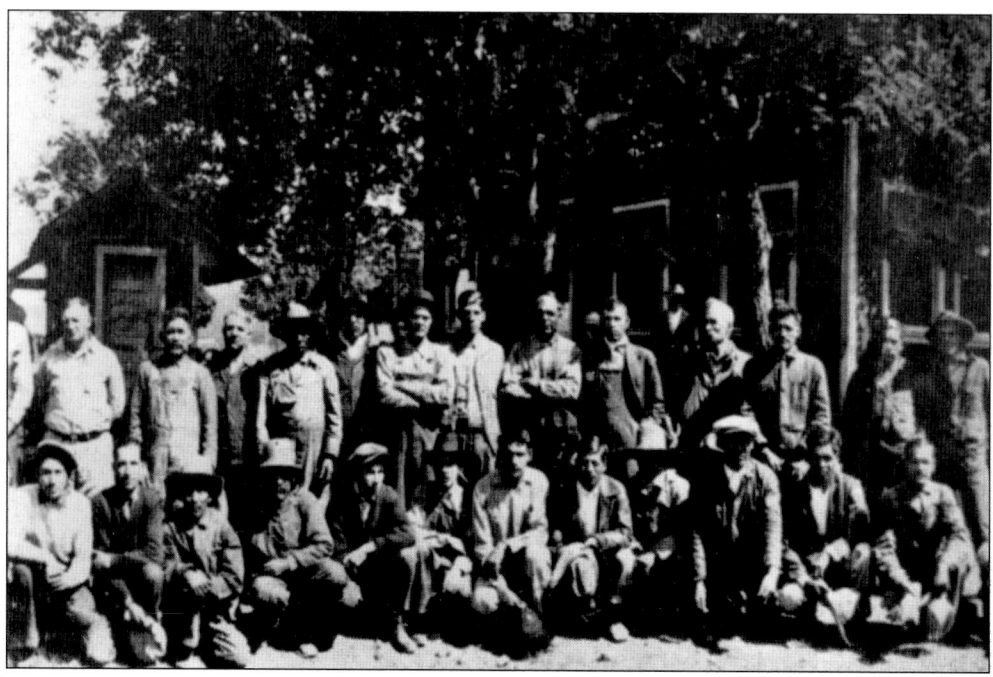

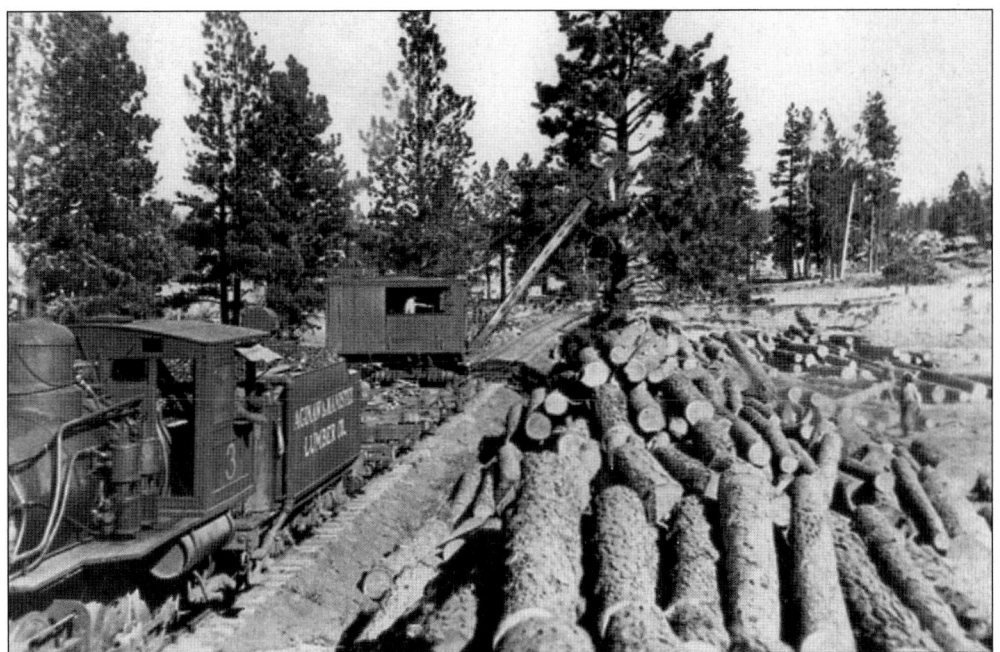

A Saginaw and Manistee logging train places its product on a docking area in the 1920s. Logging trains could often be seen heading toward Williams loaded with Ponderosa pine logs. (Courtesy U.S. Forest Service, Southwestern Region, Kaibab National Forest.)

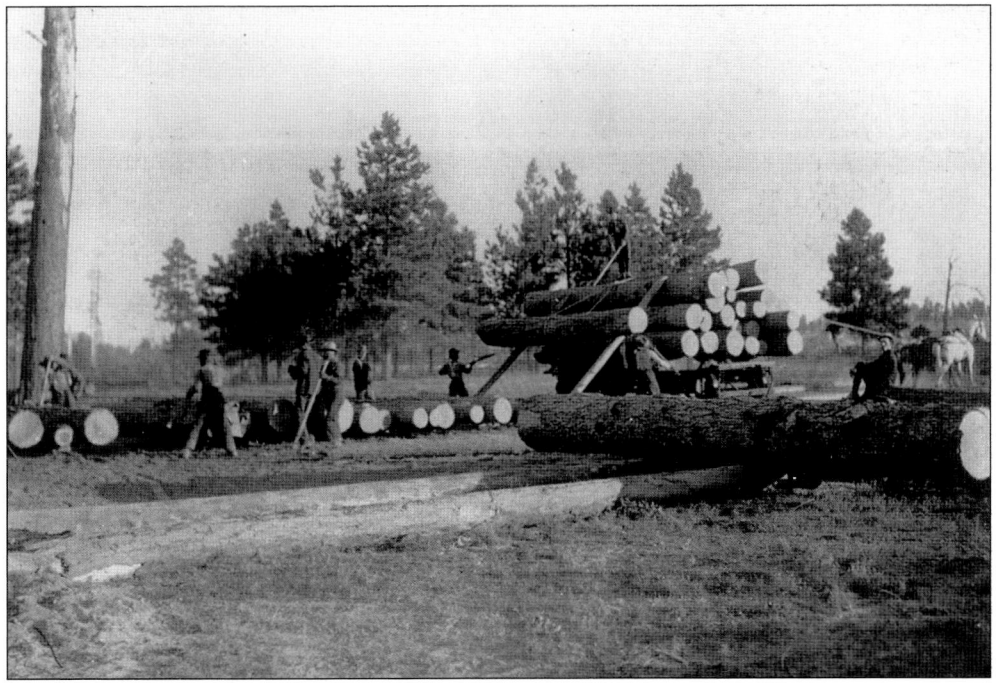

A handful of hearty lumberjacks load logs near Williams for processing at the Saginaw lumber mill. The logging industry became such an integral part of the history of northern Arizona that the nearby university in Flagstaff would name its mascot the Lumberjack. (Courtesy U.S. Forest Service, Southwestern Region, Kaibab National Forest.)

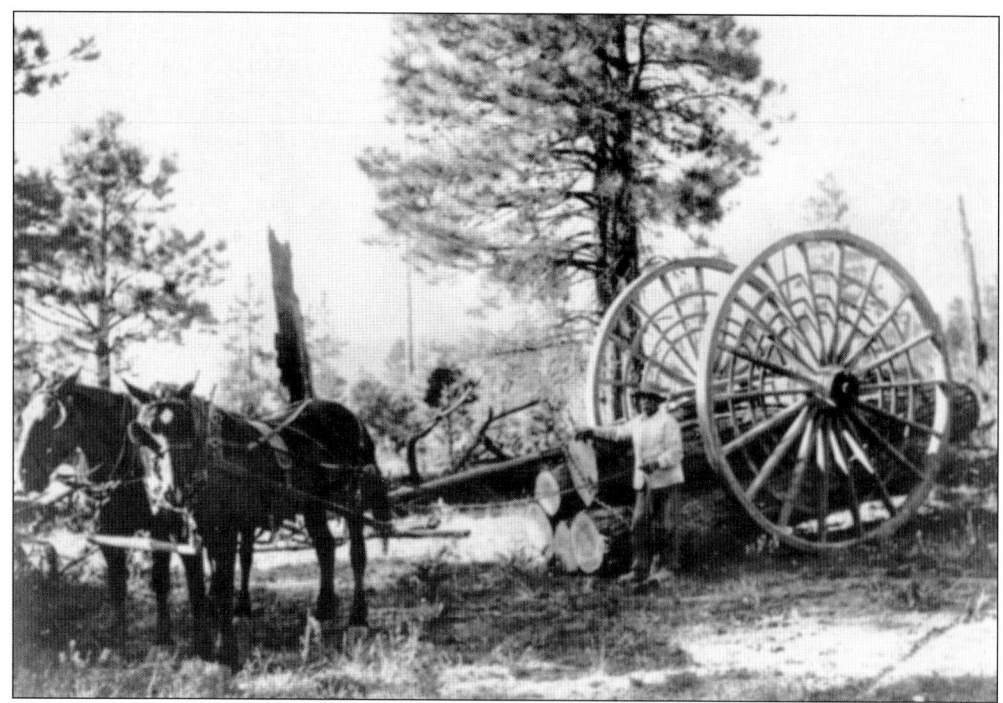

A sole lumberjack heads to Williams with his two draft horses. The horses had their work cut out for them as they hauled a large-wheeled lumber cart loaded with logs. (Courtesy U.S. Forest Service, Southwestern Region, Kaibab National Forest.)

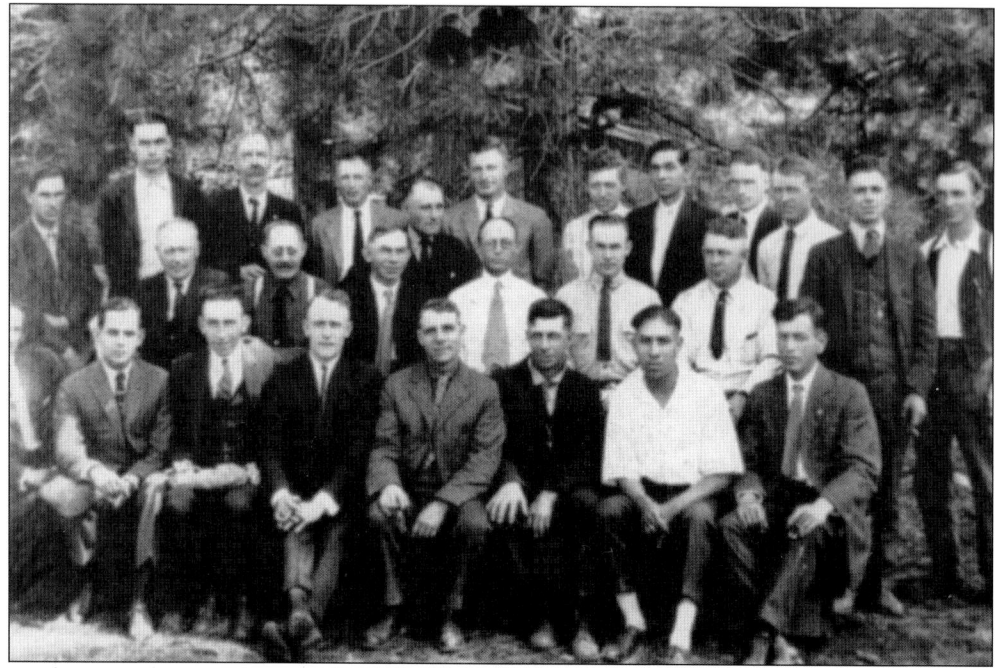

Like many large-scale industries, the Saginaw and Manistee Lumber Mill formed a safety committee. Shown in 1923, the committee was responsible for the safety and welfare of the employees who worked at the mill. (Courtesy Williams Public Library.)

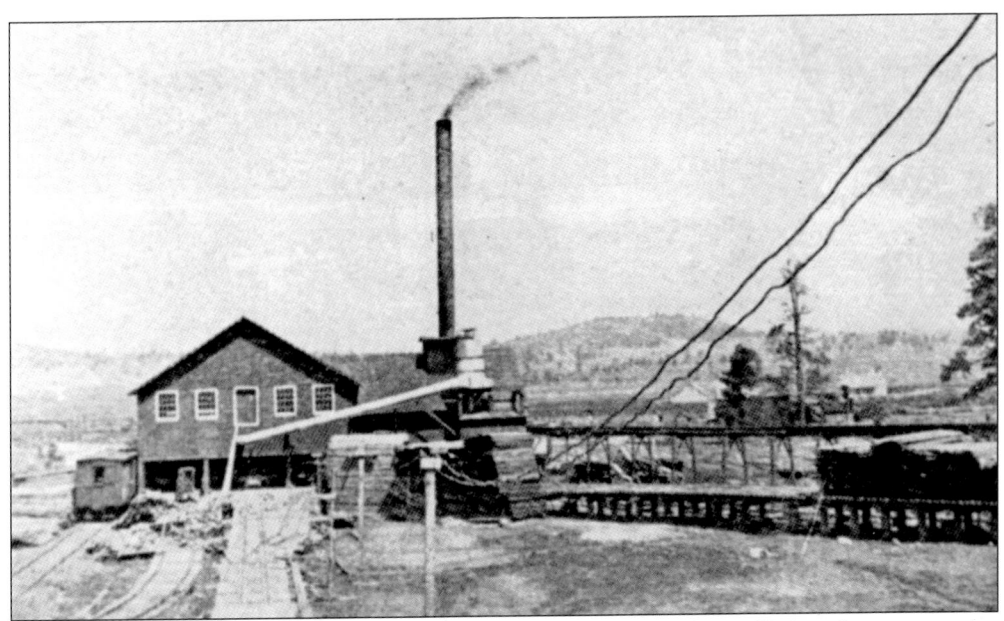

The Saginaw planing mill was destroyed by a fire around 1897. The mill's box factory was also destroyed in the blaze. Roughly eight million feet of lumber went up in smoke as a result of the conflagration. (Courtesy Williams Public Library.)

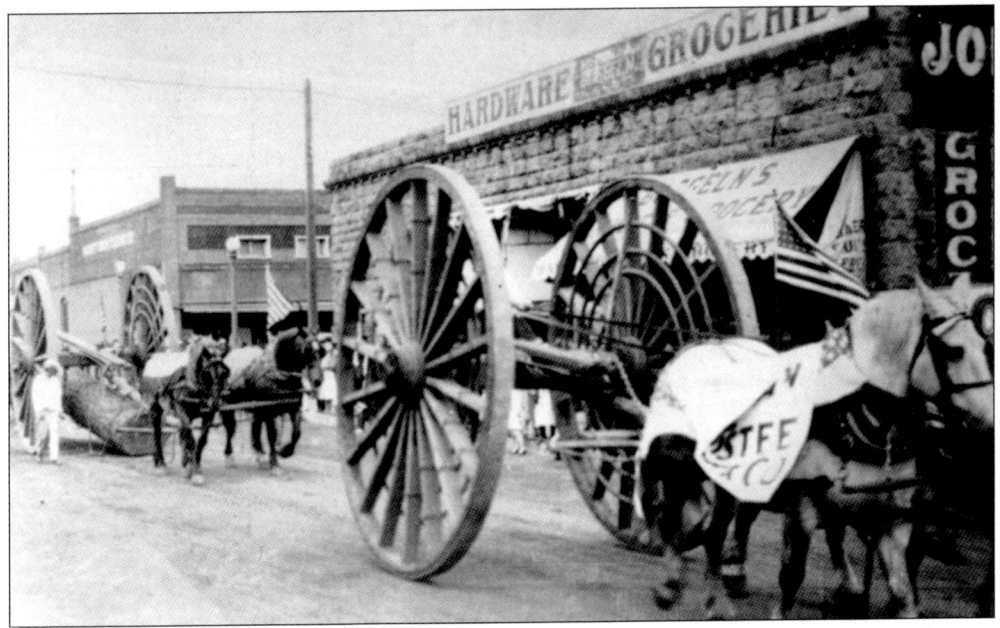

Large-wheeled Saginaw and Manistee lumber carts make their way east along Bill Williams Avenue as part of the city's Fourth of July parade in 1927. (Courtesy Williams Public Library.)

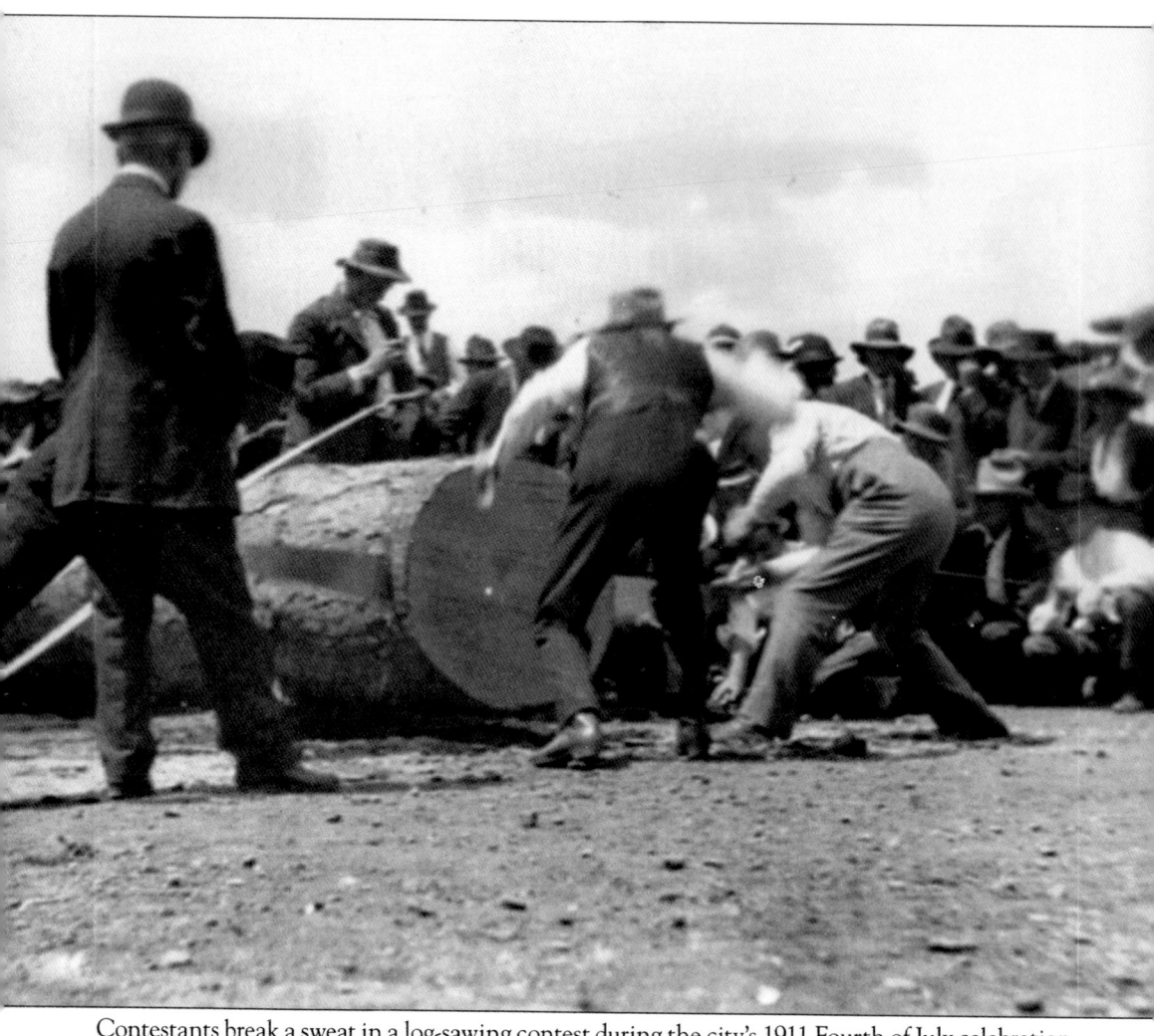

Contestants break a sweat in a log-sawing contest during the city's 1911 Fourth of July celebration. The team in this photograph managed to saw their log in 32 seconds flat. (Courtesy U.S. Forest Service, Southwestern Region, Kaibab National Forest.)

Five

FIRES AND BROTHELS
WILLIAMS BURNS AND BOOMS

Prior to the formation of the Williams Volunteer Fire Department in 1912, residents would fire five shots into the air in the event of a fire with the hopes that other locals would bring buckets of water and perhaps a water wagon. Those shots rang out often, as Williams was plagued by large fires in its early years.

The first notorious fire came in 1884, when four local businesses burned to the ground. A second fire erupted one year later, razing a total of seven buildings in all. Two blocks of what was once known as Front Street were ravaged by flames in 1895. The worst fire came in 1901 and consumed 36 businesses, 2 hotels, and 10 homes before it was finally doused. The 1901 fire caused a total of $300,000 worth of damage—a hefty sum for the time. Another fire in 1903 devoured six saloons, one restaurant, and two homes. A number of Williams families were made homeless in 1908 following a blaze that took out an entire city block as well as 12 homes.

Fires were not the only problem in Williams. The criminal element also seemed to enjoy the area. The town became known as having more opium smokers than any other town of its size in the United States. One notorious den, called Wu's Joint, operated well into 1908, when it was finally raided by a local constable and two rangers. Brothels, it seemed, were just as common as the opium dens, fires, and criminals.

Houses of ill repute could be found along Williams's Whiskey Row, including one located on the second floor in what is today known as the Red Garter Bed and Bakery. Another notorious brothel was Big Bertha's, located on the corner of First Street and Railroad Avenue. While prostitution was illegal in the Arizona Territory, ordinances were put in place to make it legal in Williams.

A night marshal was appointed in 1914 to bring justice to the wild town. Payments for his duties were paid by those he arrested. Further payment, it is said, he collected from the numerous houses of ill repute.

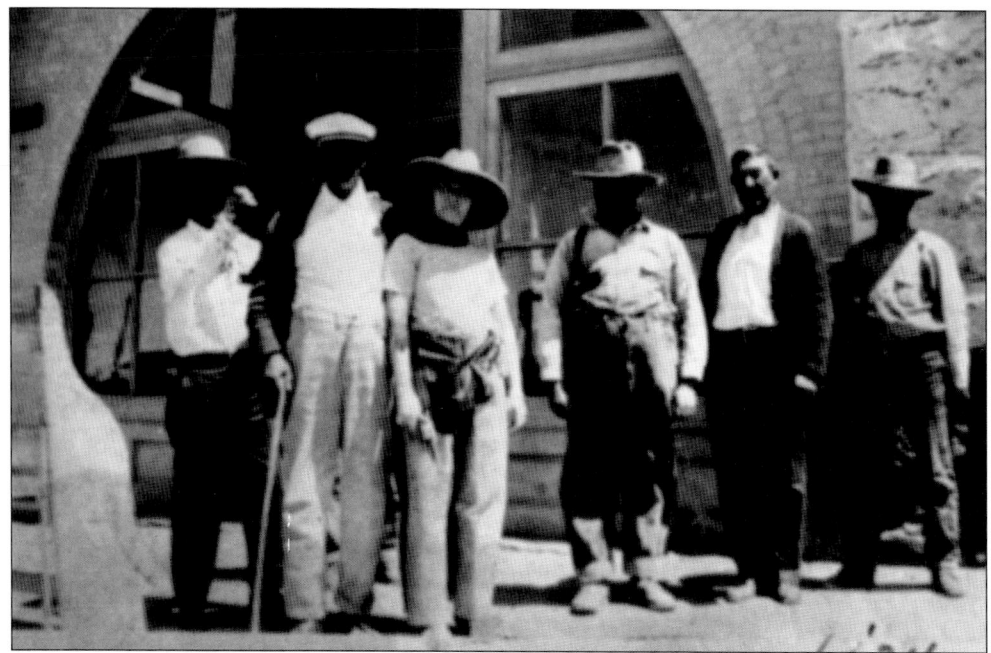

Williams saloon owner Longino Mora (second from left) stands in front of what is known today as the Red Garter building. The establishment's upstairs madam is also pictured, dressed for a rodeo weekend in her "Welcome to Williams" garb. Even the madams, it seemed, did their part for the city's chamber of commerce. (Courtesy John Holst of the Red Garter Bed and Bakery and the Mora family.)

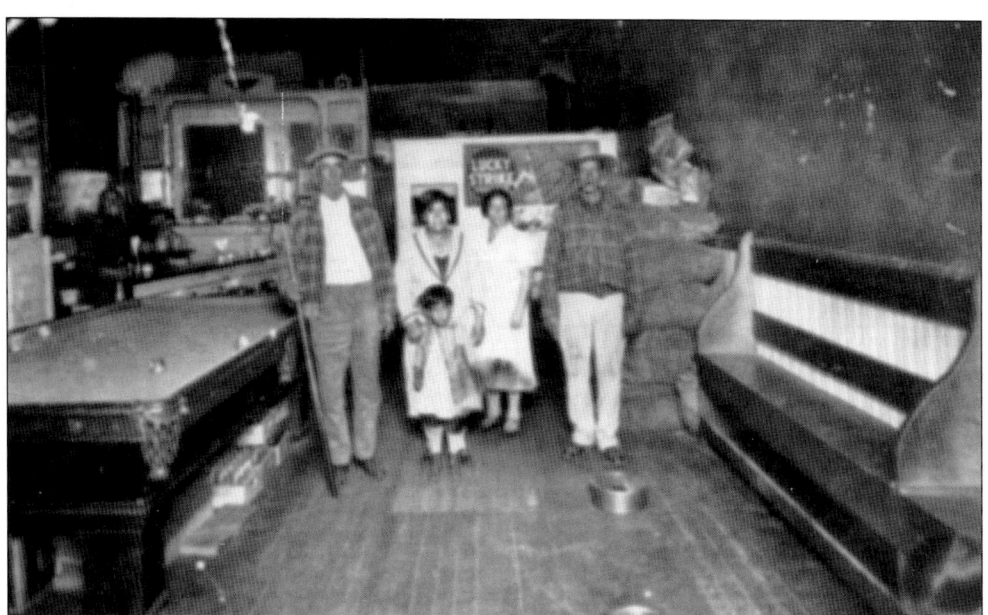

The Mora family is pictured inside their saloon in the 1930s. While the brothel ran its business upstairs, Longino Mora ran a bootlegging and gambling operation from the back of his business. (Courtesy John Holst of the Red Garter Bed and Bakery and the Mora family.)

Saloon owner Longino Mora (far right) stands on Railroad Avenue with a number of family and friends, including one of the upstairs girls. A Williams city ordinance prevented the girls from offering their services outside of a two-block area. (Courtesy John Holst of the Red Garter Bed and Bakery and the Mora family.)

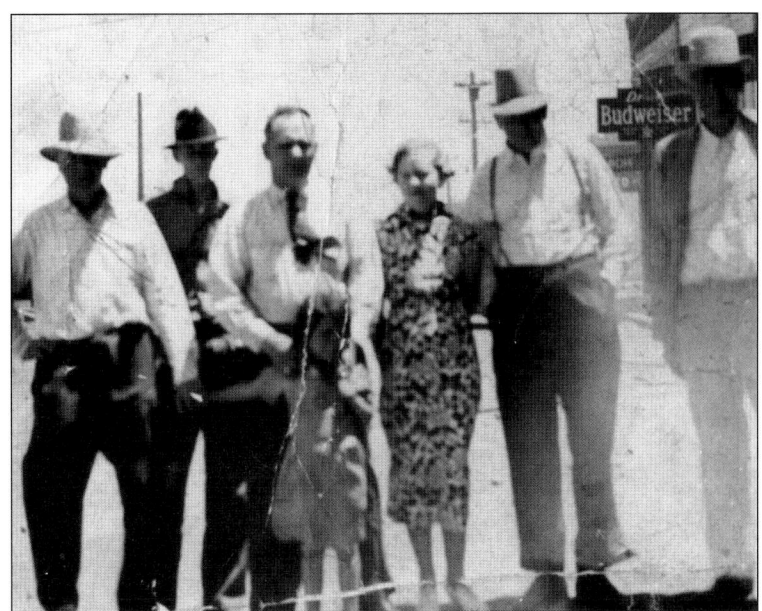

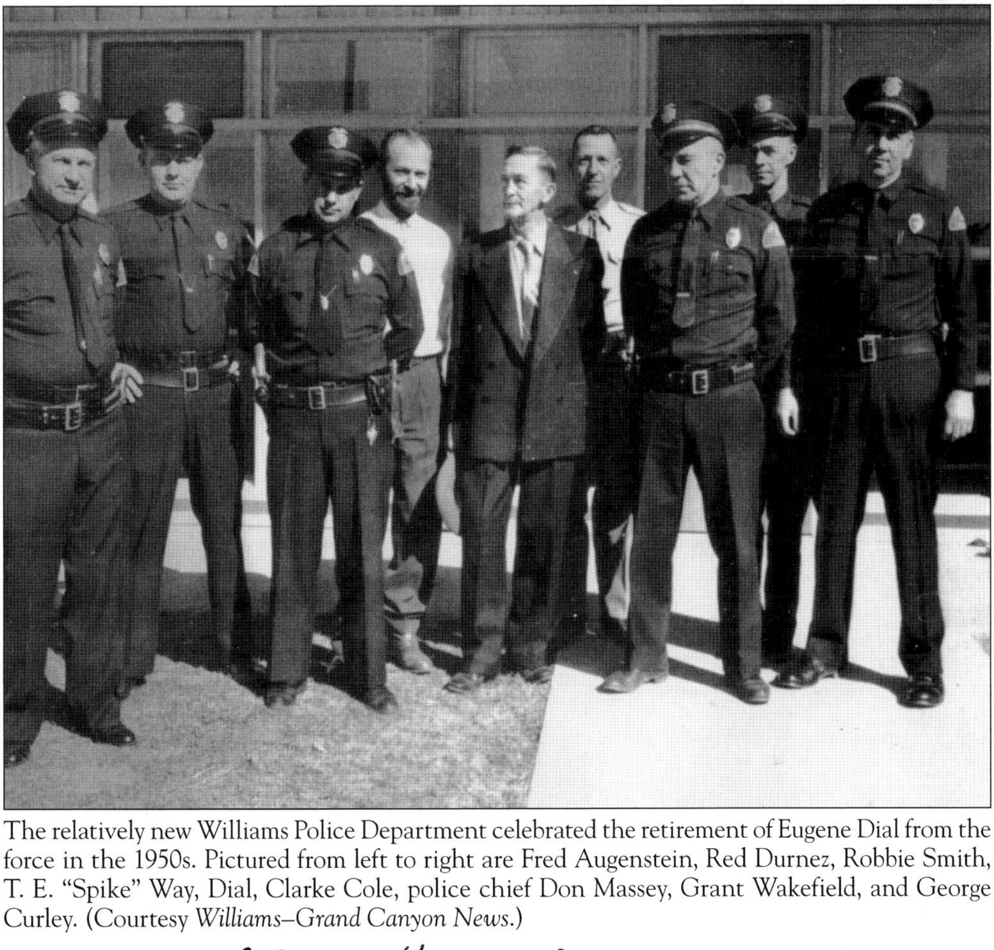

The relatively new Williams Police Department celebrated the retirement of Eugene Dial from the force in the 1950s. Pictured from left to right are Fred Augenstein, Red Durnez, Robbie Smith, T. E. "Spike" Way, Dial, Clarke Cole, police chief Don Massey, Grant Wakefield, and George Curley. (Courtesy *Williams–Grand Canyon News*.)

KATHY & ROBIN SMITH'S DAD
CRAIG

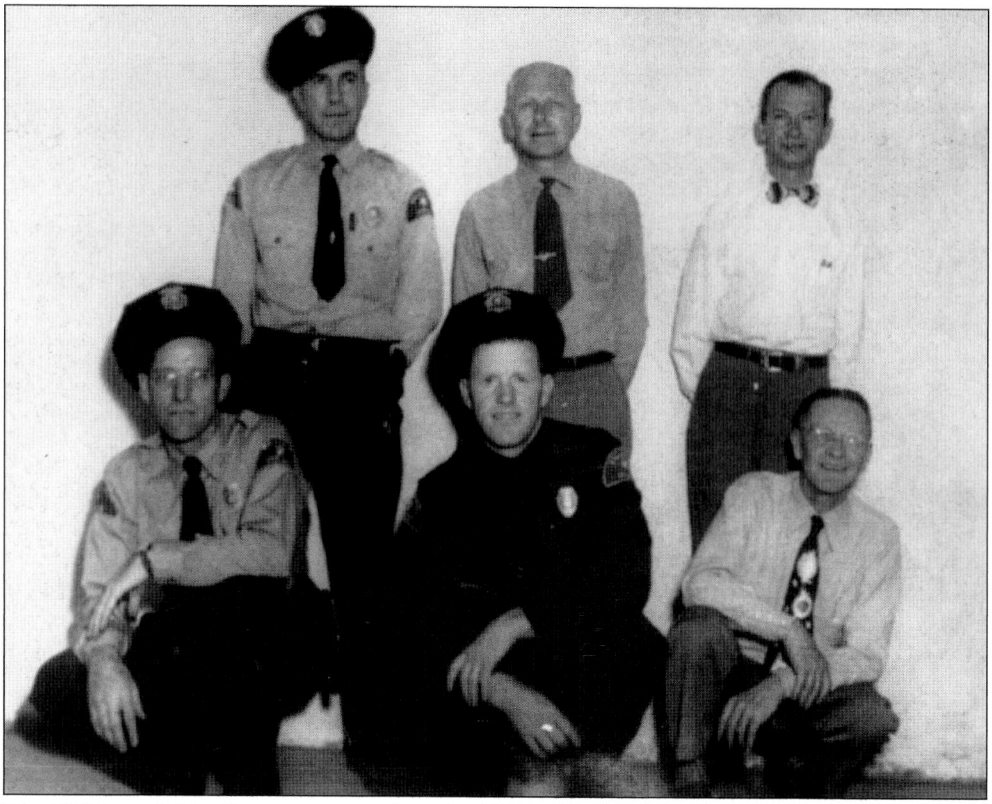

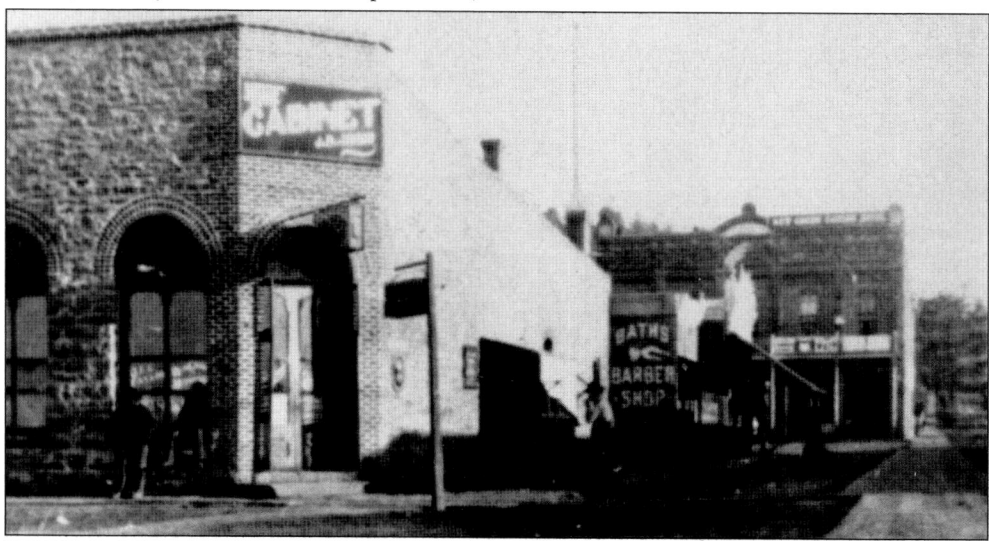

The Williams Police Force is pictured in the 1950s. A police chief would not be appointed to the city until around 1940, a man by the name of Joe McDaniels, who was subsequently shot and killed in an altercation behind the Sultana Bar. Don Massey became the first long-term chief in 1947. (Courtesy Williams Police Department.)

The Cabinet Saloon was a popular watering hole in the Williams area for travelers and residents. It was part of Williams's "Whiskey Row." Bathhouses, bars, and brothels were common sights in this part of the city. (Courtesy Williams Public Library.)

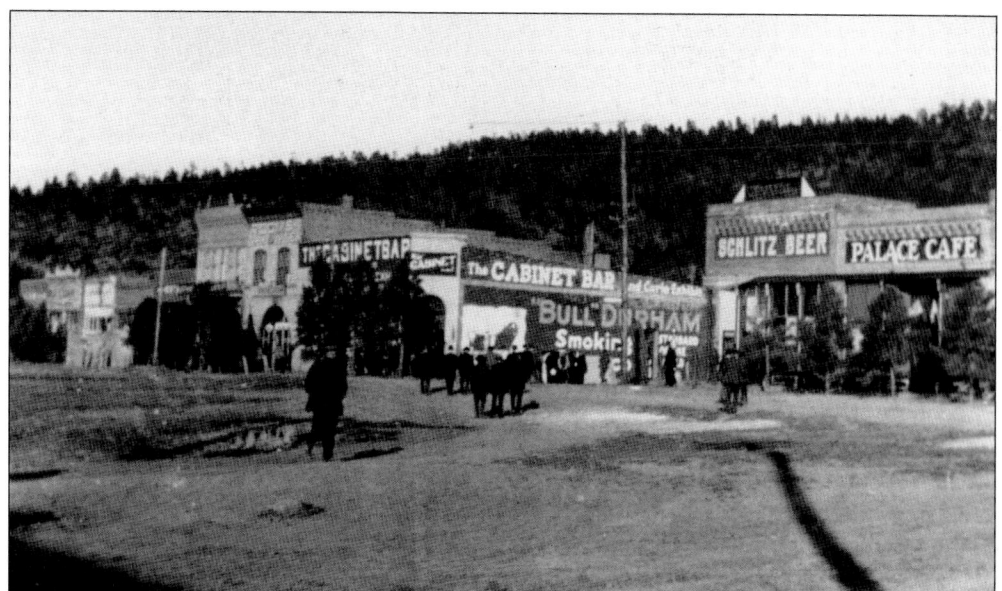

The corner of Front and Second Streets was a popular place in 1914. The Mora saloon and upstairs brothel can be seen next to the Cabinet Bar. In later years, Front Street would be renamed Railroad Avenue. (Courtesy Williams Public Library.)

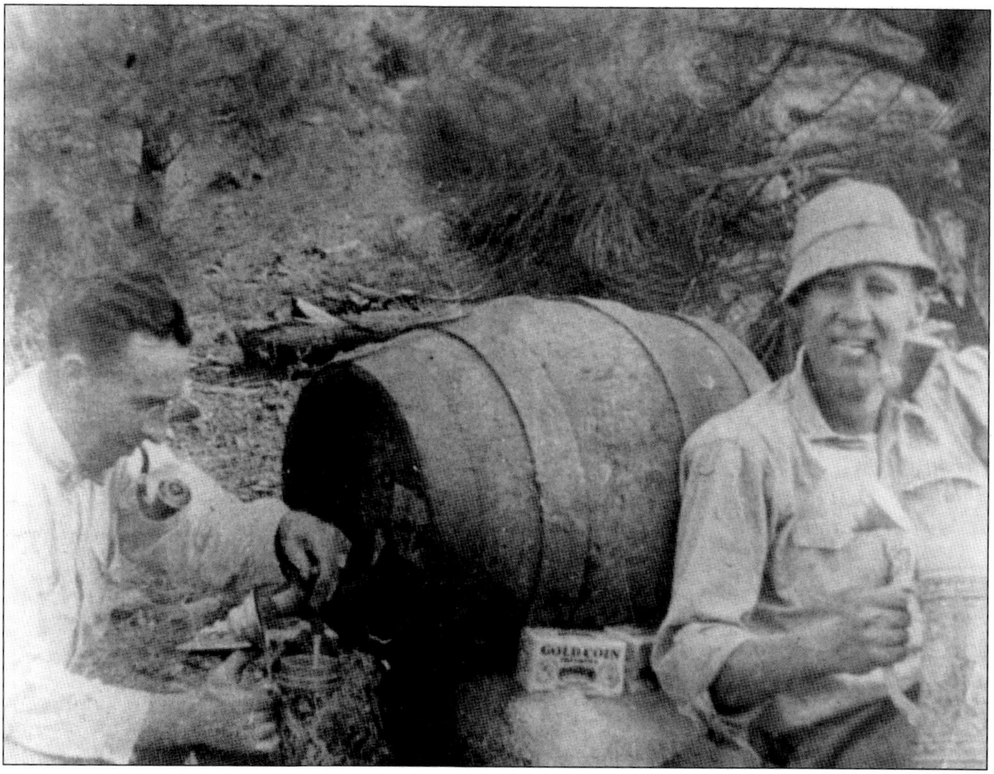

Looking more like famous crooner Bing Crosby than a bootlegger, Lilo Perrin enjoys a day outdoors with a friend. Perrin, known as the last pioneer of Williams, concocted his own brand of moonshine during the Prohibition era. (Courtesy Williams Public Library.)

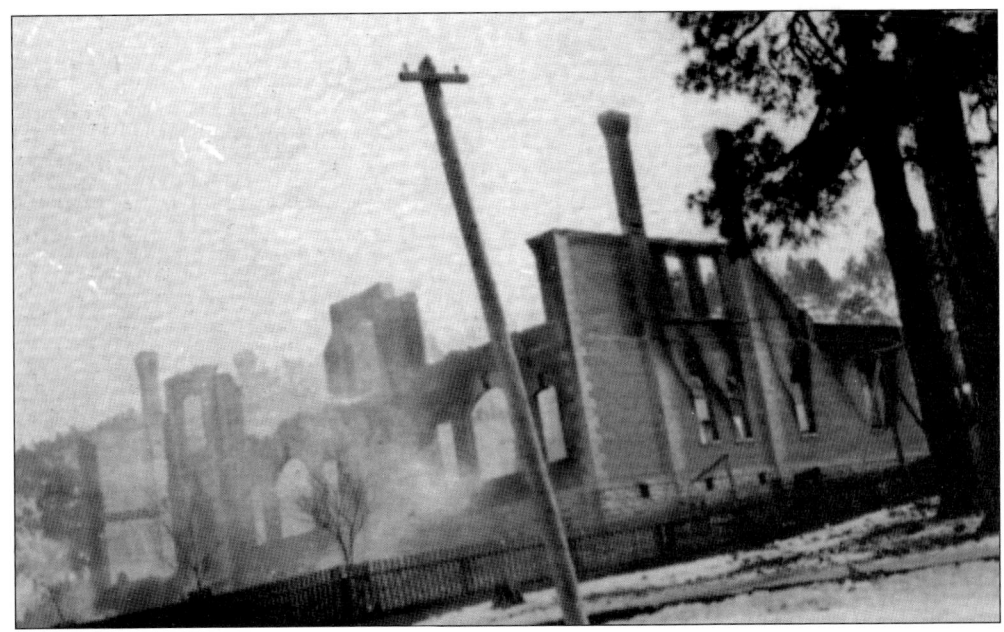

Fires continuously proved to be a thorn in the side of the residents of Williams throughout its history. This included the fire that destroyed the Williams school, which can be seen the day after it burned down in 1912. (Courtesy Williams Public Library.)

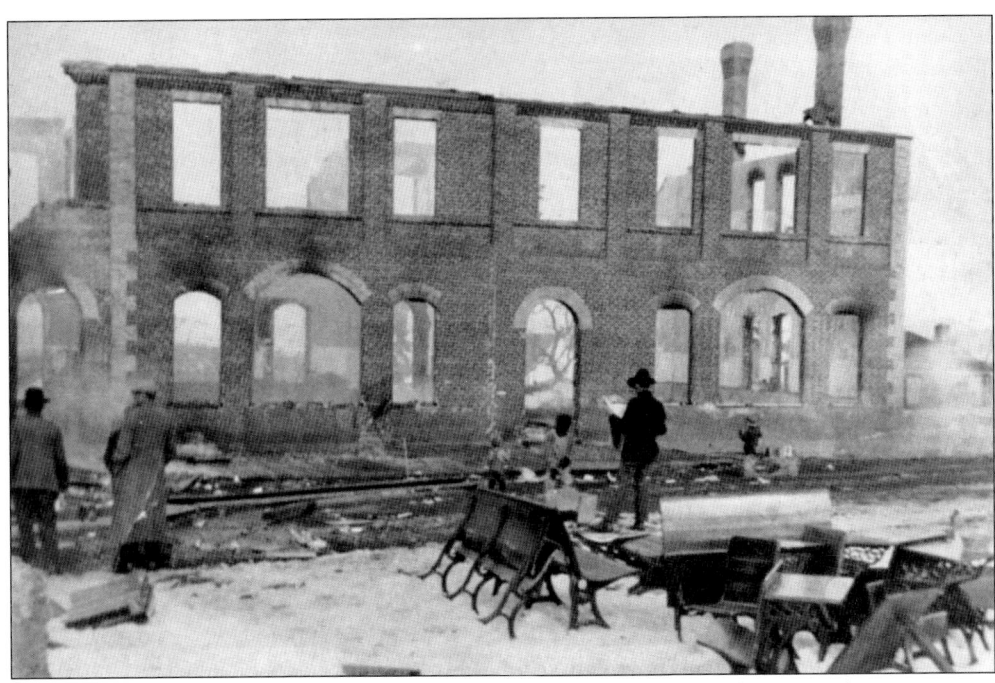

A man casually reads a newspaper while standing in front of the burned-out remains of the school in 1912. The Williams Fire Department formed that same year. (Courtesy Williams Public Library.)

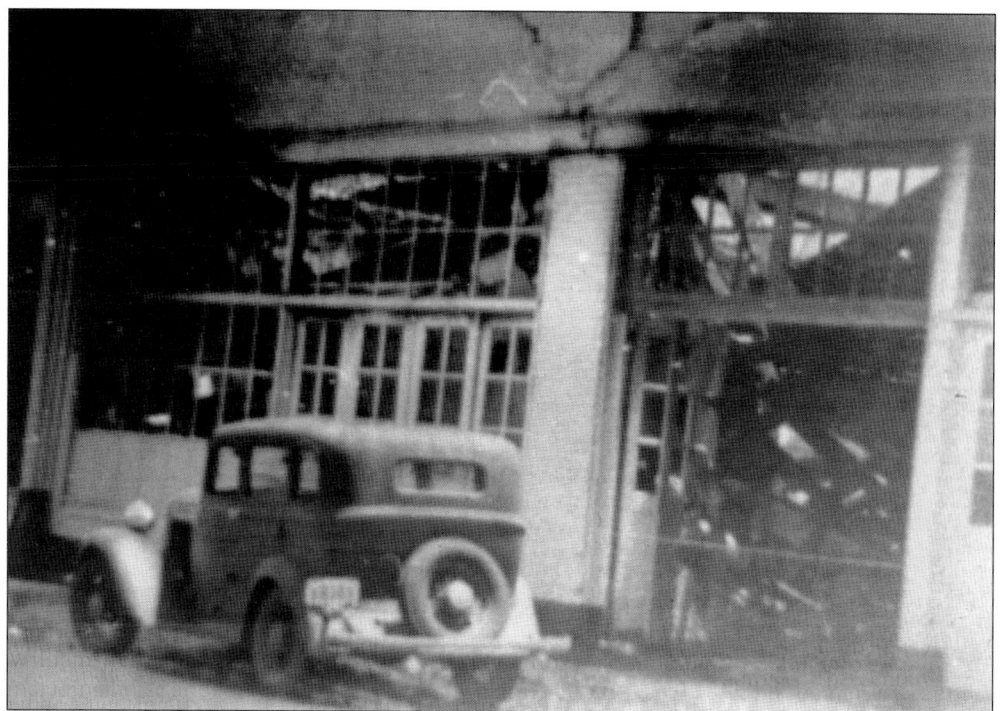

The formation of a fire department in the city helped put a stop to the uncontrolled blazes that had swept through the community at the beginning of the 20th century, though smaller fires, such as the Williams Motor Company fire of 1930, would still occur from time to time. (Courtesy Williams Public Library.)

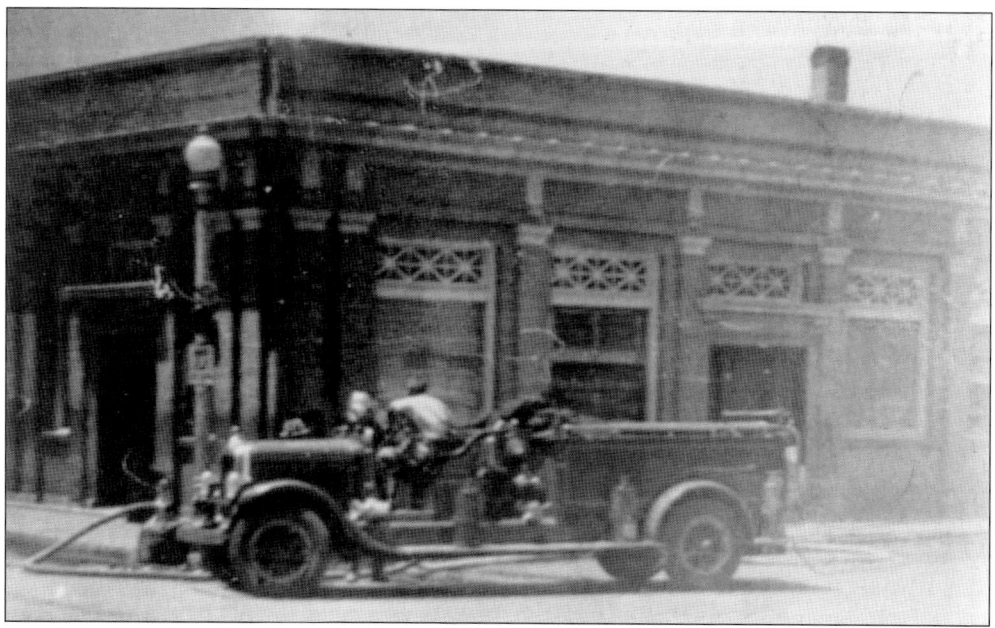

A Williams fire engine responds to a fire at the corner bank in 1930. There were 12 firefighters in Williams, as well as one Ford Model T truck with a 350-gallon water tank. (Courtesy Williams Public Library.)

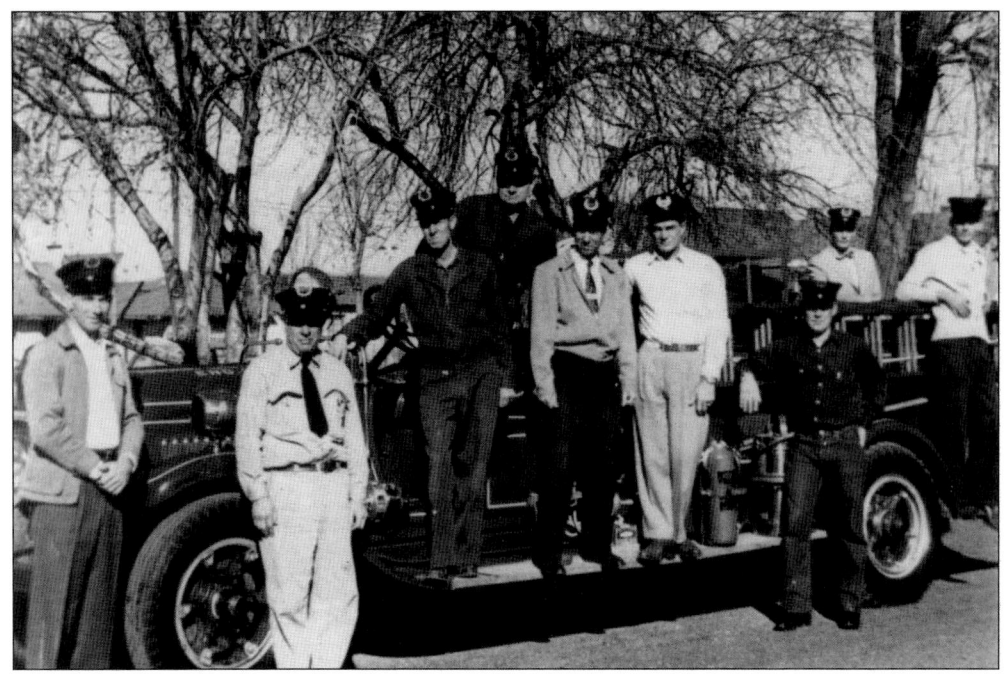

The Williams Fire Department in 1955 included (from left to right) Jim Salem, R. Cox, Seth Lilly, Bud Augenstein, Charles Way, Albert Cardani, Bill Lilly, Virgil Hengel, and Gene McDougall. (Courtesy Williams Public Library.)

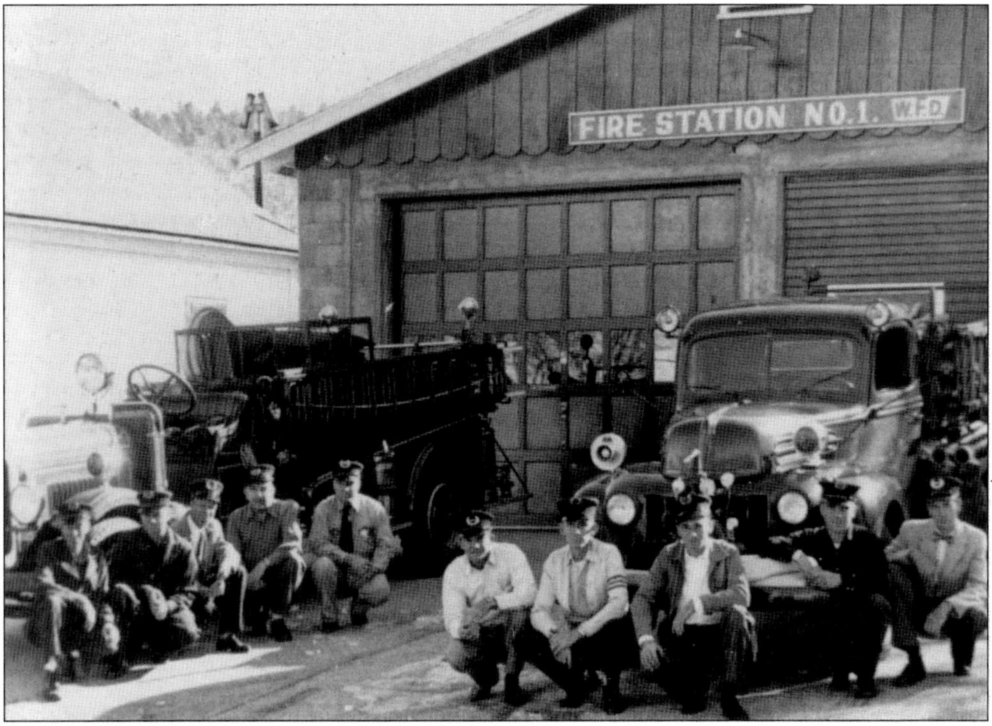

Members of the fire department show off their firefighting vehicles and the Williams Fire Department's No. 1 fire station. (Courtesy Williams Public Library.)

Six

OVER 100 YEARS OF NEWS
CITY NEWSPAPER
CHRONICLES HISTORY

The arrival of a newspaper in October 1889 meant Williams had truly become a noteworthy part of northern Arizona. The weekly paper, originally published by John F. Michael, suffered from a revolving door in its formative years. A number of publishers came and went, including a former Williams school principal, George U. Young. Young sold the newspaper in 1901 to C. A. Neal and L. H. Dawley, who in turn sold the business to C. M. Funston. Funston then sold the business to New York newspaperman J. V. Van Eaton. Williams pioneer Cormick Boyce helped fund Van Eaton's endeavor, helping to purchase the business in 1913. Later that same year, Van Eaton betrayed Boyce's generosity. After requesting an additional $600 for a new press, Van Eaton boarded a train and headed west to California. Both Van Eaton and the money vanished without a trace.

That same year, a young man by the name of Frank Evarts Wells arrived in Williams from Lawrence, Kansas. Wells, along with his wife, Ruth, and young son Evarts Jr., arrived in October 1913. Shortly thereafter, Wells took ownership of the *Williams News*. Lured to northern Arizona by his sister, Ruth Gold, Wells was no stranger to the newspaper business—he had managed a newspaper in Kansas prior to his move to Williams.

Wells went on to produce the paper for the next 50 years. He passed away two years after celebrating his 50th anniversary as editor in 1963. The newspaper would remain a family-run business, however. Evarts Wells, who had enlisted in the U.S. Navy in World War II, returned to Williams with his new wife, Cecil, and their two young sons, Ken and Brent, in 1946 in order for him to take over the family business. Evarts and Cecil soon celebrated the birth of two additional sons, Dennis and Doug Wells. Doug Wells assumed management of the newspaper in 1978 upon the death of his father. While the newspaper was sold to Western Newspapers, Inc., in 1991, Doug Wells remained publisher.

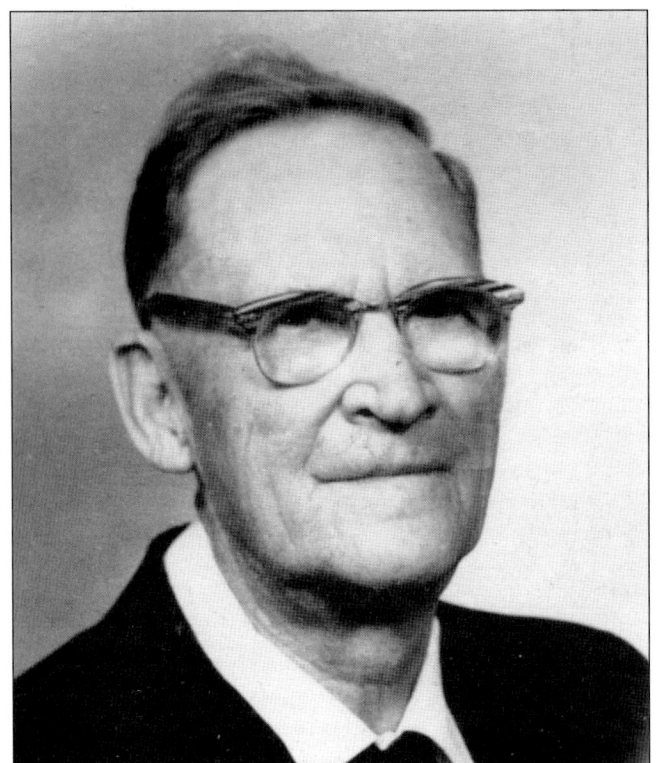

Frank Evart Wells's first day at the *Williams News* in 1913 was one of surprises. He found a former editor in the newspaper office who demanded payment for his services at gunpoint. Longtime Williams businessman Cormick Boyce helped settle the matter. (Courtesy Wells family.)

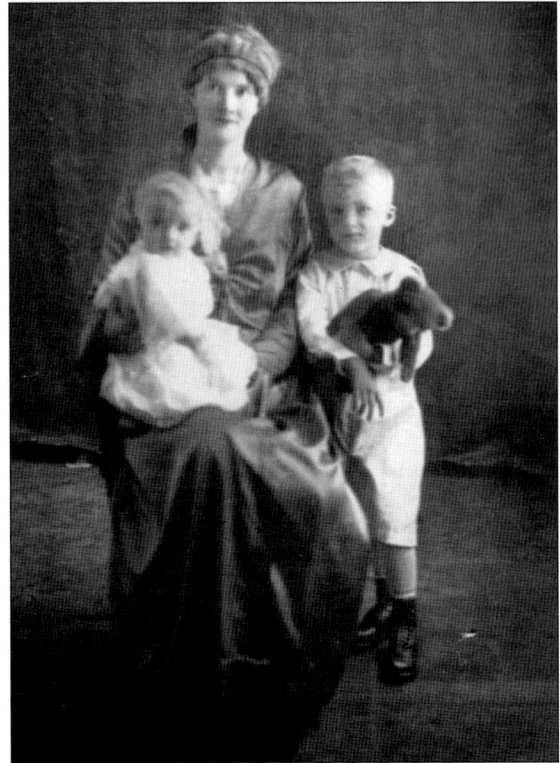

Frank Wells's wife, Ruth, is pictured with her children, Evarts Jr. and Frances. The family moved to Williams from Lawrence, Kansas, where Wells had managed a newspaper. (Courtesy Wells family.)

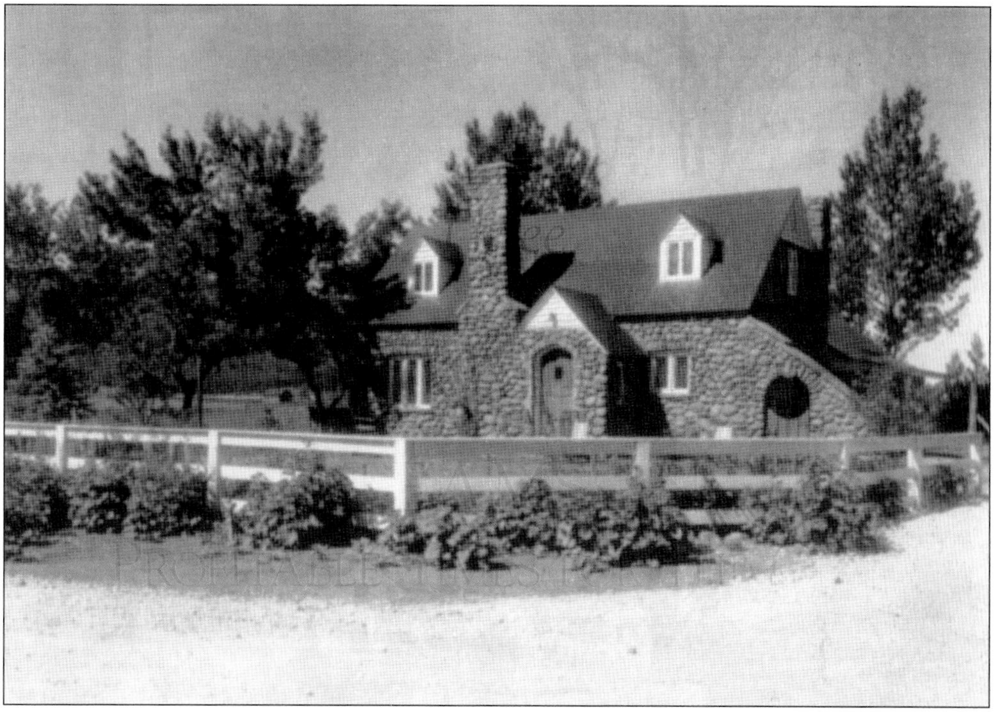

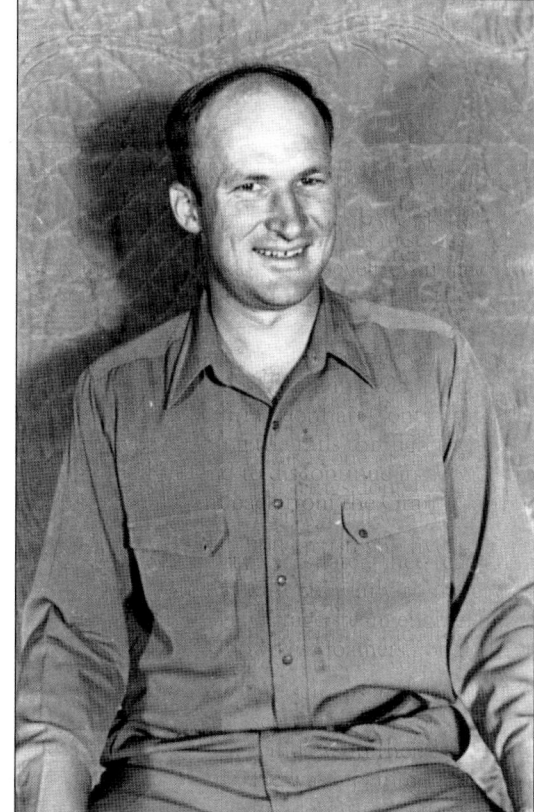

The Wells house has always been a familiar landmark in Williams. A new addition to the home was completed between 1934 and 1935. (Courtesy Wells family.)

After serving in the U.S. Navy during World War II, Evarts Wells Jr. returned to Williams in 1946 to take over the family-run newspaper. Evarts's sister, Frances Wells, also contributed to the publication, providing stories and art. (Courtesy Wells family.)

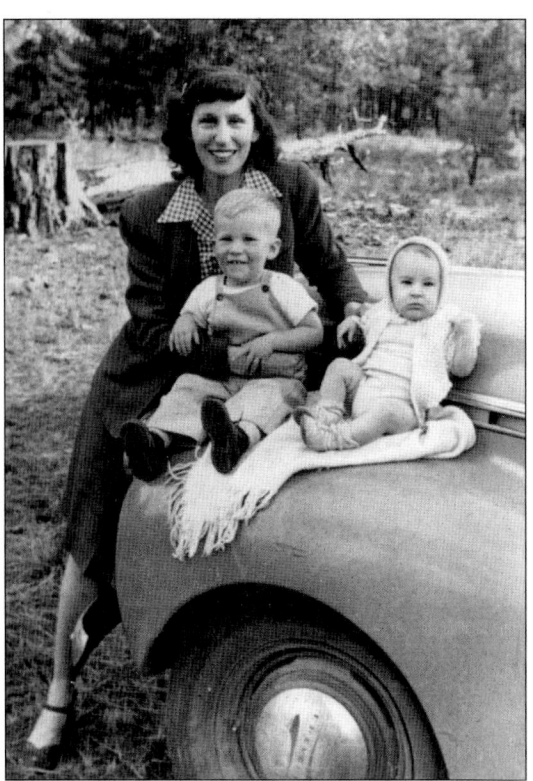

Cecil Wells, along with her first two sons, Kenneth (left) and Brent, enjoy their first summer outing in Williams in 1946. (Courtesy Wells family.)

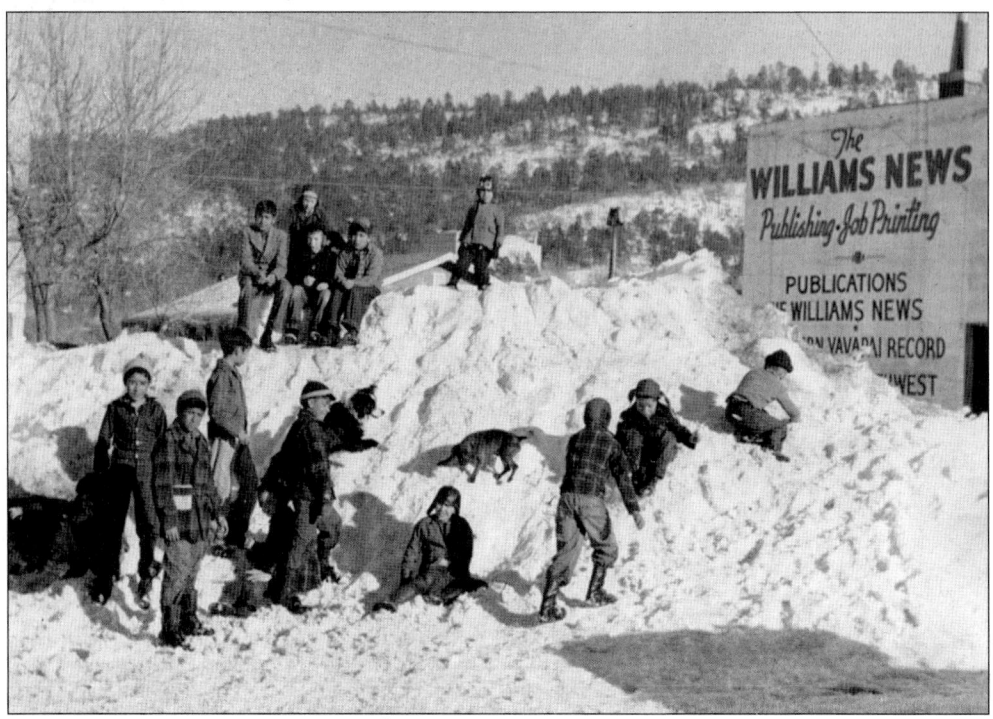

A number of Williams children, along with a curious dog, play outside the office of the *Williams News* thanks to a plentiful snowstorm in 1948. (Courtesy Wells family.)

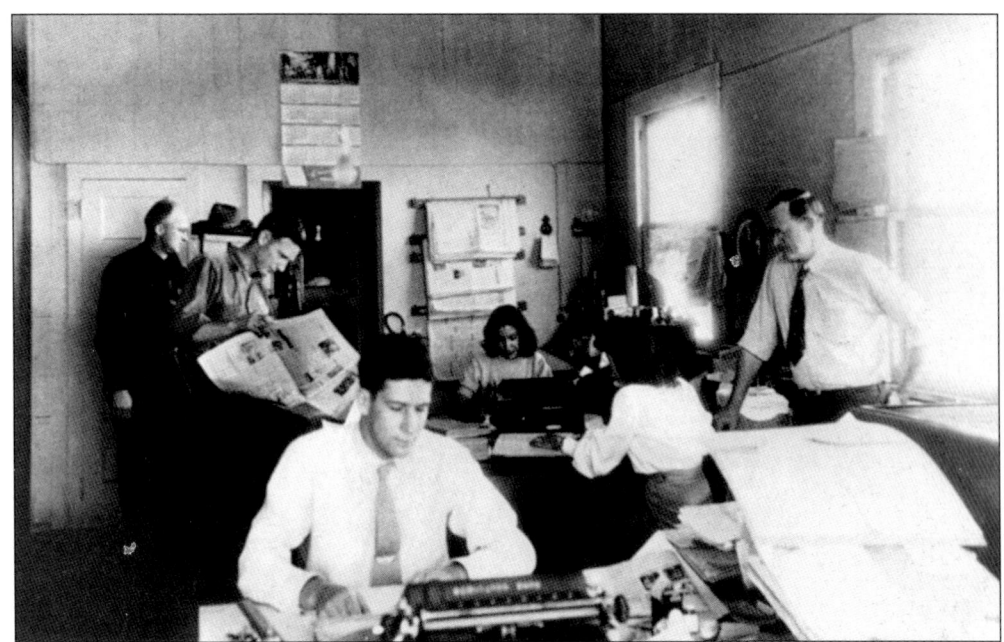

Pictured at the *Williams News* office in 1954 are (from left to right) publisher Frank Wells, Evarts Wells, reporter Don Karshan, Eldridge Trott, Gloria Negrette, and Tony Magana. (Courtesy U.S. Forest Service, Southwestern Region, Kaibab National Forest.)

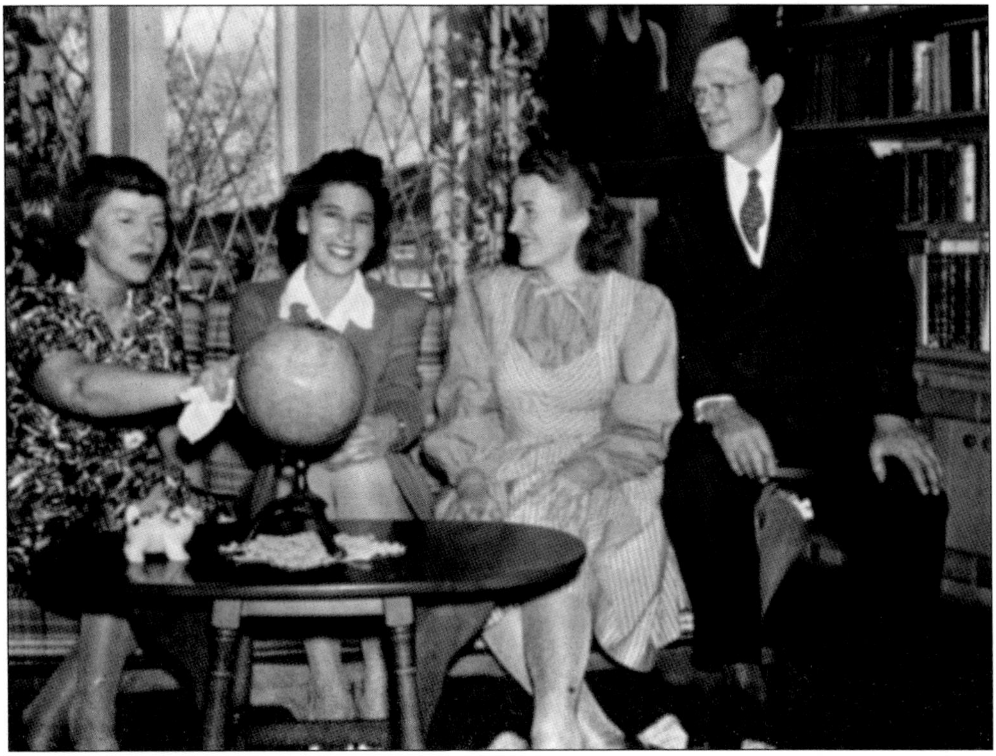

Cecil Wells entertains company inside the Wells family home. Cecil had two more sons, Doug and Dennis Wells, after the move to Williams in 1946. (Courtesy Wells family.)

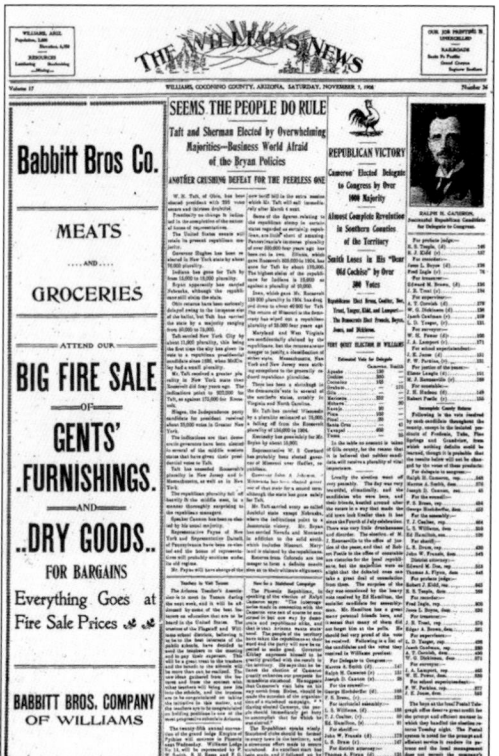

The *Williams News*, which would eventually come to be called the *Williams–Grand Canyon News*, has been published by the Wells family for more than a century. (Courtesy *Williams–Grand Canyon News*.)

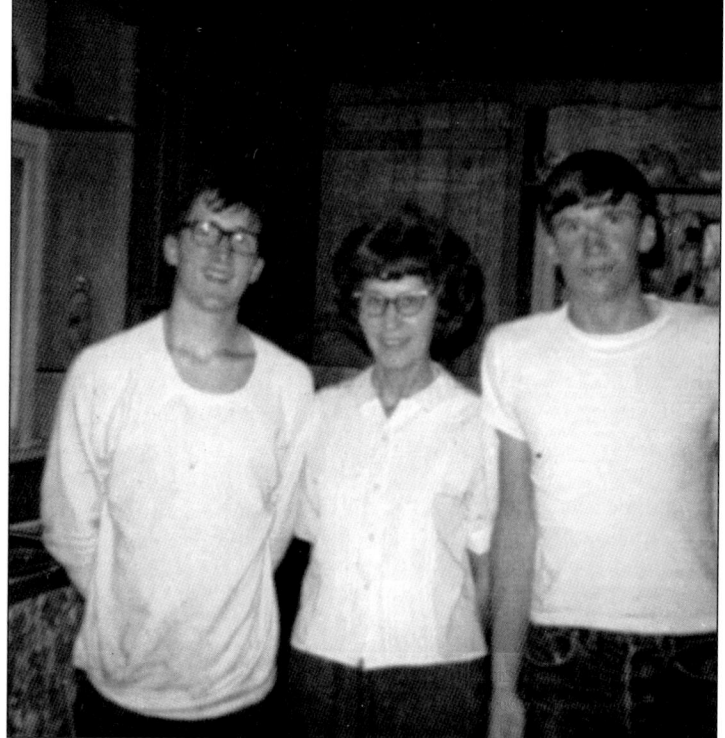

Doug Wells (left) stands with Cecil and Dennis Wells. Doug Wells would assume management of the family newspaper in 1978, following the death of Evarts Wells. (Courtesy Wells family.)

Seven

FLYING INTO THE FUTURE
H.A. CLARK PIONEERS FLIGHT IN WILLIAMS

Williams began to take off, quite literally, in the late 1930s, when local resident Hubert A. Clark purchased his first airplane, giving him the proud distinction of being the first airplane owner and pilot in Williams.

Clark spent his childhood in Oklahoma, where he enlisted in the U.S. military. His first sight of Williams came when he rode on a troop train that passed through the area during World War I. He decided to move his family to the town soon after.

The Clark family owned a number of campgrounds in Williams, though it seemed H. A. Clark's attention frequently drifted skyward.

A number of notable Americans took part in Clark's journey from a successful businessman to a successful pilot, beginning with a visit from famed pilot Jimmy Angel. Angel told Clark he was on his way to explore Venezuela. It is said that Clark, intrigued by the adventurous pilot, gave him $200 to fund his trip. Angel went on to discover the largest waterfall in the world, Angel Falls.

Clark bought his first plane in 1937, a 110-horspower Monocoupe, and soon sold that in favor of a newer model. Clark also began a local flying club and began planning an airport in the area. While Clark's airport was not the first airport in Williams, his had staying power. Webber Field was constructed within the city in 1925 and lasted only a year. The location of Clark's airport, it is said, was recommended by none other than Charles Lindbergh, who had to make an emergency landing north of the city shortly after his takeoff from Webber Field. Clark, with the help of the Williams Flying Club, constructed the first hangar at the Williams Airport in 1940.

Three years after the construction of the hangar, Clark sold his second airplane to Western singer and movie star Gene Autry. Clark purchased his third Monocoupe in 1943. Sadly, Clark died that year while flying through a thunderstorm between Williams and Texas. The Williams Airport was renamed the H. A. Clark Memorial Airfield in 1992.

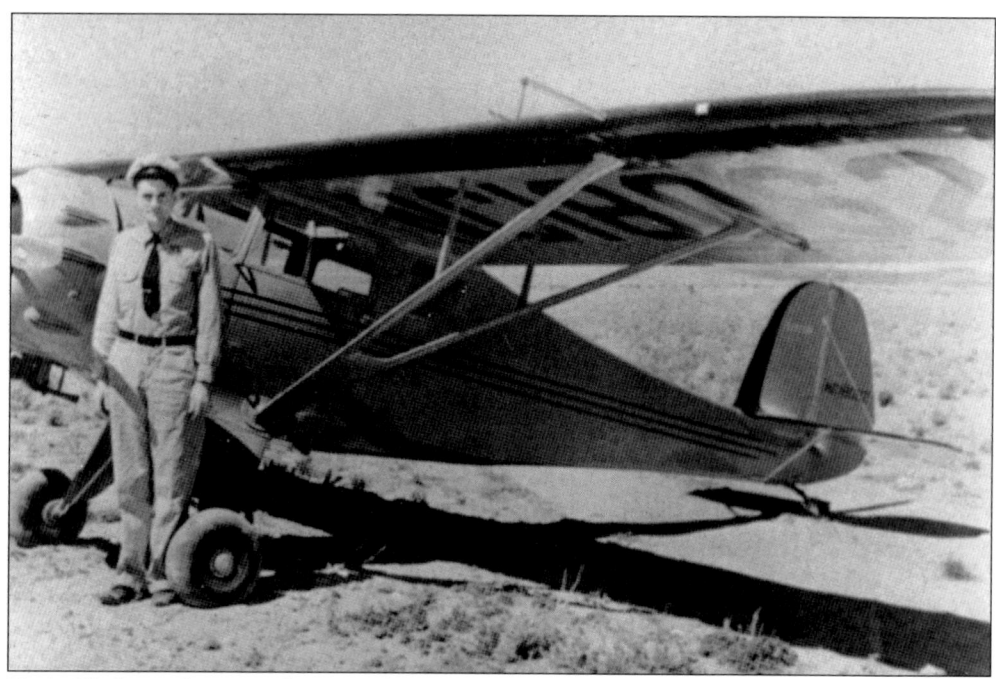

H. A. Clark stands next to his second Monocoupe. Clark became well known in the area as the first airplane owner and pilot in Williams. (Courtesy Williams Public Library.)

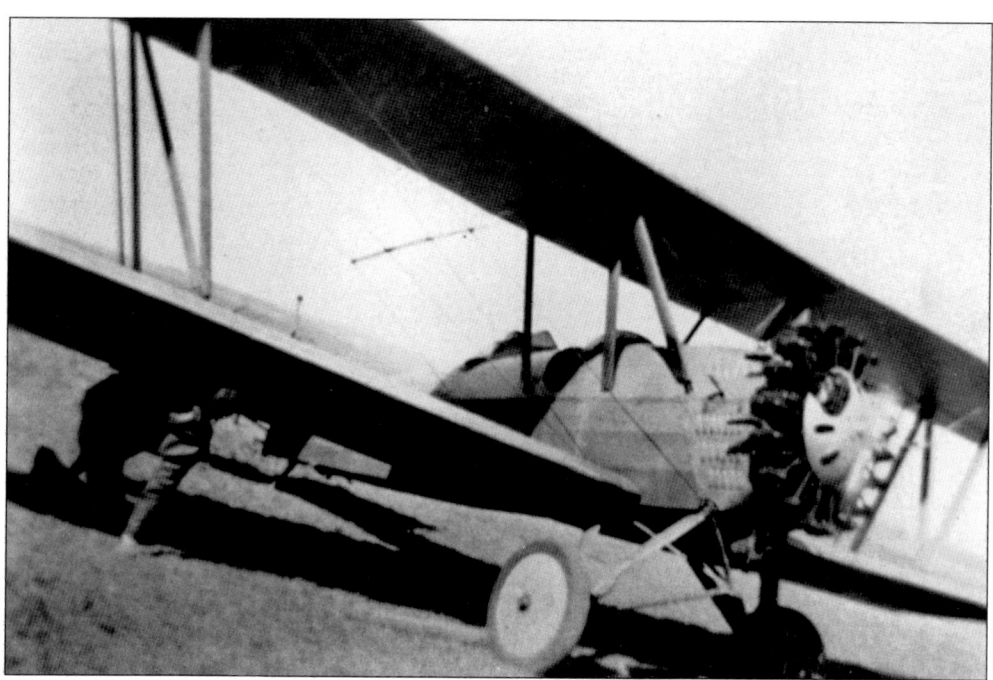

Charles Lindbergh checks on his airplane after having to land outside of the city of Williams in the 1920s. It is said that Lindbergh suggested the location of the current airstrip in Williams. (Courtesy Williams Public Library.)

Pilot George Johnson stands next to his airplane in 1939. The first hangar was built at the Williams Airport in 1940. (Courtesy Williams Public Library.)

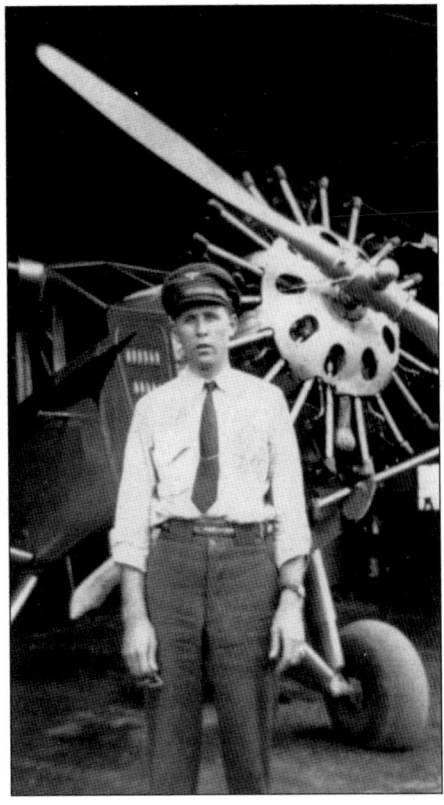

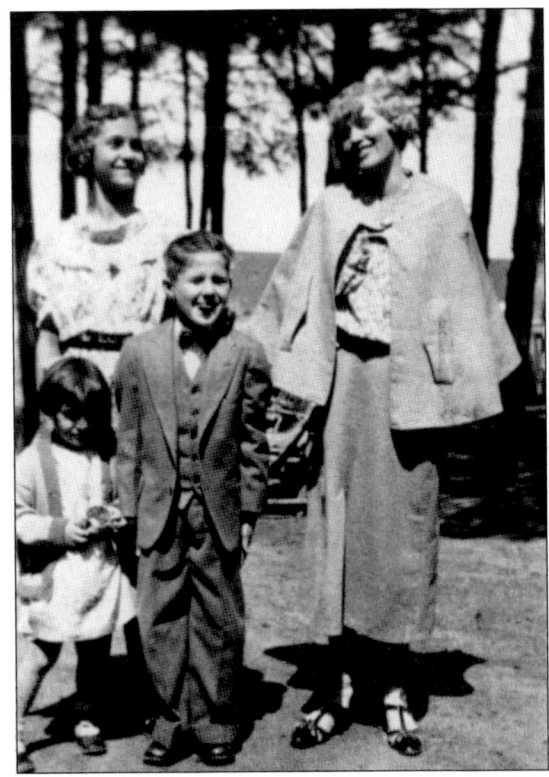

H. A. Clark's children, pictured in 1934, included (from left to right) Clara Margaret, Elinor, Hubert Jr., and Patricia Clark. Clara earned the distinction of being the first female pilot in Williams. (Courtesy Williams Public Library.)

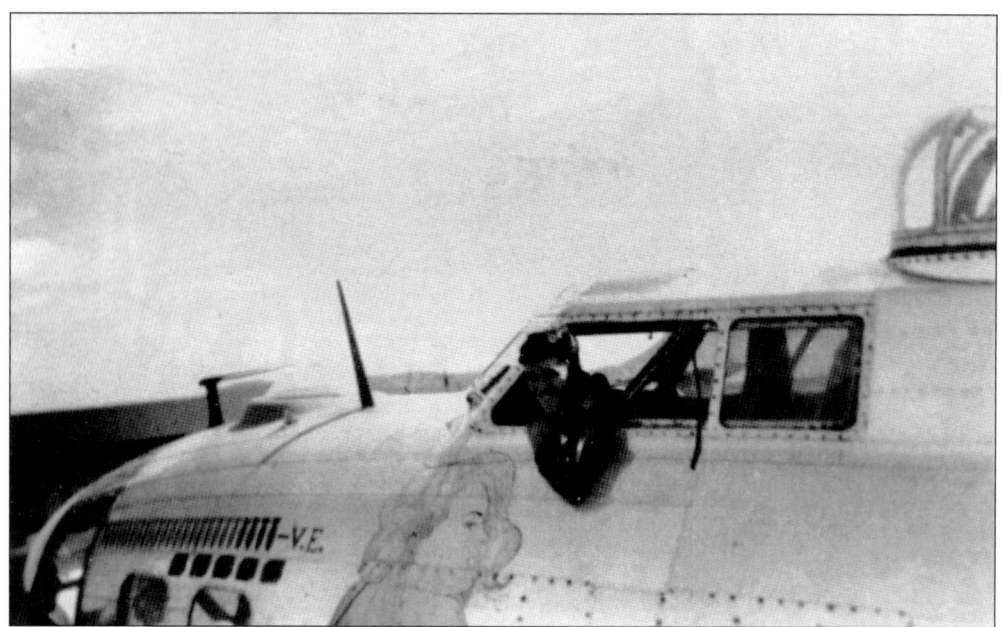

Hubert Clark Jr. sits in the cockpit of a B-17 that had to make an emergency landing at the Williams Airport in 1946. (Courtesy Williams Public Library.)

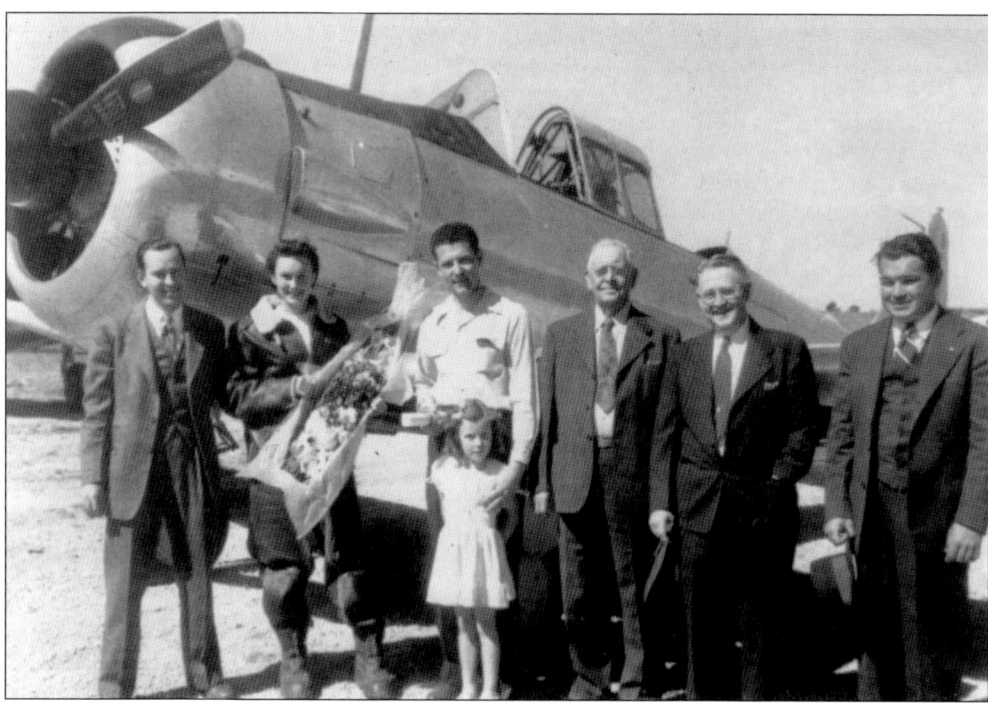

A BT-13 has landed at the Williams Airport in 1946. Pictured are Ty Tyson, Les and Penny Perkins, Charles Proctor, Fred Theroux, and others as they stand near the airstrip. (Courtesy Williams Public Library.)

Eight

HONORING OLD BILL
MOUNTAIN MEN
PUT THE CITY ON THE MAP

Seeking a way to put Williams on the map, a group of men in the Williams area hit on a grand idea in 1953. There could no better way to spotlight the town than by celebrating one of the most famous mountain men of all time, Bill Williams. Organizers originally met at Diz's Tavern to form the particulars of the group. Rod Graves, owner of Rod's Steak House along Bill Williams Avenue, became involved in the group in its early stages. The group planned the first Rendezvous Ride in 1954, in which the Mountain Men traveled from Williams to Phoenix on horseback and even muleback, in some cases.

Graves was instrumental in helping the group participate in the Jaycees Rodeo, held in the Phoenix area, at the culmination of its ride. The men continued to make the famed trip each year. They would also visit children in Phoenix-area hospitals and would stop at a number of schools to entertain the students with their wild ways.

The Bill Williams Mountain Men were soon named Arizona ambassadors and represented the state in four presidential inauguration parades. The group has been featured in *Arizona Highways* and other magazines throughout the years. Williams's events, meanwhile, were hardly without a Mountain Man or two in attendance.

Originally, the group consisted of Williams residents alone, though organizers eventually opened the club to applicants from all over the state after a dip in local membership threatened to close the club in 1970. The move proved to be a successful one for the group, which has seen more than 150 different members since it began.

There have been a wide variety of Mountain Men over the years, ranging from lawyers to doctors to farmhands. A mountain lion named Tuffy, caught by member George McNelly, also enjoyed membership status. The animal was subsequently featured in a number of Williams parades. There were two Tuffys in all. The second Tuffy attended the John F. Kennedy inaugural celebration in 1961.

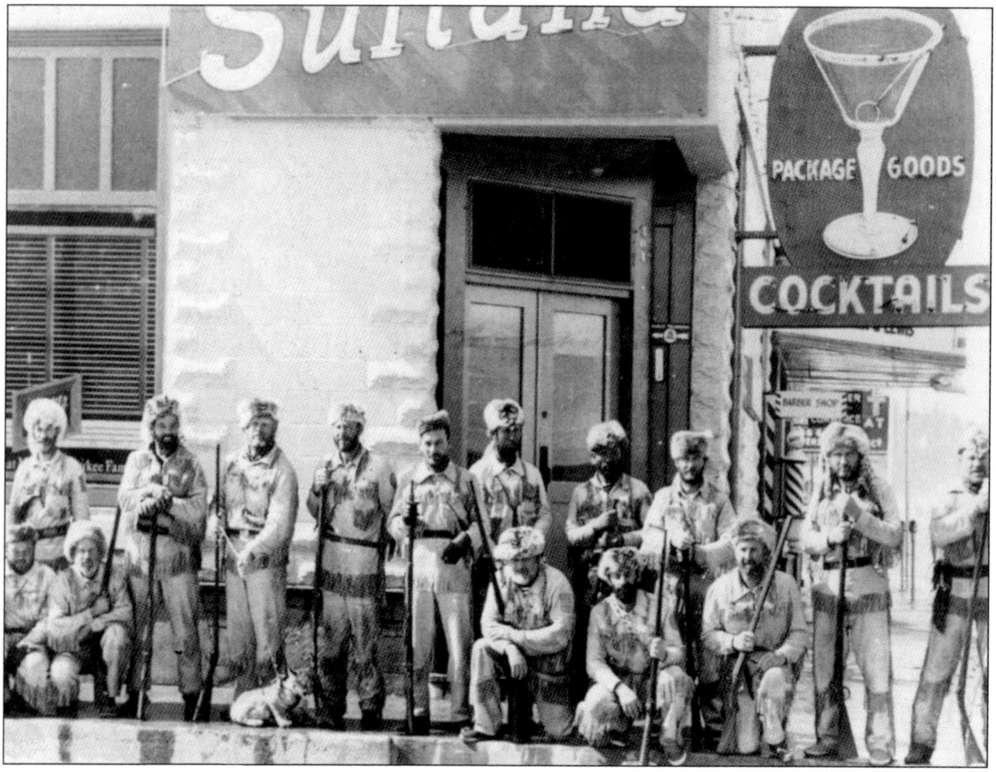

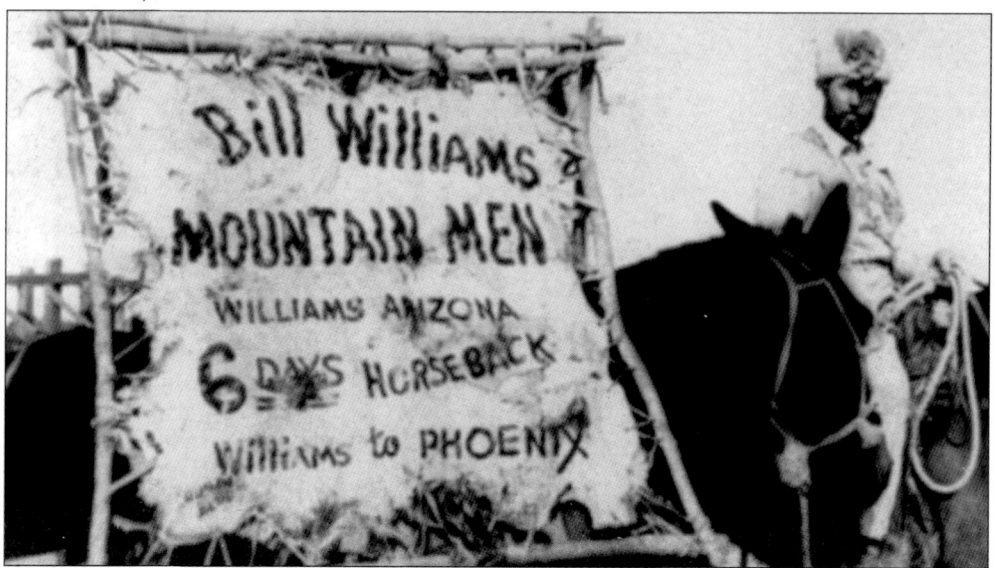

The Bill Williams Mountain Men formed in 1953. The group, pictured on a postcard from the 1950s, became hugely popular throughout Arizona. After their initial formation, the group began to hold regular meetings at Rod's Steak House along Bill Williams Avenue. (Courtesy Williams Public Library.)

A buckskin sign highlights the group's annual Rendezvous Ride from Williams to Phoenix. Mountain Man Thurman Mayes sits on horseback by the sign in 1955. (Courtesy Williams Public Library.)

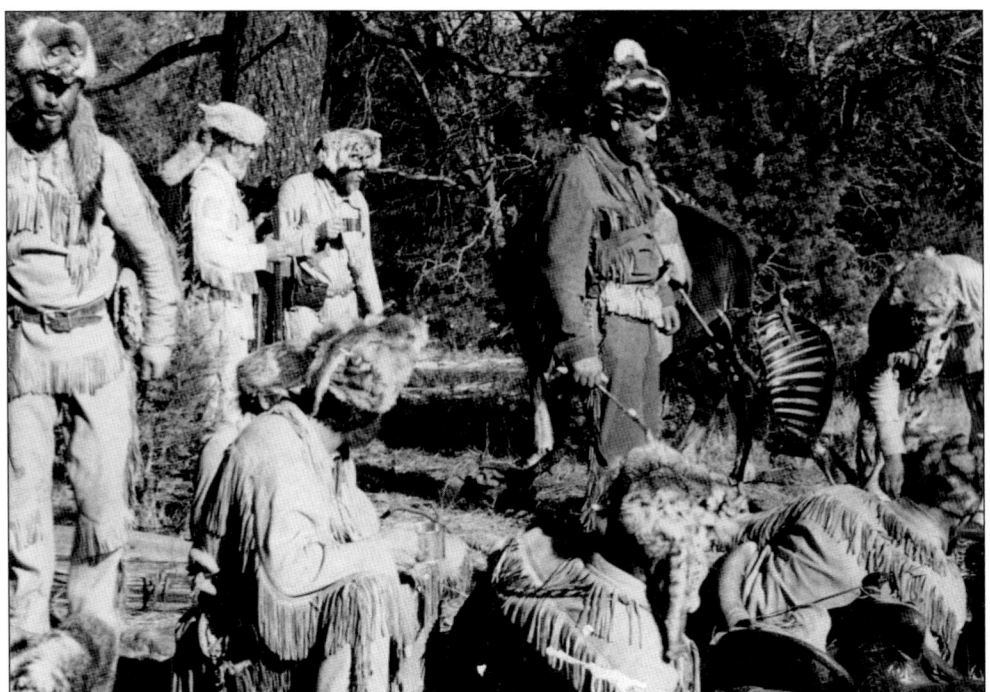

The Bill Williams Mountain Men are seen during one of their first Rendezvous Rides in the 1950s. The ride is roughly 200 miles, a distance the group traveled on either horseback or muleback. (Courtesy *Williams–Grand Canyon News*.)

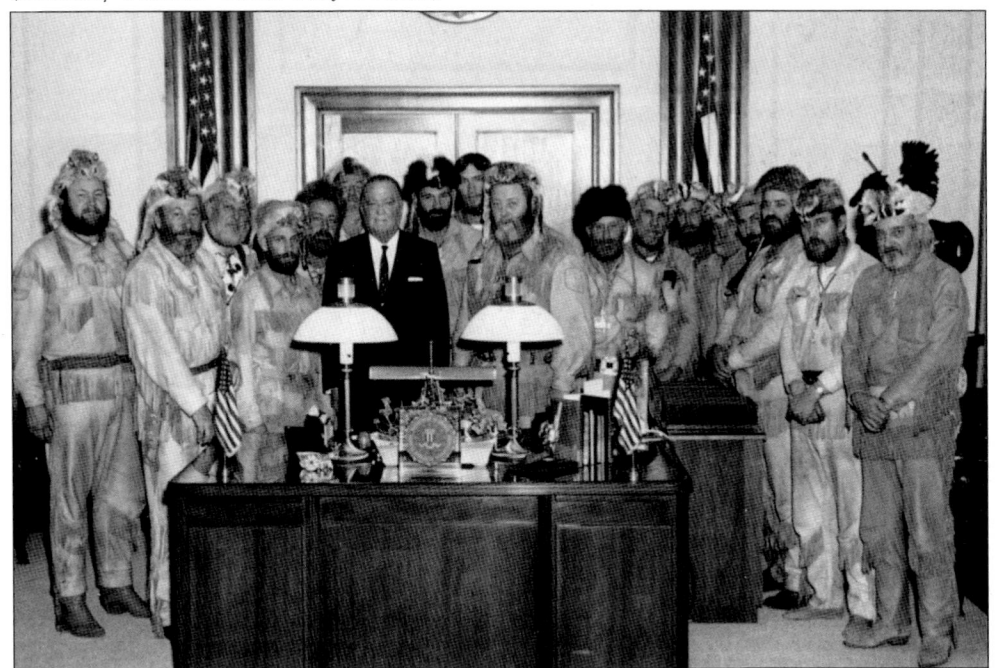

The Bill Williams Mountain Men pay a visit to J. Edgar Hoover in the FBI Building on January 19, 1965. The Mountain Men, as Arizona state ambassadors, attended a number of presidential inaugurations as well. (Courtesy Bob Dean.)

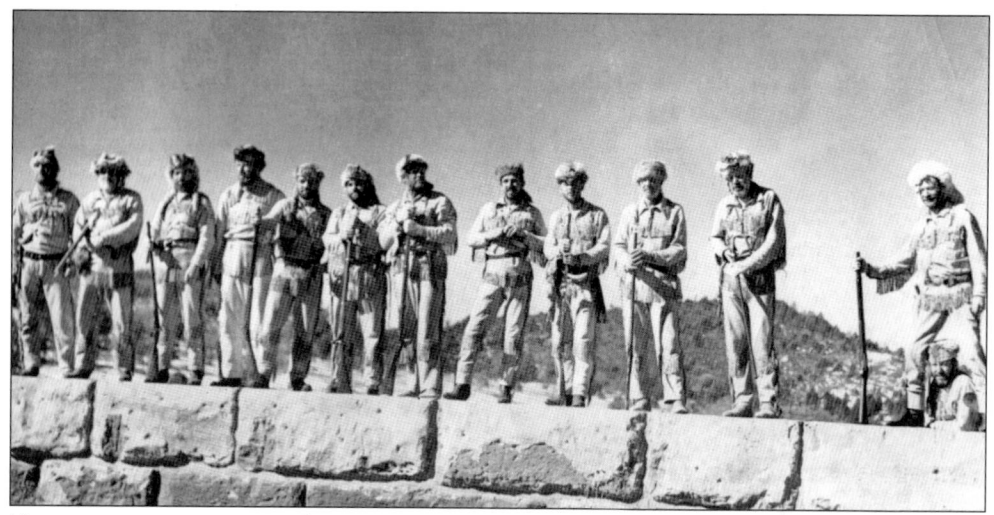

Never a group to pass up a photo opportunity, the Bill Williams Mountain Men are often seen smiling for fans with cameras at events in Williams and all over Arizona. The group stands atop the Santa Fe Dam at the top of Fourth Street in this 1950s photograph. (Courtesy Bob Dean.)

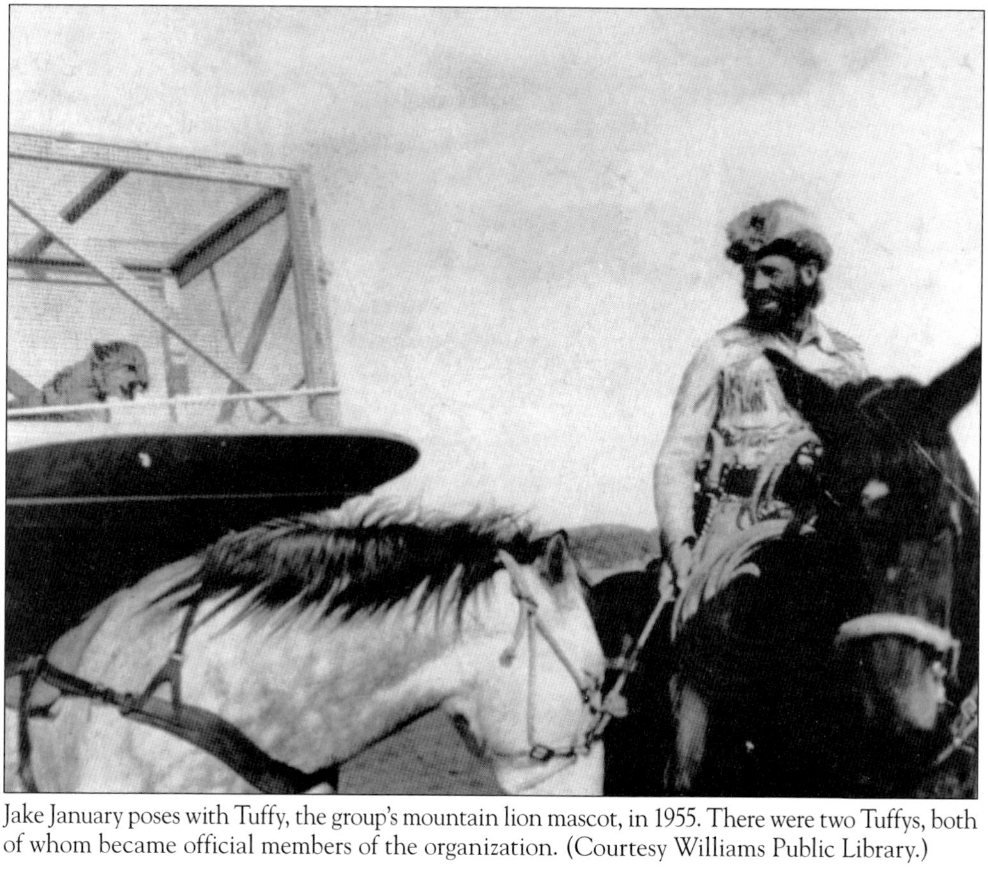

Jake January poses with Tuffy, the group's mountain lion mascot, in 1955. There were two Tuffys, both of whom became official members of the organization. (Courtesy Williams Public Library.)

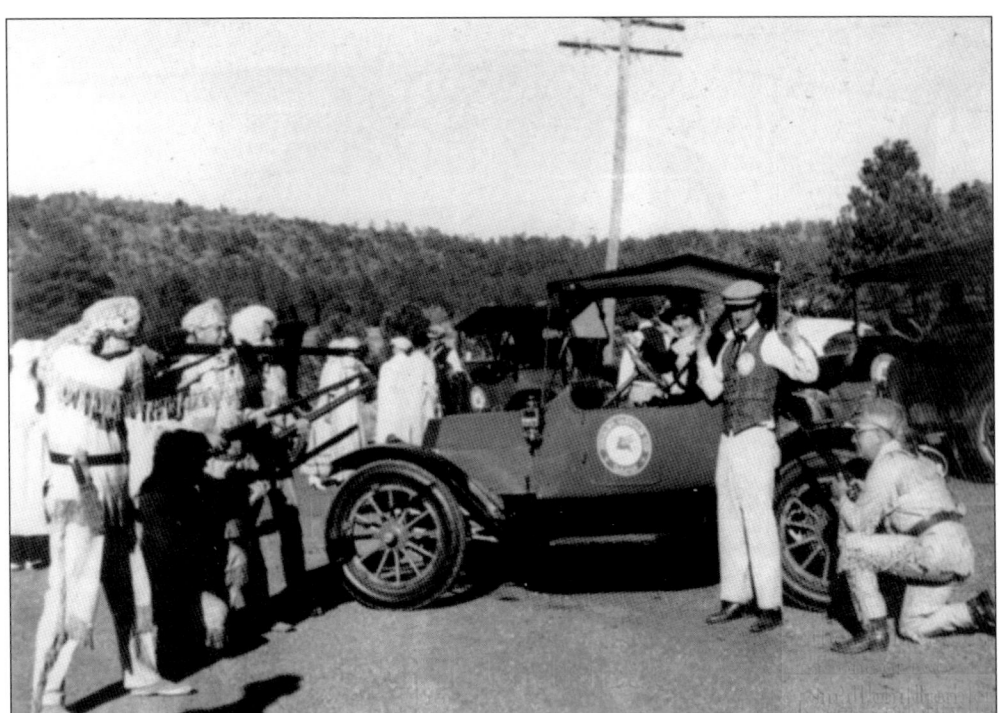

Members of the Bill Williams Mountain Men put on a mock arrest in the 1950s. Membership in the group was initially restricted to Williams residents only, though they eventually allowed members from all over the state. The group's original charter also called for only 30 members, though that number would grow in subsequent years. (Both, courtesy Williams Public Library.)

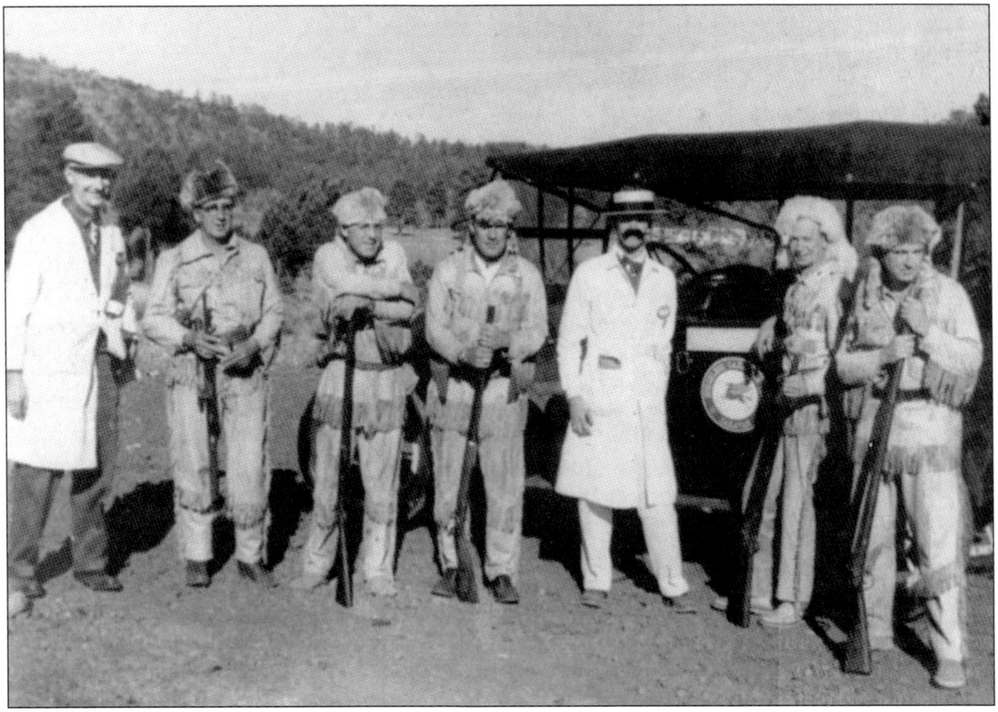

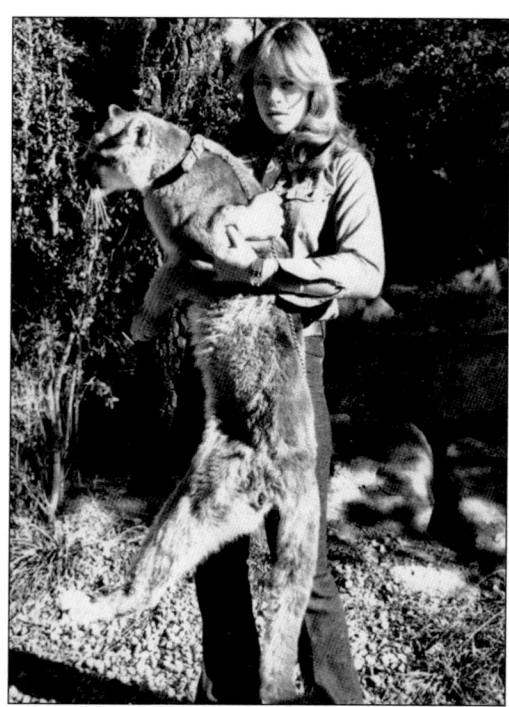

The Mountain Men were not the only people in Williams to adopt a pet lion. Williams resident Becky Bates had her own pet cat in 1978. Named Pebbles, the large mountain lion even slept on Bates's bed at night. (Courtesy Eddie Sandoval.)

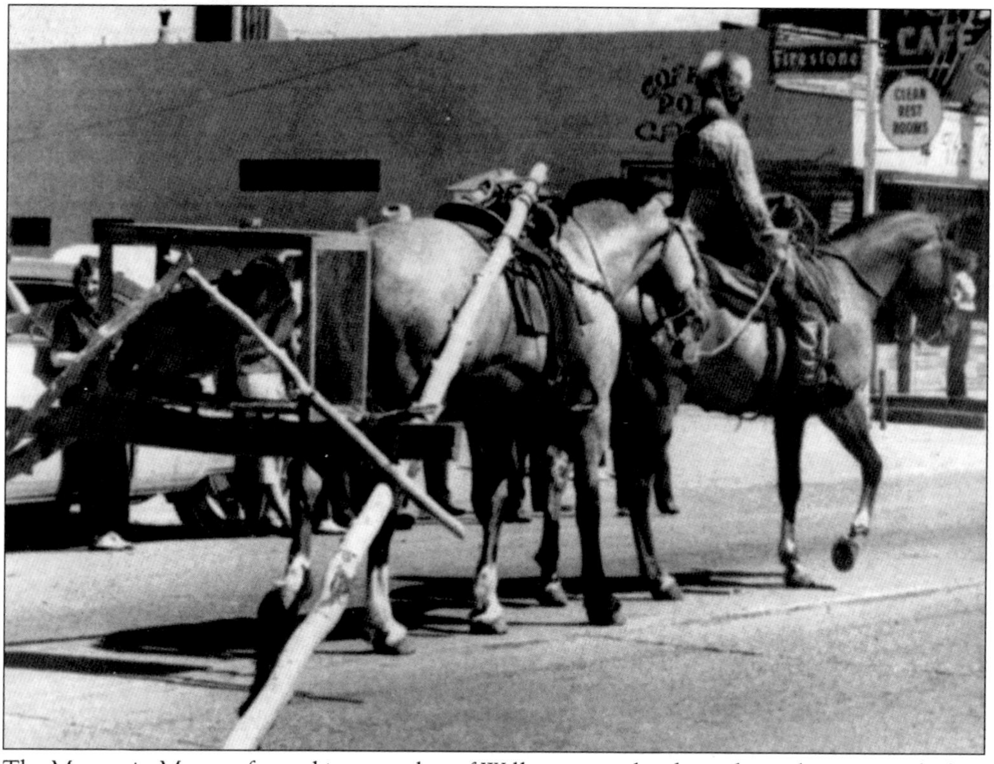

The Mountain Men performed in a number of Williams parades throughout the years and often brought Tuffy along for the ride. The group's second mountain lion attended the inauguration of John F. Kennedy in 1961. (Courtesy Williams Public Library.)

Bill Williams Mountain Man Pat Tissaw poses in his full buckskin regalia with a large elk. The original buckskin uniforms of the Mountain Men were ordered from a tailor in New York. (Courtesy Williams Public Library.)

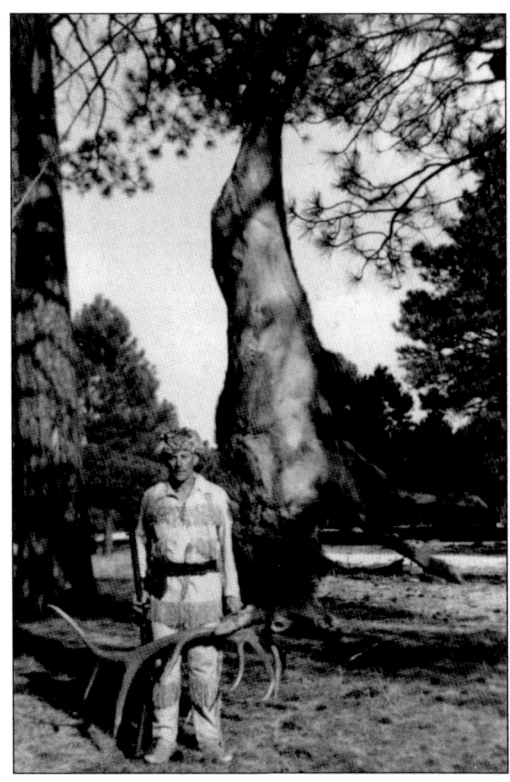

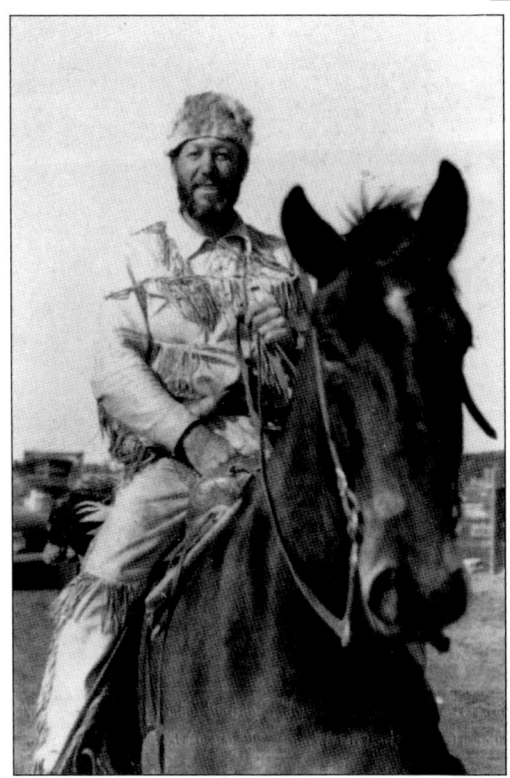

Denton Diz Dean, owner of Diz's Tavern, was one of the founding members of the Bill Williams Mountain Men. Planning for the group started at the tavern. (Courtesy Williams Public Library.)

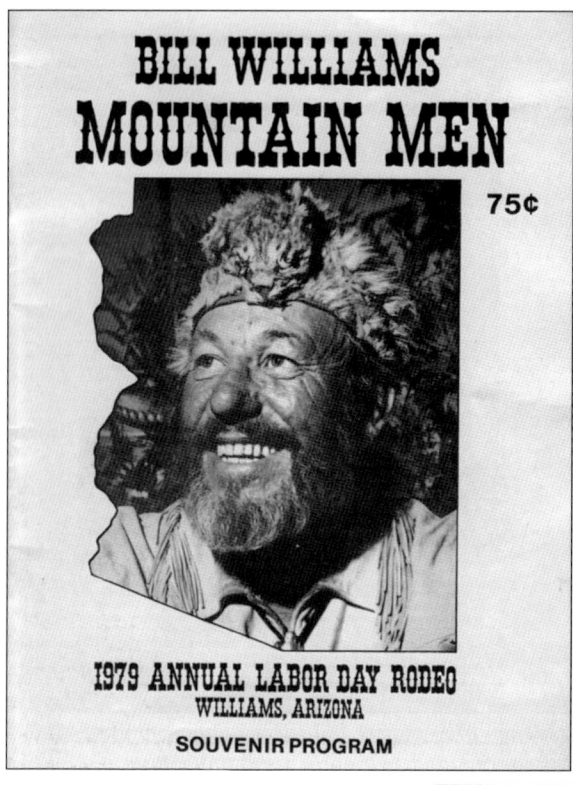

BILL WILLIAMS
MOUNTAIN MEN

75¢

1979 ANNUAL LABOR DAY RODEO
WILLIAMS, ARIZONA
SOUVENIR PROGRAM

The Labor Day Rodeo souvenir program featured the Bill Williams Mountain Men in 1979. The Mountain Men took part in a number of parades throughout Arizona. (Courtesy Bob Dean.)

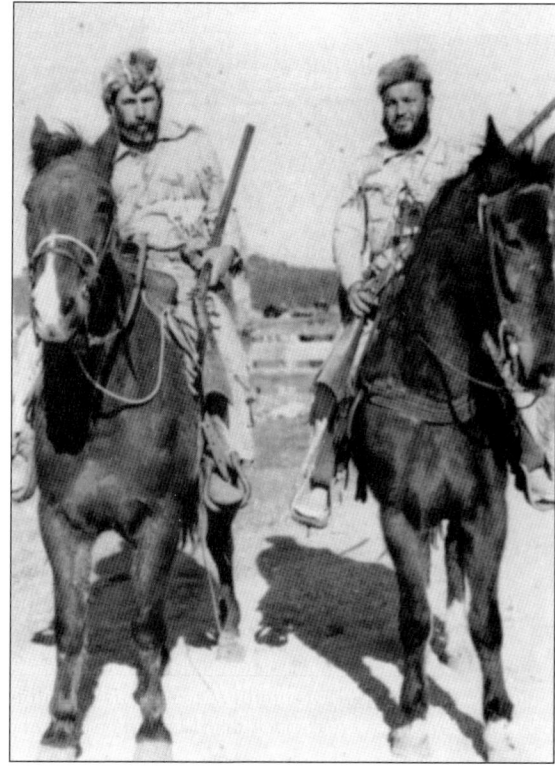

Bill Williams Mountain Men Jim Tissaw (left) and Fred Theroux were part of the group that visited hospitals and schools in the Phoenix area at the conclusion of the annual Rendezvous Ride. (Courtesy Williams Public Library.)

Nine

A PARK IS BORN
MONUMENT PARK IMMORTALIZES
BILL WILLIAMS

Area sculptor Bill Pettit worked long, laborious hours in 1979, creating what would become a beloved fixture in Williams: the bronze statue of Bill Williams in Monument Park, located at the west end of Route 66. Neither the statue nor the park was around prior to the late 1970s. Nor was one of Williams's most cherished annual events, Rendezvous Days, which celebrates the city's pioneering history of trappers, mountain men, and cowboys.

Measuring 8.5 feet tall, the statue was a labor of love for Pettit, who worked on the bronze monument for 13 consecutive months. Pettit, who had long dreamed of creating a life-sized replica of the famous Bill Williams, donated his time on the project. With the help of *Williams–Grand Canyon News* publisher Doug Wells, a committee was formed to bring the statue to life. Fund-raising efforts were started by the Bill Williams Mountain Men, and the group brought in enough money for Pettit to begin work on the project. The project cost a meager $3,500 to accomplish, thanks to Pettit's offer of free labor. Fund-raising efforts included smaller versions of the statue, which were sold to raise money for the project.

Plans for Monument Park were under way as well, thanks to a design by U.S. Forest Service architect Bill Lauger. While officials with the city of Williams had already expressed a plan to develop a park in the city, Lauger is credited with designing the "mountain-top" setting where the statue was eventually placed. He also designed the rest of the park, which extends west from the base of the Bill Williams statue.

The unveiling of the statue at Monument Park also kicked off the first annual Rendezvous Days celebration in Williams, an event that continues in Williams each summer. A number of notables attended the April 26, 1980, dedication ceremony, including then–U.S. senator Barry Goldwater, members of Bill Williams's family, Williams historian T. E. "Spike" Way, and former mayor Robert Eddingfield. The original Rendezvous Days included barbecues, a parade, and mountain men celebrations, such as a black powder shoot.

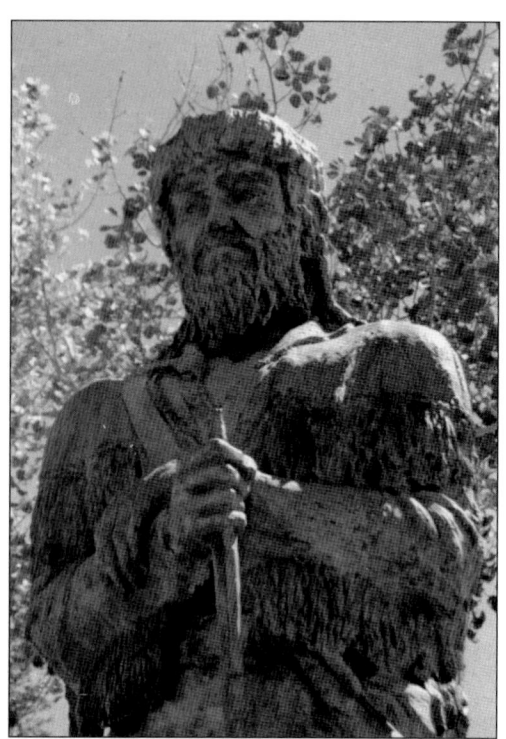

The statue of Bill Williams at Monument Park was created by area sculptor Bill Pettit in 1978. It measures 8.5 feet tall and is made from 1,000 pounds of bronze. (Courtesy the author.)

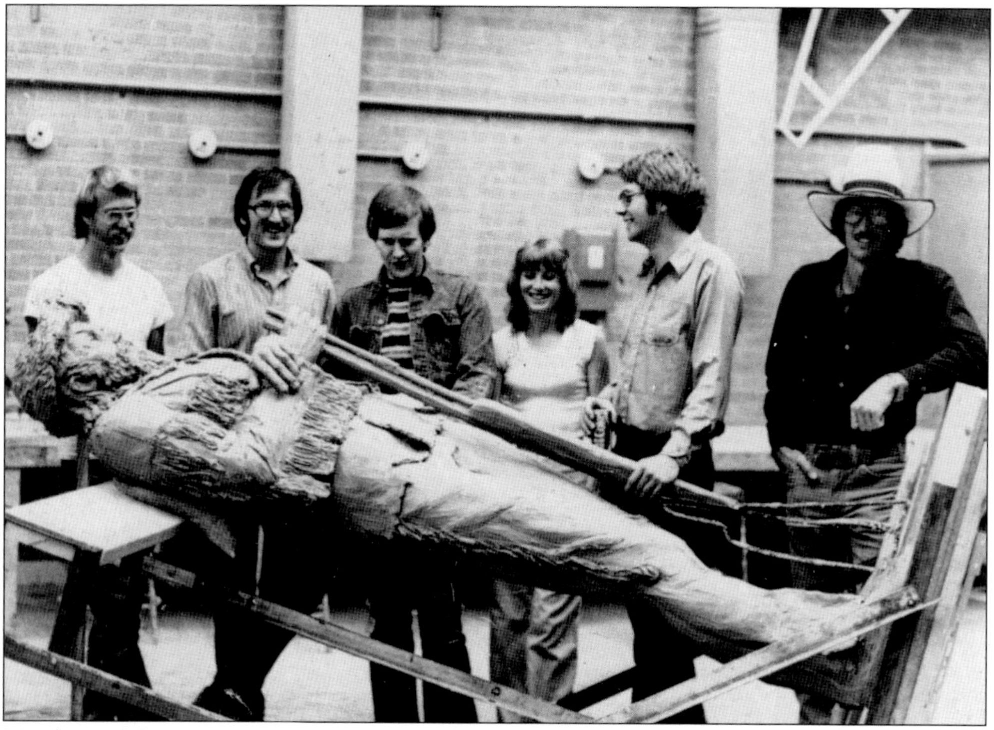

Members of the statue committee stand around the nearly finished sculpture before it is placed at Monument Park for an unveiling ceremony on April 26, 1980. (Courtesy *Williams–Grand Canyon News*.)

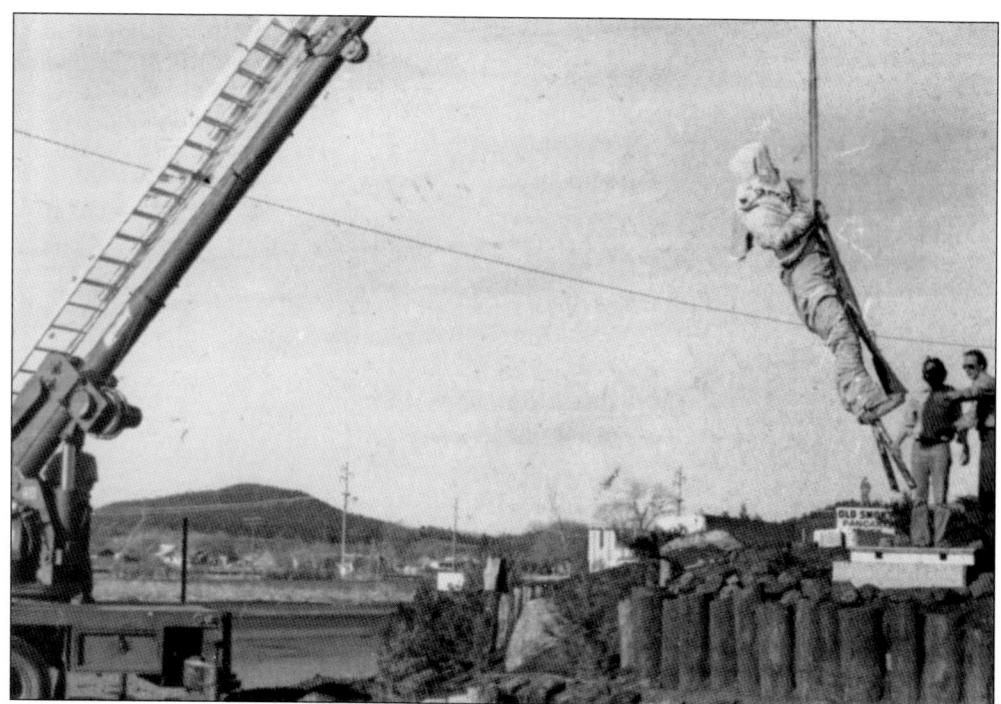

Crews lower the covered sculpture of Bill Williams into position in 1980. Monument Park was designed by U.S. Forest Service architect Bill Lauger. (Courtesy *Williams–Grand Canyon News*.)

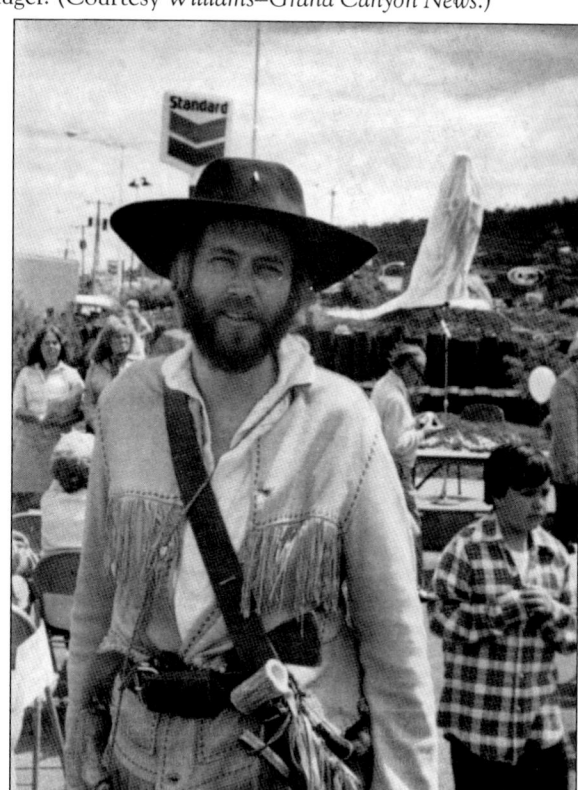

Sculptor Bill Pettit, in full buckskin attire, participated in the unveiling event, which also kicked off the first annual Rendezvous Days. The sculpture can be seen in the background, under wraps until the unveiling ceremony. (Courtesy *Williams–Grand Canyon News*.)

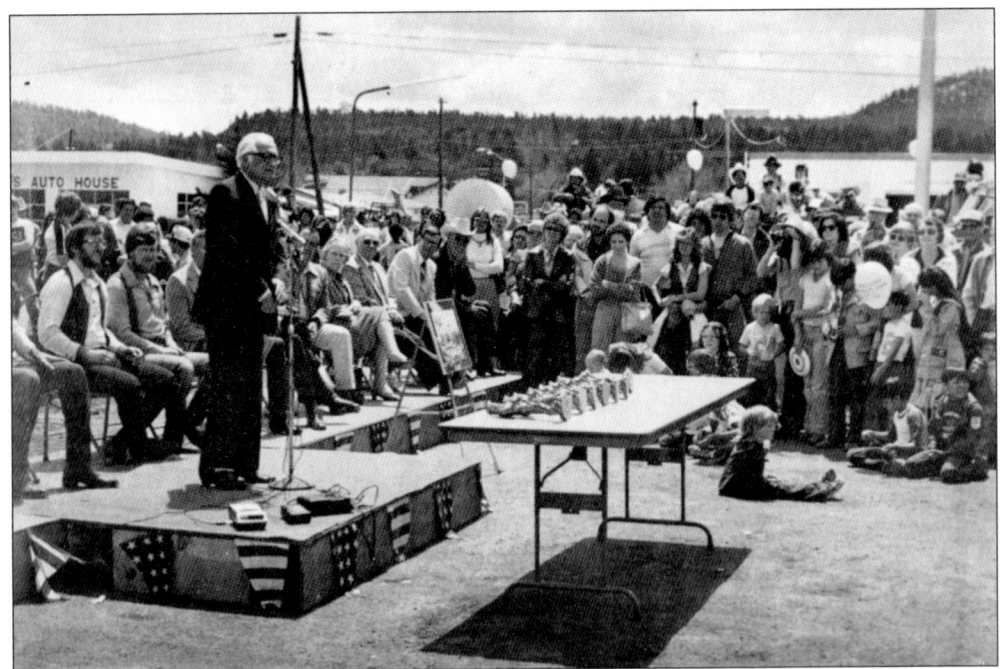

Barry Goldwater speaks to a rapt audience during the Monument Park ceremony in 1980. Commemorative statues are visible on the table in front of the small stages. The statues were sold by the Bill Williams Mountain Men to raise funds for the sculpture. (Courtesy *Williams–Grand Canyon News*.)

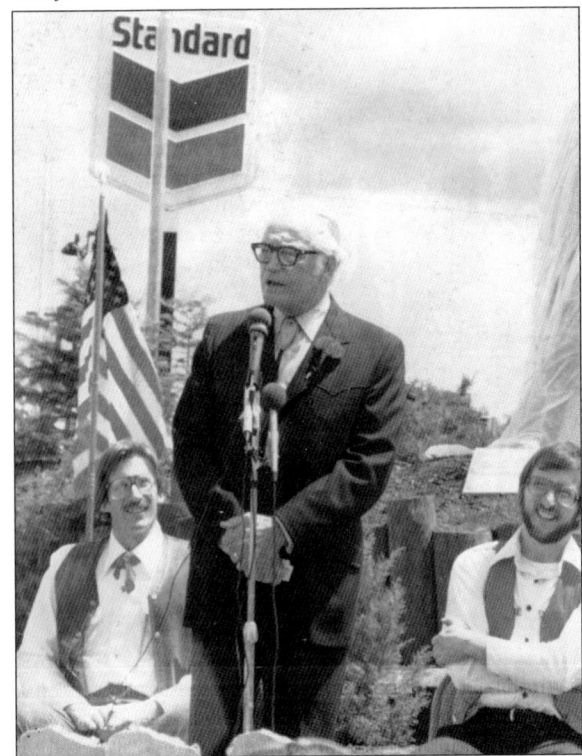

Long time Williams residents Dennis (left) and Doug Wells (right) listen to Barry Goldwater deliver his dedication speech at Monument Park. The Wells family, as part of the statue committee, was instrumental in overseeing the completion of the project. (Courtesy *Williams–Grand Canyon News*.)

Participants in the first annual Rendezvous Days celebration dressed up for the historic occasion in period costumes. (Courtesy *Williams–Grand Canyon News*.)

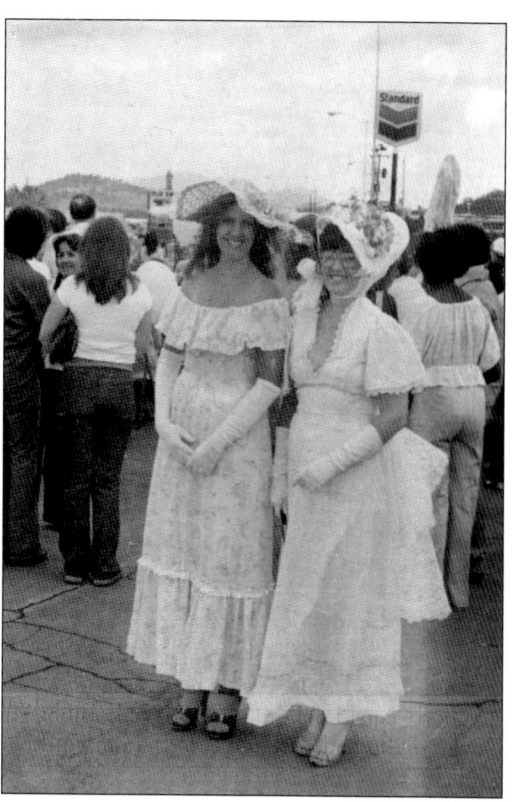

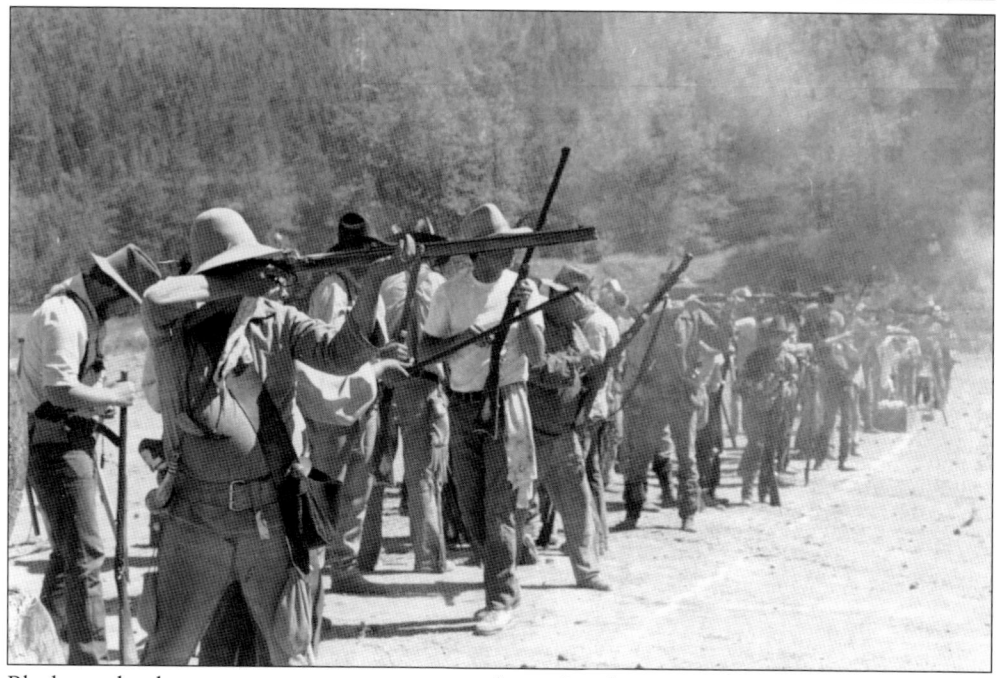

Black powder shoots were a common attraction during Rendezvous Days in Williams. Shoots were held at the aptly-named Buckskinner Park south of the downtown area. (Courtesy *Williams–Grand Canyon News*.)

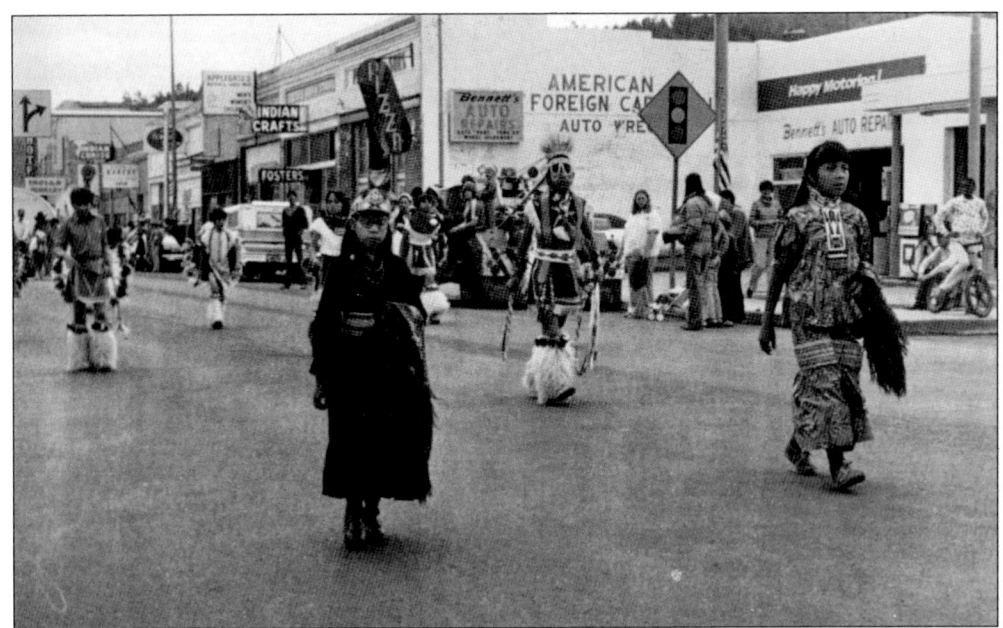

Other highlights of the annual Rendezvous Days weekend included the Rendezvous Days parade, held along Bill Williams Avenue, which would later be renamed Route 66. The parade featured a number of entries celebrating the culture of northern Arizona, including entries from a number of native tribes. (Courtesy *Williams–Grand Canyon News.*)

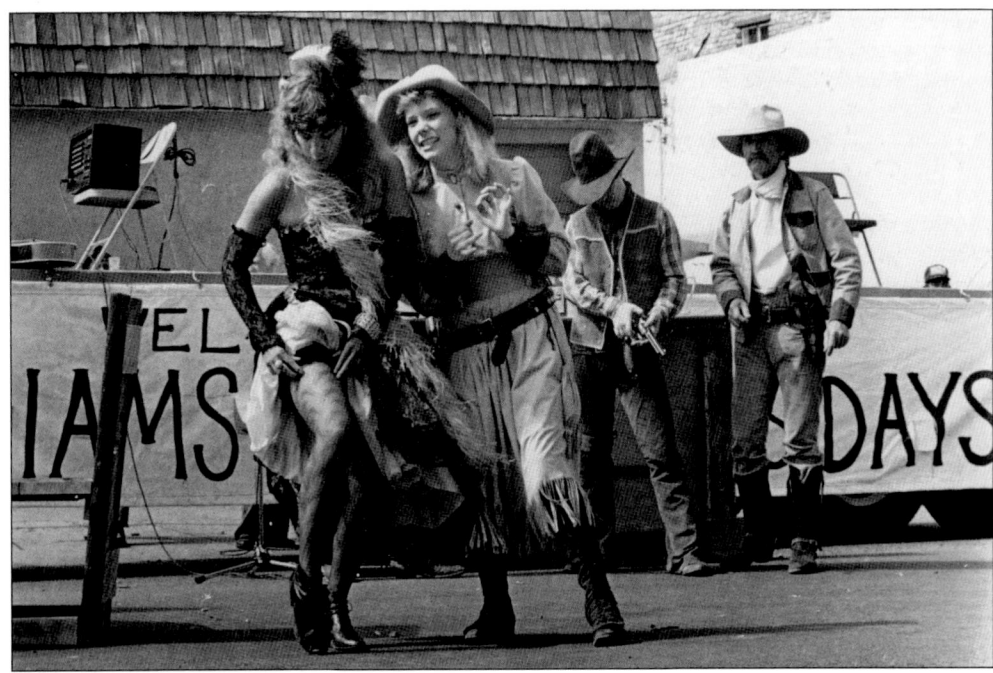

Harlots, Annie Oakleys, and cowboys were a common sight during the first annual Rendezvous Days event, held over Memorial Day weekend to honor the beginning of the summer season. (Courtesy *Williams–Grand Canyon News.*)

Ten

INTERSTATE 40 RETIRES ROUTE 66
THE DAY OF THE BIG BYPASS

Stretching from Chicago to Los Angeles, Route 66 remains one of the most fondly thought-of roads in this nation's history, if not the history of the world. Designated in 1926, the two-lane "Mother Road," as it is commonly called, served travelers in the United States for years. When cars got faster and more frequent, newer roads were built, including Interstate 40, which eventually spelled the end of Route 66.

Williams retains a unique distinction for Route 66 enthusiasts, as it was the last Route 66 town to be bypassed by the interstate. City officials in 1984 knew full well that the bypass would be a historic occasion and quickly set to work planning for the inevitable circumvention. A dedication ceremony was held on October 13, 1984, to mark the passage in history.

Singer Bobby Troupe, composer of the song "Get Your Kicks on Route 66," was named grand marshal for the momentous affair. Troupe cut a dedication ribbon during the ceremony with giant scissors made in a local shop class. Bill Ordway, director of the Arizona Department of Transportation (ADOT), and Charles Miller, state engineer for ADOT, were also on hand for the bypass festivities. A number of local and state dignitaries were also on site to stress an upbeat message on what they hoped would be a positive future for Williams, despite the fact that many business owners feared the city would soon go bust as a result of the bypass.

Surviving hardships, however, came as nothing new to Williams residents, who had already managed through fires, the closure of logging companies, and other adversities. The town soon bounced back, thanks to the restoration of the Grand Canyon Railway and the revival of Route 66 enthusiasm. Years after the bypass, city officials renamed Bill Williams Avenue to Route 66 amidst efforts to support interest in the city as a Mother Road landmark. By 2007, the Williams–Forest Service Visitor Center, formerly known as the information center, celebrated a record-breaking year in visitation, recording more than 110,000 visitors. That number, by all indications, is one that continues to grow.

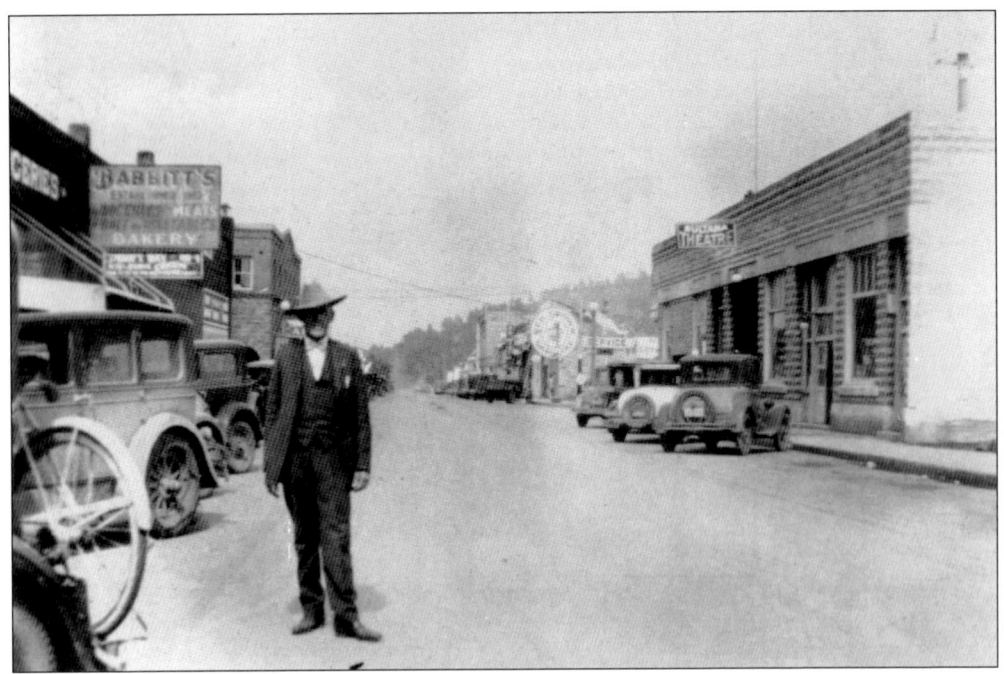

This view of Bill Williams Avenue in 1931 shows a block of the downtown area between Fourth and Third Streets, which included the Babbitt's Store and the Sultana Theater. Resident John Manning stands in the foreground. (Courtesy Williams Public Library.)

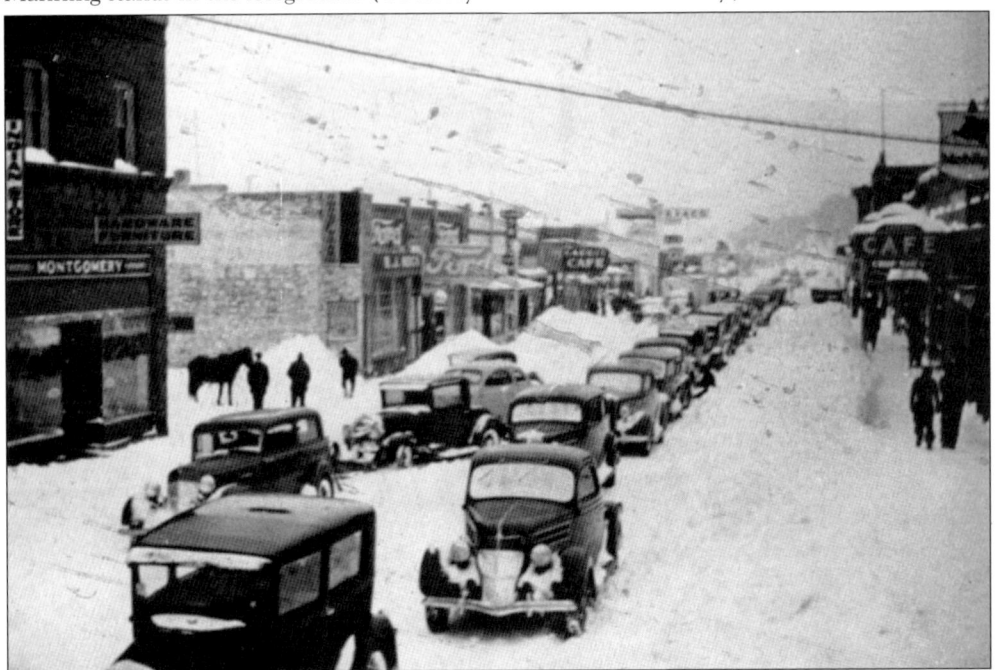

A large snowstorm in 1937 brought traffic to a standstill along Bill Williams Avenue between Third and Second Streets. Traffic flow on Route 66 was later changed to one direction, turning Bill Williams Avenue to eastbound traffic and Railroad Avenue to westbound traffic. (Courtesy Williams Public Library.)

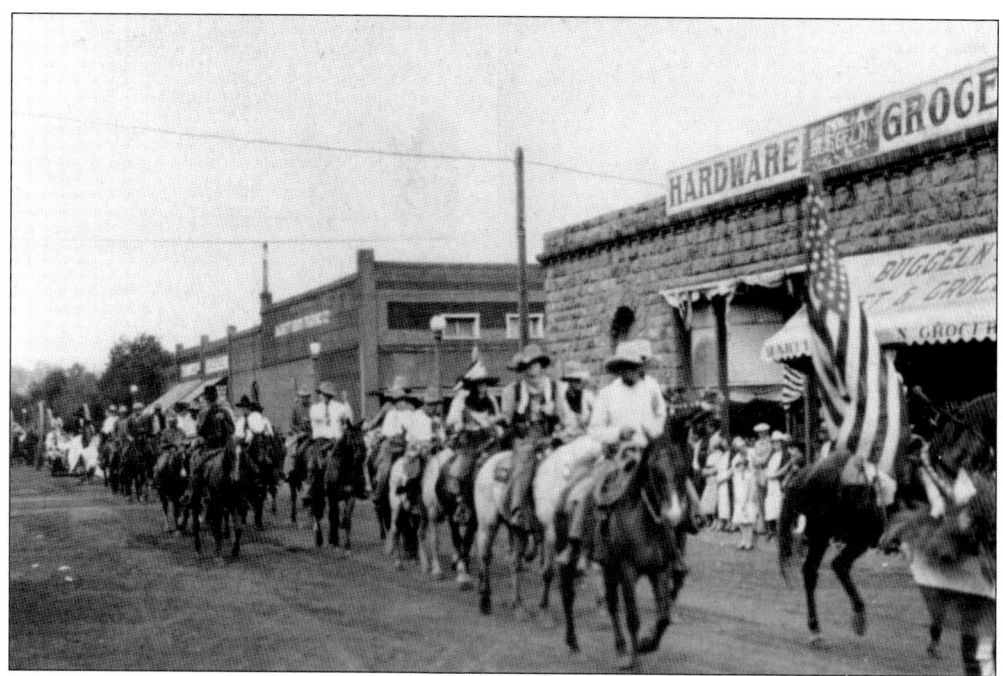

Parades have always been a common and anticipated sight along Bill Williams Avenue, such as this 1927 Fourth of July parade. (Courtesy Williams Public Library.)

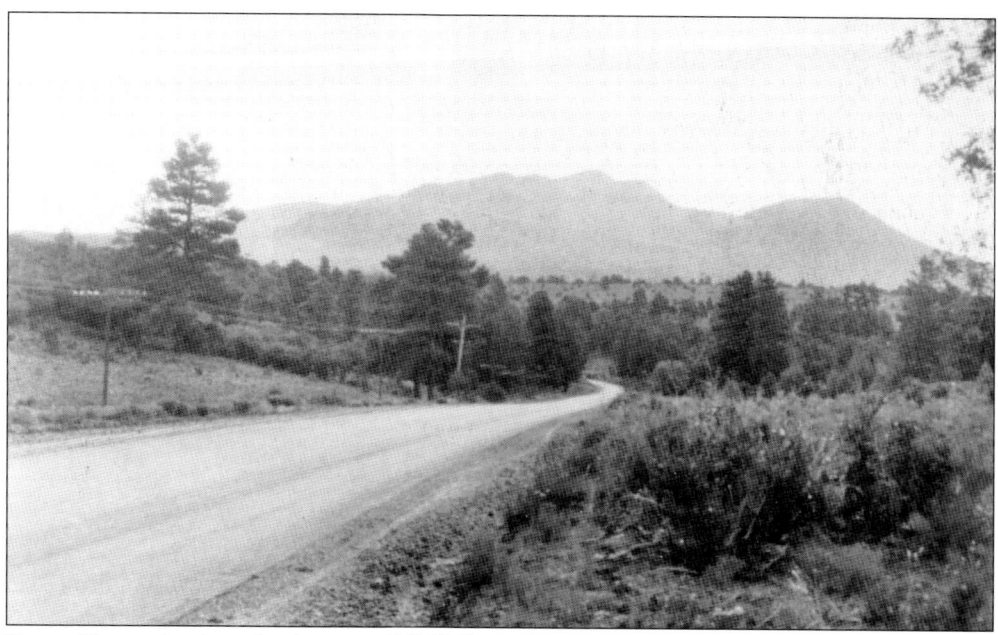

Route 66 stretches into the distance. Bill Williams Mountain can be seen in the background. Oil paving of the highway began between Ash Fork and Flagstaff, a stretch that included Williams, in 1928. (Courtesy Williams Public Library.)

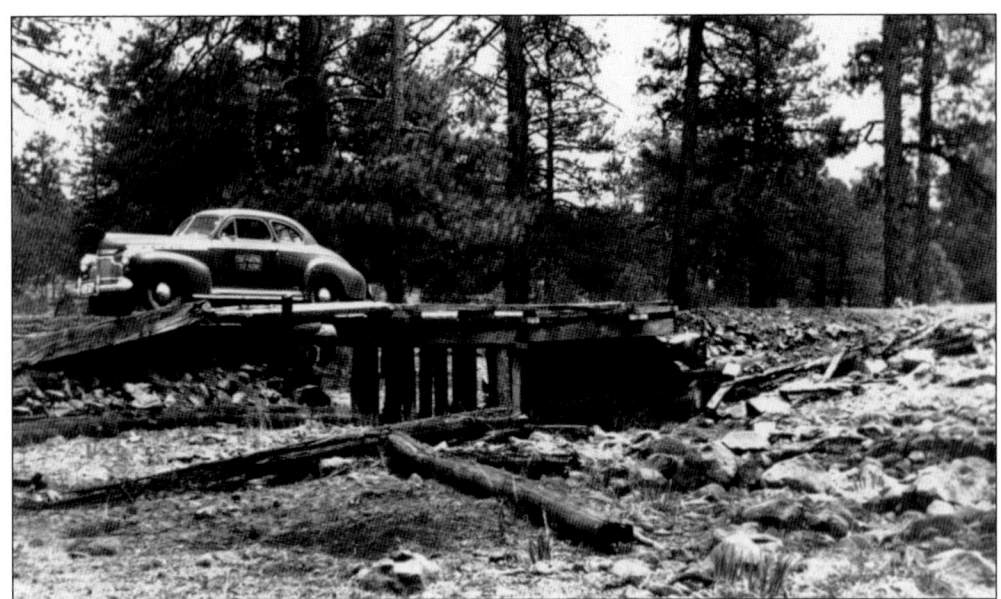

A vehicle with the Arizona Highway Department travels over a creaky bridge on Route 66 in the 1940s. Officials with the city of Williams were concerned with a number of other roads in and out of the community at the same time Route 66 entered the picture in the 1920s, including roads to the Grand Canyon and Verde Valley. (Courtesy George Garcia.)

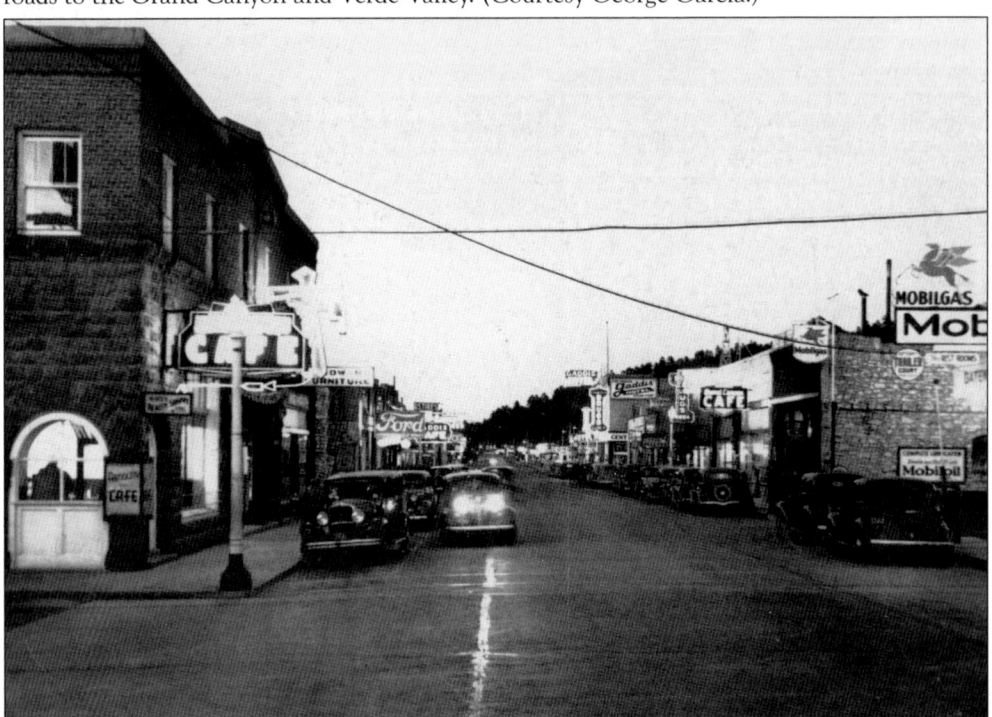

Headlights shine along a wet road in downtown Williams in 1938. The popularity of the automobile led to a decision by officials with the U.S. Forest Service to create a road on Bill Williams Mountain in the 1920s that eventually connected to Route 66. The road became known as the Bill Williams Loop Road. (Courtesy Williams Public Library.)

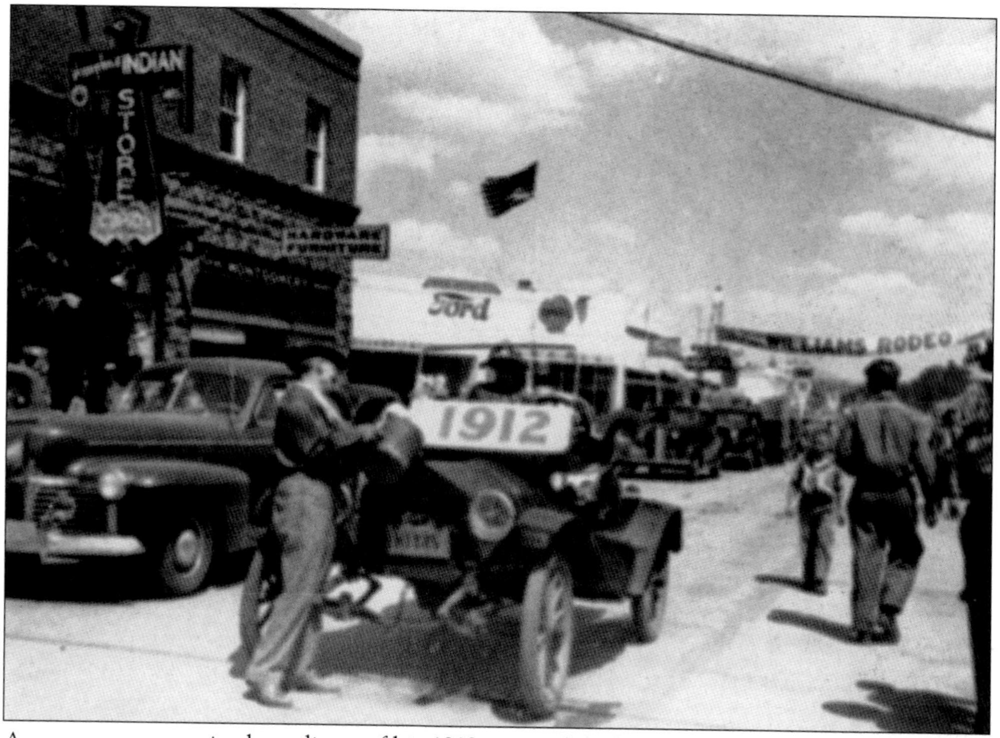

A man pours water in the radiator of his 1912 automobile during the 1941 Labor Day Parade in downtown Williams. (Courtesy Williams Public Library.)

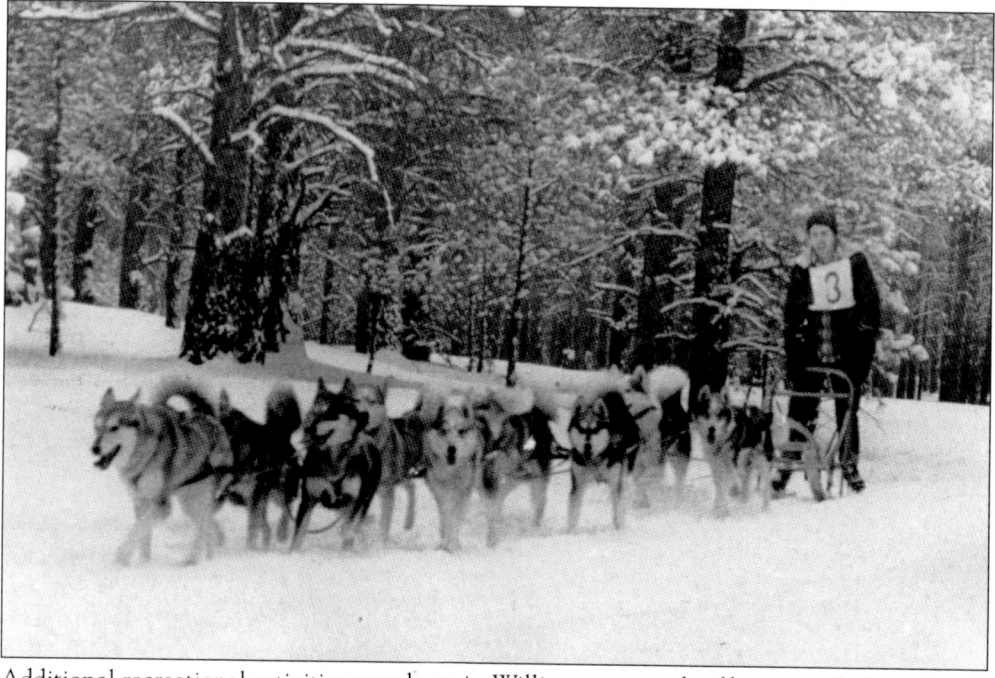

Additional recreational activities were born in Williams as a result of better roads that allowed access to many areas surrounding Williams. One such activity in the 1950s, dogsled racing, became a frequent affair in Williams. (Courtesy Williams Public Library.)

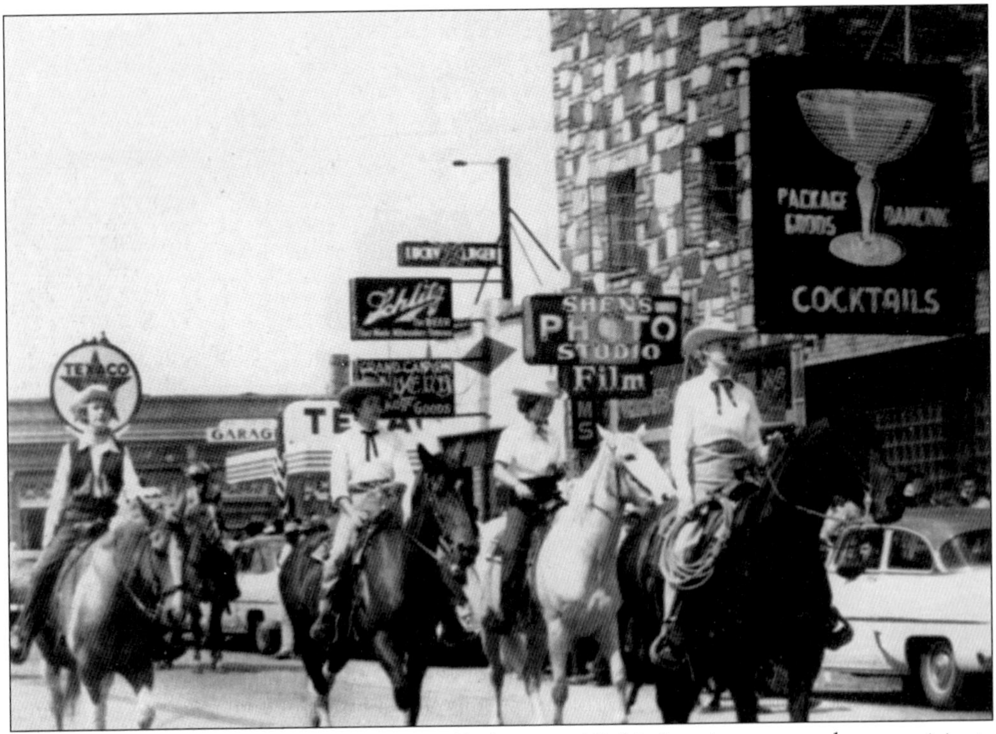

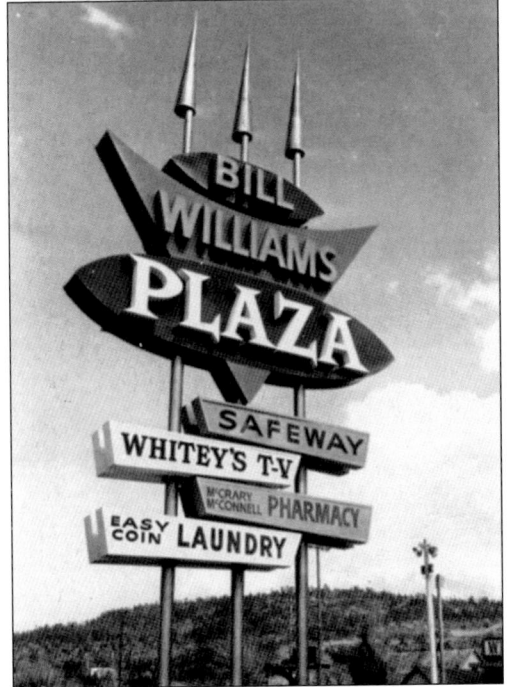

From left to right, Catherine Mayes, Connie Dickson, and Robin Laurie, among others, participate in the annual Williams Rodeo Labor Day parade in the 1950s. The group made their way down Route 66, passing alongside the Canyon Club bar between Second and First Streets. (Courtesy Williams Public Library.)

A flashy 1950s sign tells Route 66 travelers that they have arrived at the Bill Williams Plaza. The plaza was located along Bill Williams Avenue near Seventh Street. (Courtesy Williams Public Library.)

The Sultana Theater once was a popular spot for locals in Williams, including teens, who could find a quiet spot to take their dates. While movies are no longer shown there, the theater building is still a part of the downtown landscape. (Courtesy Williams Public Library.)

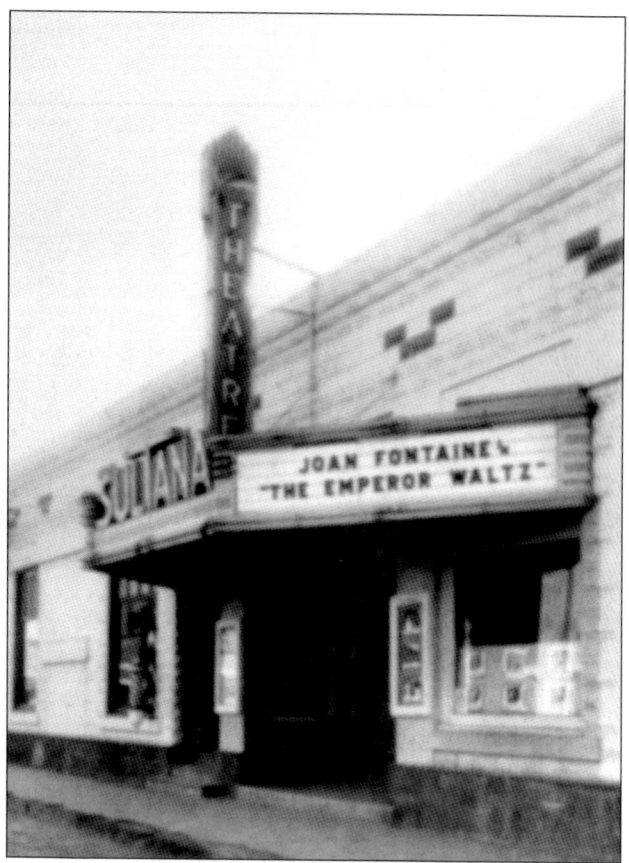

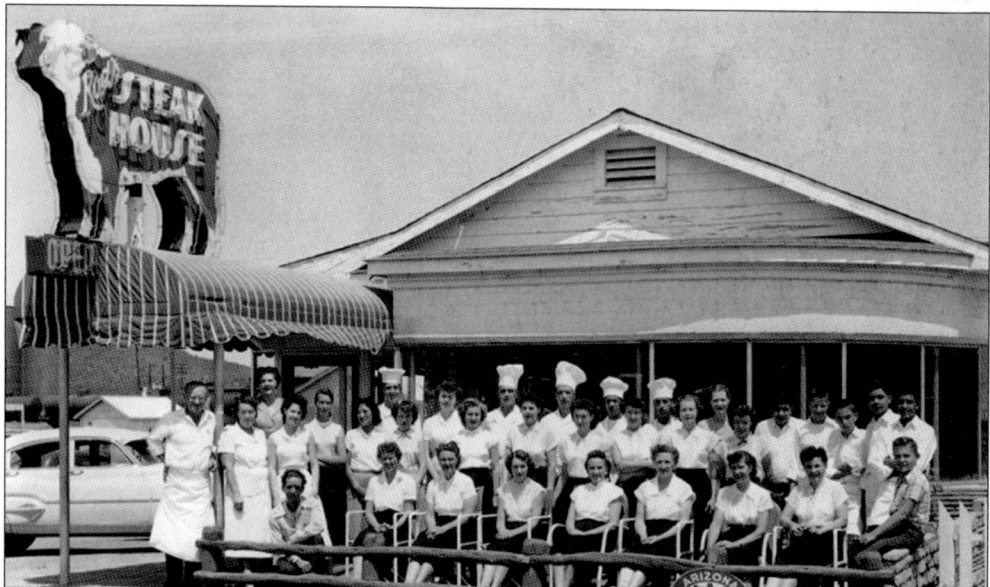

Rod's Steak House, originally owned by Rod Graves, became a well-known stopping place for travelers along Route 66. The restaurant is immediately recognizable thanks to a large steer that stands on the sidewalk outside. (Courtesy *Williams–Grand Canyon News*.)

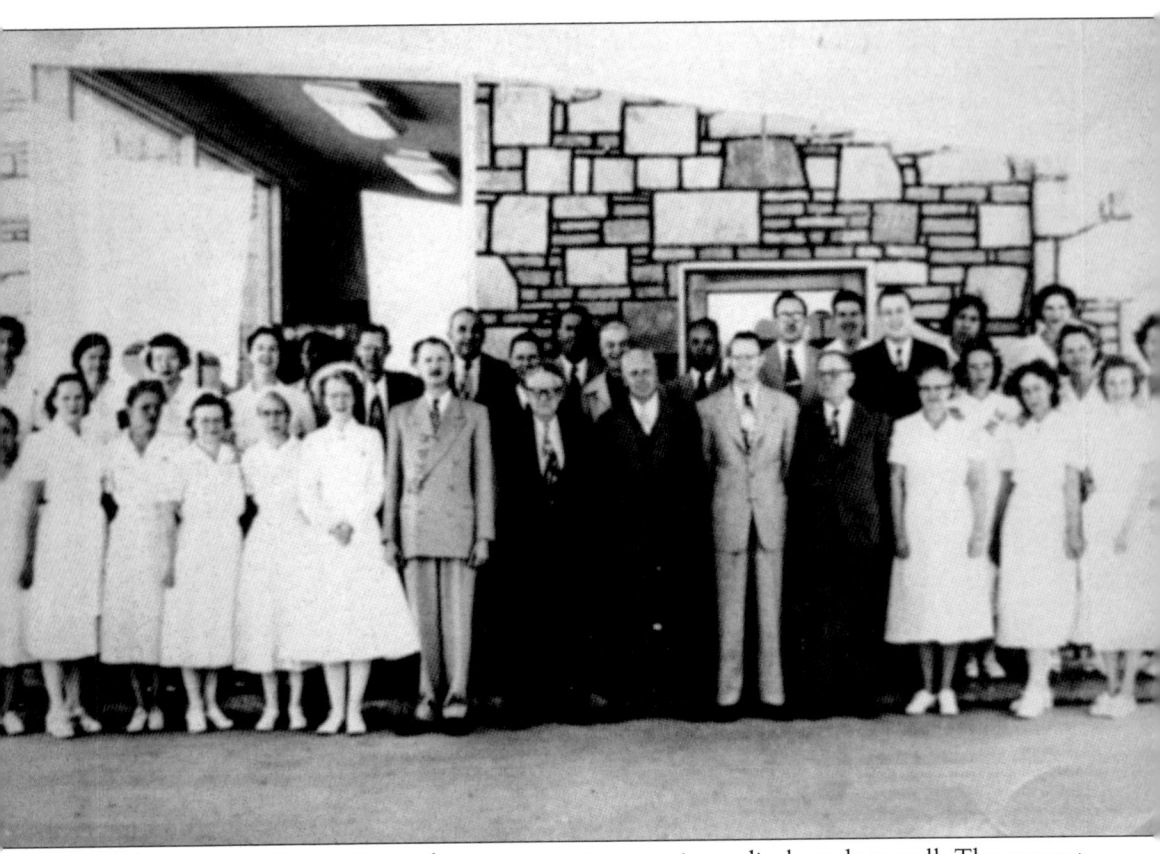

The increase in Route 66 travelers meant an increase in medical needs as well. The current Williams Health Care Center was officially opened for business on Sixth Street on May 11, 1950. (Courtesy Williams Public Library.)

ADOT employee Victor Leon looks over a scale model of the Interstate 40 bypass through Williams in 1975. By October 1984, that bypass of Route 66 through Williams became a reality. (Courtesy George Garcia.)

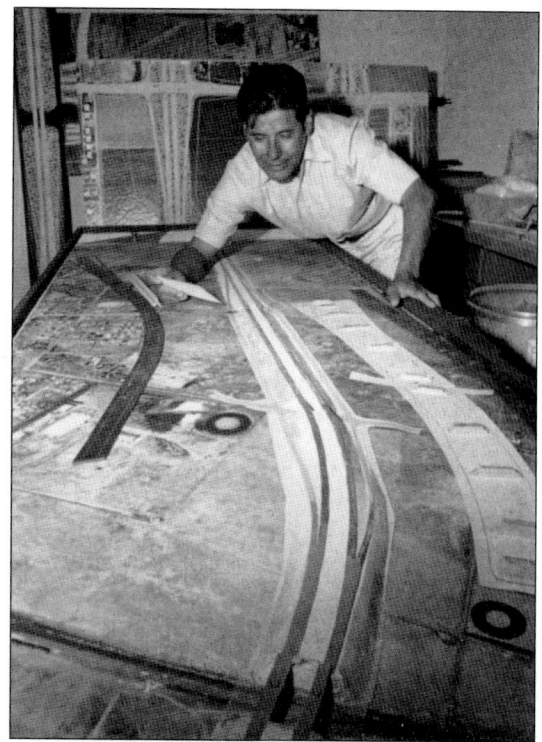

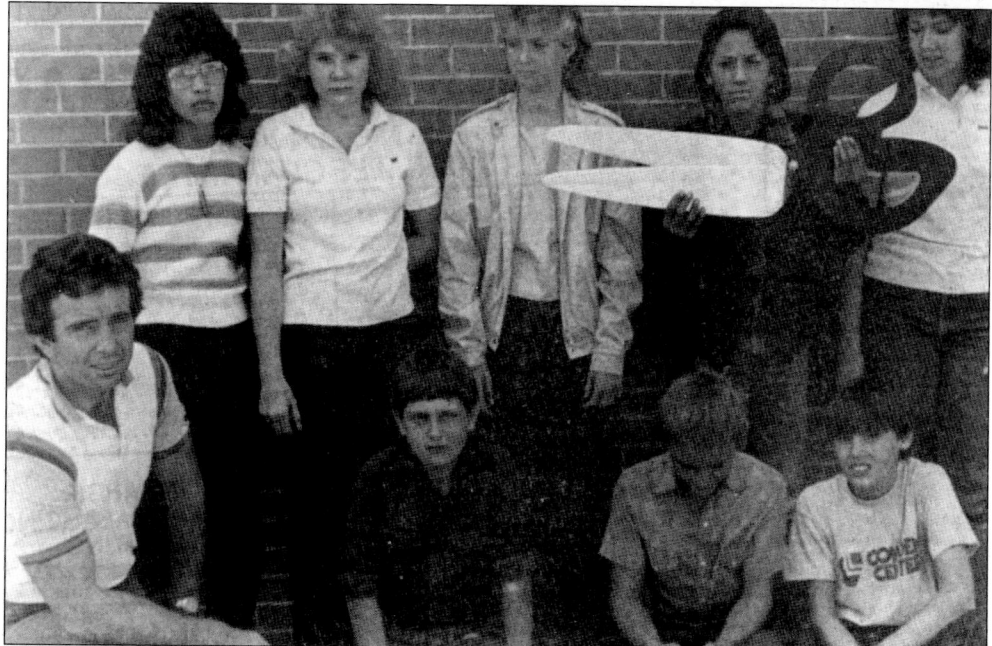

Shop teacher Bill Sutton (kneeling, far left) poses with his students, from left to right, (kneeling) George Davis, Jack Johnson, and Shawn McClary; (standing) Melissa Chavez, Susan Logan, Janine Russel, Frankie Serrano, and Rita Salz in 1984. The class made giant scissors from a pattern designed by artist Bonnie Dent that were used by Bobby Troupe to cut a dedication ribbon during the bypass ceremony. (Courtesy *Williams–Grand Canyon News*.)

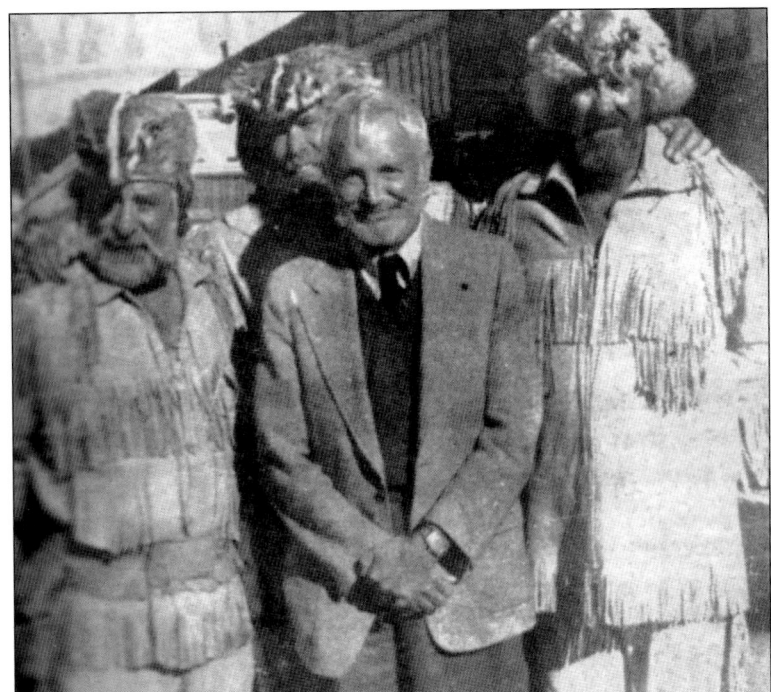

Singer Bobby Troupe (center) poses with members of the Bill Williams Mountain Men during the festivities in 1984. Troupe, famous for his "Get Your Kicks on Route 66" tune, turned 66 at almost the same time as the dedication. (Courtesy *Williams–Grand Canyon News.*)

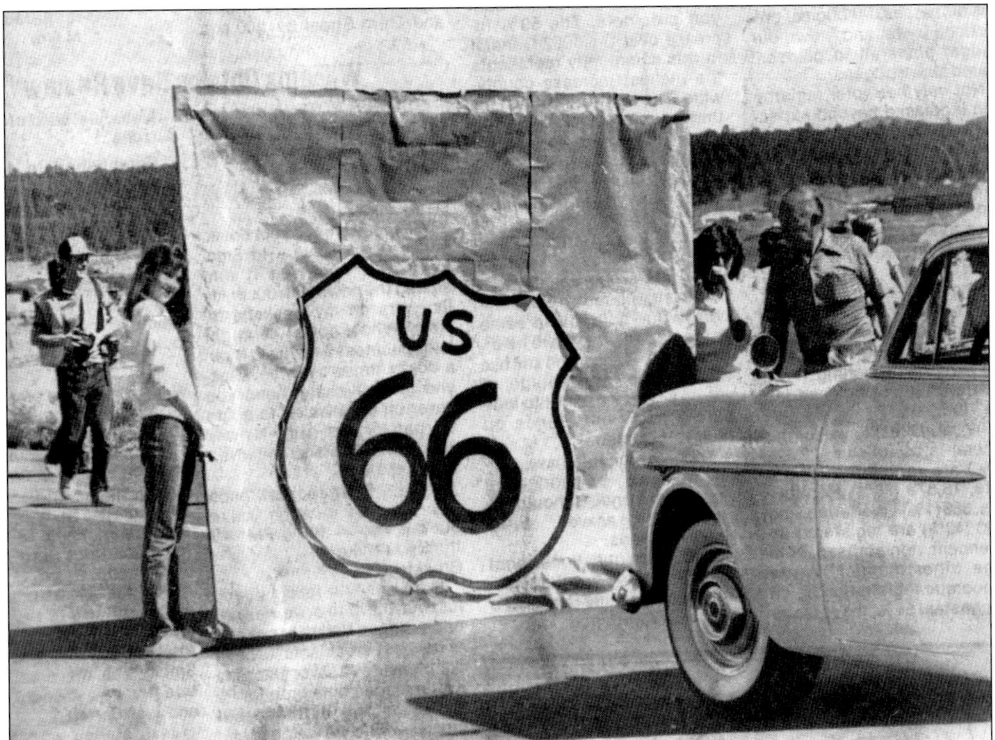

Tammy Andredo (left) and Samantha Sandoval (right) of Williams hold a giant Route 66 banner in 1984. Williams resident Ken Mowbray drove through the banner in his Packard automobile. (Courtesy *Williams–Grand Canyon News.*)

BIBLIOGRAPHY

Fuchs, James R. *A History of Williams, Arizona*. Tucson, AZ: University of Arizona Press, 1955.
Richmond, Al. *Rails to the Rim*. Centennial edition. Flagstaff, AZ: Grand Canyon Railway, 2001.
———. *The Story of the Grand Canyon Railway*. Revised edition. Flagstaff, AZ: Grand Canyon Railway, 1995.
Wells, Frank Evarts. *The Story of "Old Bill Williams."* 11th edition. Williams, AZ: Williams News Press, 1957.
Williams–Grand Canyon News. Williams, Arizona. Rendezvous Days Special Edition, 1980.
Williams–Grand Canyon News. Williams, Arizona. Special Editions, 1989, 1999.

ABOUT THE AUTHOR

Having lived in Williams for 15 years, Patrick Whitehurst has written numerous stories about the city for a number of northern Arizona publications. His stories range from news reporting to humor columns. A graduate of Northern Arizona University with a degree in journalism and a former Williams talk show host, Whitehurst currently works as a reporter for the *Williams–Grand Canyon News*.

ACROSS AMERICA, PEOPLE ARE DISCOVERING SOMETHING WONDERFUL. *THEIR HERITAGE.*

Arcadia Publishing is the leading local history publisher in the United States. With more than 4,000 titles in print and hundreds of new titles released every year, Arcadia has extensive specialized experience chronicling the history of communities and celebrating America's hidden stories, bringing to life the people, places, and events from the past. To discover the history of other communities across the nation, please visit:

www.arcadiapublishing.com

Customized search tools allow you to find regional history books about the town where you grew up, the cities where your friends and family live, the town where your parents met, or even that retirement spot you've been dreaming about.

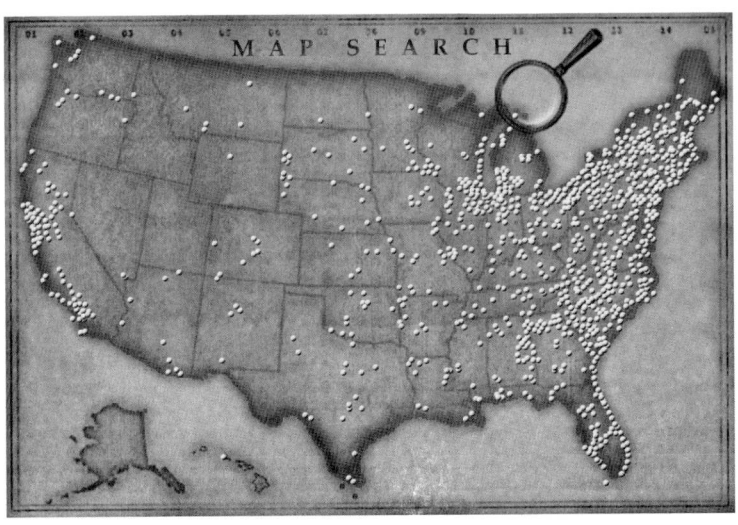